W9-BYT-429

S50

THE MARRIAGE SCENARIOS

By the same author

Fanny and Alexander

From the Life of the Marionettes

The Serpent's Egg

PANTHEON · BOOKS · NEW · YORK

THE MARRIAGE

SCENES FROM A
MARRIAGE
FACE TO FACE
AUTUMN SONATA

SCENARIOS

Ingmar Bergman

Translated · from · the · Swedish · by · Alan · Blair

Compilation copyright © 1983 by Random House, Inc.

English translation Copyright © 1974, 1976, 1978
by Alan Blair

All rights reserved under International and Pan-American
Copyright Conventions. Published in the United States by
Pantheon Books, a division of Random House, Inc., New
York, and simultaneously in Canada by Random House of
Canada Limited, Toronto. *Scenes from a Marriage* originally
published in Sweden as *Scener ur ett äktenskap* by P.A.
Norstedt & Söner, Stockholm. Copyright © 1973 by Ingmar
Bergman. *Face to Face* originally published in Sweden as
Ansikte mot ansikte by P.A. Norstedt & Söner, Stockholm.
Copyright © 1976 by Ingmar Bergman. *Autumn Sonata*
originally published in Sweden as *Höstsonaten* by P.A.
Norstedt & Söner, Stockholm. Copyright © 1978 by
Cinematograph, Fårö, Sweden. The photographs in this
book were taken by Arne Carlsson and Lars Karlsson.

This selection first published in the United States by
Pantheon Books, a division of Random House, Inc.,
in 1983.

Library of Congress Cataloging-in-Publication Data
Bergman, Ingmar, 1918–
The marriage scenarios.
(Pantheon modern writers)
Contents: Scenes from a marriage—Face to face—
Autumn sonata.
I. Title.   II. Series
[PT9875.B533A23   1988]   791.43'75   88-17901
ISBN 0-679-72032-4 (pbk.)

Manufactured in the United States of America
First Pantheon Modern Writers Edition

CONTENTS

Scenes from a Marriage

P R E F A C E

To prevent the constrained reader from getting lost in the text I have decided—contrary to my habit—to write a commentary on the six scenes. Those who are offended by such guidance should skip the following lines.

First scene: Johan and Marianne are conventional and set in their ways and believe in material security. They have never found their middle-class way of life oppressive or false. They have conformed to a pattern which they are prepared to pass on. Their former political activity is a confirmation of this rather than a contradiction.

In the first scene they present a pretty picture of an almost ideal marriage, which is confronted moreover with an inferno-like relationship. They are smug in a quiet way, convinced that they have arranged everything for the best. The air is thick with makeshift solutions and well-meant platitudes. Peter and Katarina appear as lunatics to be pitied, while Johan and Marianne have arranged for the best in this best of worlds. All the same, at the end of this scene they receive a slight setback. They are faced with a choice. A sore, apparently trifling, breaks open, heals, and forms a scar, but under the scar an infection has formed. That's my idea anyway. If someone else wishes to think differently, that's fine.

Second scene: Everything is still ideal, almost splendid. Small worries are solved in joking agreement. Their professions and working environments are presented. Marianne is aware of a vague anxiety. She can't define it, still less pin it down, but instinctively she feels that something is wrong between her and Johan. She makes a lame and not very successful effort to repair the dimly sensed rift. Johan has several mysterious telephone calls. One evening when they've been to the theater and seen *A Doll's House* (what else would they have seen?), there is a sudden feeling of discord between them; they try to make light of it and finally sweep it under the rug.

Third scene: The blow falls. In rather a brutal way Johan announces that he is in love with another woman and is going to leave. He is full of vital eagerness to act and oxidized by the cheerful selfishness of the new infatuation. Marianne is thunderstruck. Utterly defenseless. Totally unprepared. Within a few minutes she changes in front of our eyes into a bleeding and trembling sore. Humiliation and perplexity.

Fourth scene: They meet again after quite a long time. Things have started to go wrong for Johan, though it is not noticeable. On the contrary. As for Marianne, there are signs of recovery, though they are extremely vague and are mixed up with the past: her ties to Johan, the ulcerous loneliness, the longing for everything to be as it was before. Their encounter is painful and clumsy in its mixture of reconciliation and aggressiveness. For brief moments they reach one another through isolation and aloofness. Everything is fragile, infected, ragged. This is a very sad scene.

Fifth scene: Now there is a terrible blowup. Marianne is finding her feet again and Johan is losing his grip on reality. They have the bright idea of starting divorce proceedings together and of engaging the same lawyer. One evening in early summer they meet at Johan's office to sign the divorce papers. Suddenly everything explodes and they give vent to all the aggressions, all the hate, all the mutual boredom and rage that they have been suppressing for years. Bit by bit they are dehumanized and at last they become really nasty and behave like maniacs who have only one thought in their minds: to maul each other physically and mentally. In these efforts they are even a degree worse than Peter and Katarina in the first scene, who have a certain routine in their inferno and are, as it were, more professional in their savagery. Johan and Marianne have not yet learned this extreme restraint. In short, they want to destroy one another, and they very nearly succeed.

Sixth scene: My idea now is that two new people begin to emerge from all this devastation. Maybe that is a little too optimistic but I can't help it, that's how it turned out. Both Johan and Marianne have walked through the vale of tears and made it rich in springs. They are beginning to acquire a new knowledge of themselves, in a manner of speaking. This is not just a matter of resignation, but concerns love too. For the first time, Marianne sits down and listens to her troublesome mother. Johan looks at his own situation with forgiveness and is good to Marianne in a new and adult way. Everything is still in confusion and nothing is any better. All relations are muddled and their lives are incontestably based on a heap of wretched compromises. But somehow they are now citizens of the world of reality in quite a different way from before. At least I think so. There's no solution at hand, anyway, so there's no happy ending. Nice as it would have been to arrive at one. If for no other reason, to annoy all artistically sensitive people, who, disgusted by this quite understandable work, will be aesthetically sick after the very first scene.

What more is there to say? This opus took three months to write, but rather a long part of my life to experience. I'm not sure that it would have turned out better had it been the other way round, though it would have seemed nicer. I have felt a kind of affection for these people while I've been occupied with them. They have grown rather contradictory, sometimes anxiously childish, sometimes pretty grown-up. They talk quite a lot of rubbish, now and then saying something sensible. They are nervous, happy, selfish, stupid, kind, wise, self-sacrificing, affectionate, angry, gentle, sentimental, insufferable, and lovable. All jumbled up. Now let's see what happens.

I.B.

Fåro, May 1972

FIRST SCENE

INNOCENCE AND PANIC

CHARACTERS

Johan
Marianne
Karin and Eva, their daughters
Mrs. Palm, the interviewer
Photographer
Peter
Katarina

MARIANNE *and* JOHAN *are being interviewed in their home. They are sitting, rather stiffly and on their best behavior, beside each other on a sofa. Quite a sofa, at that. It's round and curved and Victorian and upholstered in green; it has friendly arms, soft cushions, and carved legs; it is a monstrosity of coziness. A handsome oil lamp can be glimpsed on a table. The background consists of massive bookshelves. On another table are tea, toast and jam, and sherry. The interviewer,* MRS. PALM, *is sitting with her back to the camera. She has set up a small tape recorder among the plates and cups. A bearded photographer moves about the room, popping up and disappearing.*

MRS. PALM *(Gaily)* We always begin with a standard question. To get over the first nervousness.

JOHAN I'm not particularly nervous.

MARIANNE Nor am I.

MRS. PALM *(Still more gaily)* All the better. The question is: How would you describe yourselves in a few words?

JOHAN That's not an easy one.

MRS. PALM Not so difficult either, surely?

JOHAN I mean, there's risk of a misunderstanding.

7

MRS. PALM   Do you think so?

JOHAN   Yes. It might sound conceited if I described myself as extremely intelligent, successful, youthful, well-balanced, and sexy. A man with a world conscience, cultivated, well-read, popular, and a good mixer. Let me see, what else can I think of . . . friendly. Friendly in a nice way even to people who are worse off. I like sports. I'm a good family man. A good son. I have no debts and I pay my taxes. I respect our government whatever it does, and I love our royal family. I've left the state church. Is this enough or do you want more details? I'm a splendid lover. Aren't I, Marianne?

MRS. PALM   *(With a smile)*   Perhaps we can return to the question. How about you, Marianne? What do you have to say?

MARIANNE   Hmm, what can I say . . . I'm married to Johan and have two daughters.

MRS. PALM   Yes . . .

MARIANNE   That's all I can think of for the moment.

MRS. PALM   There must be something . . .

MARIANNE   I think Johan is rather nice.

JOHAN   Kind of you, I'm sure.

MARIANNE   We've been married for ten years.

JOHAN   I've just renewed the contract.

MARIANNE   I doubt if I have the same natural appreciation of my own excellence as Johan. But to tell the truth, I'm glad I can live the life I do. It's a good life, if you know what I mean. Well, what else can I say . . . Oh dear, this is difficult!

JOHAN   She has a nice figure.

MARIANNE   You're joking. I'm trying to take this thing seriously. I have two daughters, Karin and Eva.

JOHAN   You've already said that.

MRS. PALM *(Giving up)*   Perhaps we can take up the question again later. By the way! What about a picture with your daughters? Here on the sofa with mother and father?

MARIANNE   They'll be home from school soon.

MRS. PALM   Oh, good. Well, let's start with a few facts. I'd like to know your ages.

JOHAN   I'm forty-two. But you wouldn't think so to look at me, would you?

MARIANNE   I'm thirty-five.

JOHAN   Both of us come from almost indecently middle-class homes.

MARIANNE   Johan's father is a doctor.

JOHAN   And my mother's the motherly type. Very much so.

MARIANNE   My father's a lawyer. It was decided from the outset that I was to be a lawyer too. I'm the youngest of seven children. Mother ran a big household. Nowadays she takes it easier.

JOHAN   She does?
(Polite smiles)

MARIANNE   The funny thing about us both is that we actually get along very well with our parents. We see quite a lot of each other. There has never been any friction to speak of.

MRS. PALM   Perhaps we'd better say something about your professions.

JOHAN   I'm an associate professor at the Psychotechnical Institute.

MARIANNE   I specialized in family law and am employed by a law firm. Most of my work has to do with divorces and so on. The interesting thing is that the whole time you're brought into contact with—

PHOTOGRAPHER *(Popping up)* Will you look at each other, please. Like that, hold it . . . I just want to . . . Sorry . . .

MARIANNE   It's awful, I feel like such a fool.

MRS. PALM   Only at first. How did you meet?

MARIANNE   Let Johan tell you.

JOHAN   Good Lord, *that's* interesting!

MARIANNE   At any rate, it wasn't love at first sight.

JOHAN   Both of us had a large circle of friends and we used to meet at all sorts of parties. Also, we were politically active for several years and we went in for amateur dramatics quite a lot as students. But I can't say we made any very deep impression on each other. Marianne thought I was stuck-up.

MARIANNE   He was having a much-discussed affair with a pop singer and that gave him a certain image and made him insufferable.

JOHAN   And Marianne was nineteen and married to a fool, whose only saving grace was that he was the apple of his rich father's eye.

MARIANNE   But he was awfully kind. And I was madly in love.

Besides, I got pregnant almost at once. And that also meant something.

MRS. PALM   But how was it that . . .

JOHAN   That we two came together? That was Marianne's idea, actually.

MARIANNE   My child died soon after it was born and then my husband and I got a divorce, rather to our relief. Johan had been dropped by that pop singer and was a little less stuck-up. We were feeling a bit lonely and tousled. So I suggested trying to make a go of it. We were not in the least in love with one another, we were just miserable.

JOHAN   We got along very well together and really got down to our studies.

MARIANNE   So we started living together. Our mothers never batted an eye, though we thought they'd be terribly shocked. Not at all! In fact, they became good friends. Suddenly we were accepted as Johan and Marianne. After six months we got married.

JOHAN   Besides, by then we were in love.

MARIANNE   Terribly.

JOHAN   We were considered an ideal married couple.

MARIANNE   And so it has gone on.

MRS. PALM   No complications?

MARIANNE   We've had no material worries. We're on good terms with friends and relations on both sides. We have good jobs that we like. We're healthy.

JOHAN   And so on and so on, to an almost vulgar degree. Security, order, comfort, and loyalty. It all has a suspiciously successful look.

MARIANNE   Naturally, like other people, we have our differences. That goes without saying. But we agree on all the important things.

MRS. PALM   Don't you ever quarrel?

JOHAN   Oh yes, Marianne does.

MARIANNE   Johan is very slow to anger, so it calms me down.

MRS. PALM   It sounds fantastic. The whole thing.

MARIANNE   Someone was saying to us just last night that the very lack of problems is in itself a serious problem. I suspect it's true. A life like ours always has its dangers. We're well aware of that.

JOHAN   The world is going to the devil and I claim the right to mind my own business. Every political system is corrupt. It makes me sick to think of these new salvation gospels. Whoever controls the computers will win the game. I hold the unpopular view of live and let live.

MARIANNE   I don't agree with Johan.

MRS. PALM   Oh, what do you think then?

MARIANNE   I believe in fellow-feeling.

MRS. PALM   What do you mean by that?

MARIANNE   If everyone learned to care about each other right from childhood, the world would be a different place, I'm certain of that.

PHOTOGRAPHER   Don't move! Keep that expression. That's it. Thank you.

MARIANNE   Here are Karin and Eva. I'll tell them to tidy themselves.
(MARIANNE *hurries out and is heard talking to her daughters.* JOHAN *fills his pipe and exchanges a rather uncertain but polite smile with the interviewer, who sips her cold tea and is at a momentary loss for a question*)

JOHAN   To tell you the truth, it's not such a simple matter.

MRS. PALM   What do you mean?

JOHAN   We used to think that nothing could happen to us. Now we know better. That's the only difference.

MRS. PALM   Are you afraid of the future?

JOHAN   If I stopped to think I'd be petrified with fear. Or so I imagine. So I don't think. I'm fond of this cozy old sofa and that oil lamp. They give me an illusion of security which is so fragile that it's almost comic. I like Bach's "St. Matthew Passion" though I'm not religious, because it gives me feelings of piety and belonging. Our families see a lot of each other and I depend very much on this contact, as it reminds me of my childhood when I felt I was protected. I like what Marianne said about fellow-feeling. It's good for a conscience which worries on quite the wrong occasions. I think you must have a kind of technique to be able to live and be content with your life. In fact, you have to practice quite hard not giving a damn about anything. The people I admire most are those who can take life as a joke. I can't. I have too little sense of humor for a feat like that. You won't print this, will you?

MRS. PALM   No, I'm afraid it's a little too complicated for our women readers. If you forgive my saying so.
(*Pause*)

JOHAN   What shall we talk about now?

MRS. PALM   Oh, I have lots of questions. (MARIANNE *comes in and sits down on the sofa with her daughters,* EVA, *12, and* KARIN, *11. They're a little stiff, giggly, embarrassed, and delighted, combed and dressed to have their picture taken. Mutual how-do-you-dos. Grouping and regrouping conducted by the photographer.* JOHAN *clutches his pipe. When the picture of the family group has been taken the children are allowed to disappear into the kitchen and have their afternoon cup of cocoa and cheese sandwich.* JOHAN *excuses himself, saying that he must make a phone call, and vanishes, more quickly than politely.* MRS. PALM *seizes the opportunity. After all, it is a woman's magazine*) I don't think you and I have met since our school days.

MARIANNE   Do you often see our old schoolmates?

MRS. PALM   Actually I don't. (*Going right to the point*) I gather that you and Johan have a good life together. Haven't you? I mean, you're really happy. Aren't you? Everything you tell me sounds simply marvelous. But then why shouldn't some people be granted perfection.

MARIANNE   I don't know that we've got perfection. But we do have a good life. I mean, we're happy. Oh yes, we're happy.

MRS. PALM (*Seizing on this*)   How would you define the word happiness?

MARIANNE   Must I really?

MRS. PALM (*Gravely*)   This is a woman's magazine, Marianne.

MARIANNE   If I thought up something to say about happiness, Johan would only laugh at me. No, I can't. You must hit on something yourself.

MRS. PALM (*Roguishly*)   Don't try to wriggle out of it now.

MARIANNE   I suppose happiness is being content. I don't long for anything. Except for the summer, of course. *(Pause)* I wish it could always be like this. That nothing ever changed.

MRS. PALM *(Her appetite whetted)* What do you have to say about fidelity?

MARIANNE   Well, really!

MRS. PALM   You must help me put some body into this. Johan's awfully sweet, but I didn't get much out of him.

MARIANNE   Fidelity?

MRS. PALM   Yes, fidelity. Between man and woman. Of course.

MARIANNE   Fidelity. Hmm, what can one say about that . . .

MRS. PALM   In your profession you must surely have come across—

MARIANNE   I wonder if fidelity can exist other than as a matter of course. I don't think fidelity can ever be a compulsion or a resolution. You can never promise anyone fidelity. Either it's there or it isn't. I like to be faithful to Johan, therefore I am faithful. But naturally I don't know how it will be tomorrow or next week.

MRS. PALM   Have you always been faithful to Johan?

MARIANNE *(Coldly)*   Now I think we're getting *too* personal.

MRS. PALM   Forgive me. Now I have only one last question, while Johan is on the phone. What do you have to say about love? You *must* say something about love. It's part of this series to give your views on love.

MARIANNE   And if I don't want to?

MRS. PALM   Then I'll have to make up something myself and it won't be half as good.

MARIANNE   No one has told me what love is. And I'm not even sure it's necessary to know. But if you want a detailed description, you can look in the Bible—Paul told us what love is. The trouble is, his definition squashes us flat. If love is what Paul says it is, then it's so rare that hardly anyone has known it. But as a set piece to be read out at weddings and other solemn occasions, those verses are rather impressive. I think it's enough if you're kind to the person you're living with. Affection is also a good thing. Comradeship and tolerance and a sense of humor. Moderate ambitions for one another. If you can supply those ingredients, then . . . then love's not so important.

MRS. PALM   Why are you so upset?

MARIANNE   In my profession I'm dealing the whole time with people who have collapsed under impossible demands for emotional expression. It's barbarous. I wish that . . .

MRS. PALM   What do you wish?

MARIANNE   I don't know. I can't see through this problem, so I'd rather not talk about it. But I wish that people . . . that we were not forced to play a lot of parts we don't want to play. That we could be simpler and gentler with each other. Don't you think so too?

MRS. PALM *(Alert)*   That life could be a little more romantic!

MARIANNE   No, I didn't mean that actually. In fact, I meant just the opposite. You see how badly I express myself. Can't we talk about food and children instead? It's something a bit more concrete, anyway.

MRS. PALM   Perhaps we did digress.

MARIANNE   Yes, I think we did.
(*Polite smile*)

MRS. PALM   Well, how do you manage both job and home?

———

JOHAN *and* MARIANNE *have asked* PETER *and* KATARINA *to dinner. Their daughters do the serving. Spirits are high.* JOHAN *is reading aloud from a woman's magazine.*

JOHAN (*Reading aloud*)   "Marianne has folksong-blue eyes that seem to light up from within. When I ask her how she manages both job and home she gives a little introspective smile as though she were keeping a sweet secret and answers rather evasively that she copes all right, that she and Johan help each other. 'It's a question of *mutual understanding*,' she says suddenly, brightening as Johan comes in and sits down beside her on the handsome heirloom sofa. He puts a protective arm around her shoulders and she snuggles up to him with a smile of security and trust. So I leave them, and I can't help noticing that they are secretly pleased when I go, so that they can once more be alone together. Two young people, strong, happy, with a constructive attitude toward life in general, but who have never forgotten all the same to give love first place."
(*As* JOHAN *finishes reading there is spontaneous applause. Then they take another helping from the casserole and pour out more wine*)

MARIANNE   We regretted it and nearly died when we read the masterpiece, and wanted to change it all, but the editor said it was too late, unfortunately. There had been some mistake and the article had already gone to press.

JOHAN   We thought seriously of complaining to the authorities, but our mothers and daughters thought it was all wonderful, so we let it go. What chiefly riled me was that it said nothing about *my* eyes. Katarina! Take a look! Can't you see any secret glow in my eyes?

KATARINA   They look more like pools of darkness to me. Awfully sexy, actually.

PETER   Katarina has fallen hard for you of late.

KATARINA   Will you elope with me, Johan?

MARIANNE   I think a change would do Johan good. He's been so awfully conjugal for ten years now and never been unfaithful.

PETER   Are you so sure?

MARIANNE   I made up my mind at the outset to believe everything he said. Didn't I, Johan?

PETER   There, you see, Katarina?

KATARINA   Yes, but I'm sure Johan lies much more cleverly than you do, my silly old darling.

JOHAN   I'm afraid I have no imagination.

PETER   That's just the point. People with no imagination tell better lies than those with too much.

KATARINA   Peter dolls up his stories with far too many details. Sometimes I'm really touched.

MARIANNE   By the way, I read Peter's article in the *Technical Magazine*. Even I understood what it was about.

PETER   It was Katarina who wrote it.

JOHAN   Are you so clever, Katarina?

PETER   I was in Germany when they called up, so Katarina sat down then and there and wrote the article, and read it to me on the phone.

MARIANNE   But why does it say it's your article when Katarina wrote it?

KATARINA   It's not an instance of keeping women in their place. We always work together, you know.

JOHAN   How I envy you.

PETER   You wouldn't say that if you knew what goes on between us. To be honest, things are goddamn lousy right now. Skoal, Katarina. It doesn't matter my saying that when we're with Johan and Marianne, does it?

MARIANNE   What is it, Katarina?

KATARINA   Nothing. Nothing at all. It's just that I think Peter's so damned clumsy sometimes.

PETER   *Clumsy* was the word. I take a pride in being clumsy. And imaginative. I'm an all-round stinker, in fact, but I really can't help that.

JOHAN   Well, let's enjoy ourselves and not go into life's injustices.

PETER   No, we musn't forget—bearing in mind the recent magazine interview—that we're, so to speak, under a happy roof and are not to make any emotional stains. Skoal, Marianne. Even if I don't envy you your domestic bliss, I wish I had your skill with food—you're a marvelous cook.

MARIANNE   Katarina's much better than I am.

KATARINA   The trouble is, Peter thinks I poison the food.

PETER   It's a standing joke in our house.

KATARINA   You do understand it's a joke, don't you?

PETER   A pretty sick one, if you ask me.

JOHAN *(Changing the subject)*   Shall we go into the living-room? There's coffee and cake for dessert.

MARIANNE   No, Katarina, please don't bother. The girls will clear the dishes and wash up. I've bribed them, you see. They like earning money. They're saving up for their summer vacation.

JOHAN   Would you like a cigar, Peter? I have some rather special ones.

PETER   No, thanks. I've given up smoking.

JOHAN   You don't say! Congratulations!

KATARINA   It has played such havoc with his nerves that I've begged him to start again. But now he won't smoke, just to annoy me. I can't stop, I've given up trying. I'll become as wrinkled as a mummy and I'll die of cancer, but never mind. Marianne dear, do you have an aspirin? I've had the most ghastly headache all day. No, I'll come with you. Then the boys can sit and exchange dirty stories in peace. (MARIANNE *and* KATARINA *go off to the bathroom, which is very elegant with marble and gilded taps, lots of mirrors, two sinks, and every imaginable luxury.* KATARINA *sits on the edge of the tub)* I only wanted to get away. I felt myself getting tipsy and then I'm awfully irritable. Poor Peter. It makes him feel like a cornered rat and he starts talking officialese and rolling his eyes.

MARIANNE   You can lie on the bed for a while if you like.

KATARINA No, it's all right. It's so quiet and peaceful here. You're kind, Marianne.

MARIANNE You both seem to be going through a bad stretch just now.

KATARINA (*With a laugh*) Yes, you could call it that.

MARIANNE Why don't you separate for a while?

KATARINA On the contrary, Marianne. We're going abroad on a long business trip. Our whole livelihood is based on our sticking together. We have everything together, you see. Peter has made over everything to me, and our business in

Italy depends entirely on what we do together. Then there are all these new synthetic materials that keep coming along and that we have to test. And I have to adjust my color schemes and patterns and Peter's so brilliant with his analyses. The whole lot would collapse if we split up. We just can't afford to.

MARIANNE   Then can't you work together and live your own private lives?

KATARINA   Do you think we haven't tried? You know that.

MARIANNE   Yes, that's true.

KATARINA   Peter says he's impotent with other women. I don't know whether he's lying, but I think he's telling the truth on that point. He goes nearly crazy if I refuse him. And the funny thing is that he's such a tender and expert lover. I quite enjoy having sex with him. Provided, of course, I have someone else.

MARIANNE   Then you don't now?

KATARINA   No. I've finished it off.

MARIANNE   You poor thing.

KATARINA   Jan couldn't cope with leading a double life. And leading a double life is the only thing I *can* cope with. So now all hell's broke loose, you see. Sometimes I hate Peter so much that I could torture him to death. When I can't sleep I lie thinking up the most extraordinary ways of tormenting him.
(*Laughs*)

MARIANNE   Is there no way out?

KATARINA   I can't see any.

MARIANNE　Have you talked to Peter?

KATARINA　How sweet you are.

MARIANNE　What does he say?

KATARINA　He says I can do whatever I damn well please. The only thing that interests him slightly is to see just how much we can degrade each other. He calls it our dehumanizing process.

MARIANNE　Do you think he needs a doctor?

KATARINA　He went and had himself analyzed for a while, but he got fed up and said the psychiatrist was an idiot.

MARIANNE　Can't you just walk out on him?

KATARINA　One morning when I woke up the bed was empty. Do you know where he'd gone?

MARIANNE　No.

KATARINA　He was standing out on the ledge, eight floors up, looking down into the street. When I asked him to come in, he said not to worry. I said I wished he would commit suicide. His reply to that was that I wasn't getting out of it all that easily.

MARIANNE　But wasn't there a time when things were good between you?

KATARINA　I'll tell you something that surprises even me. In the middle of it all I feel a hopeless affection for him. I think I understand his misery and disgust and panic and that aching void he feels. And I have an idea that in some strange way he knows things about me that no one else does. He says jokingly that I look like a woman but am a man inside.

(Laughs) In one way he's right. Shall we go back? I'm much better now.

(They rejoin JOHAN *and* PETER, *who have been playing chess in the living room. But* JOHAN *was soon beaten and both tired of it.* JOHAN *serves drinks of various kinds.* MARIANNE *lights a fire)*

PETER *(Rather drunk)*   Actually it's all too goddamn touching.

JOHAN   What is?

PETER   Your marriage. Johan and Marianne. Marianne and Johan. It's so moving it brings a lump to your throat. In fact it makes you want to stick a pin into your beautiful balloon. Skoal to you both!

KATARINA   You've been married for ten years, haven't you?

MARIANNE   We've just had our tenth anniversary.

PETER   And no skeletons in the closet.

JOHAN *(Laughs)* Well, you never know.

KATARINA   No, you never know.

MARIANNE   Both Johan and I like to keep things tidy.

PETER   Do you hear that, Katarina? We've been a bit too slov-
enly, you and I. But now we'll get down to it, won't we,
Katarina? Next week I'll call up Marianne and make an
appointment and she can arrange our divorce.

KATARINA *(Also rather drunk)*   Unfortunately Peter will have
changed his mind before he has sobered up. That's when the
calculating machine starts going clickety-clack. This is what
it says: I'll agree to a divorce if Katarina gives up her claim
on the assets in Switzerland. And my reply is: It's actually
my money. I'm the one who earned it. Then Peter answers
that he's the one who has multiplied it, and I can have the
whole goddamn factory. Thanks, I say, that's nice of you,
what do I want with a factory in Italy that gets to be more
and more of a gamble with every increase in labor costs? So
Peter says, well, you can take the whole damn kit and caboo-
dle in Sweden with apartment and country place and weekend cottage and boats and cars and paintings and stocks and
bonds. And I say, how sweet of you to let me shoulder a
gigantic load of taxable assets. I'm sorry to take up our nice
time together with such trivial matters, but when Peter
starts talking about settling, I know exactly how much he
has had to drink and exactly how much further it will go
before the insults.

PETER   It's just what I'm always saying. Katarina is a businessman, with equal stress on both words. What's more, she's a brilliant artist. What's more, she has an IQ of I don't know what. Pretty, too. She's a paragon, all gift-wrapped. How this monster of perfection has ever allowed me to get between her legs is a mystery.

KATARINA   I think we'll phone for a cab and go home now, Peter. It can't be very pleasant for Johan and Marianne to witness this scene.

PETER *(Carried away)*   Johan and Marianne have red ribbons around their tummies and big bows on their backs, just like the marzipan pigs of our childhood. It's very good for their morale to peep into the bottom-most pit of hell. I wonder whether there's anything more horrible than a husband and wife who hate each other? What do you think? Perhaps child abuse is worse. But then Katarina and I *are* two children, for Chrissake. Right inside Katarina a little girl's sitting and crying because she has fallen and hurt herself and no one has come to comfort her. And I'm sitting in the corner and haven't grown up, and am crying because Katarina can't love me even though I'm nasty to her.

KATARINA   There's one thing to be grateful for. And that is that you can be certain there's nothing worse than this. That's why I think we're ready for divorce.

PETER   Provided you listen to reason. Provided we simultaneously in each other's presence and together with reliable witnesses sign all the papers. So that one of us can't cheat the other. We'll call you this week.

MARIANNE   I'd be glad to help you. And we have an excellent business lawyer at the office. Borglund, you may have heard of him. He can help you with the financial arrangements.

PETER   Well, Katarina, what do you say?

KATARINA   Even if we agree about the money you'll never let me go. I know that.

PETER   Do you imagine you're so indispensable, my dear Katarina? What has suddenly given you that idea? It would be interesting to know. Do tell me.

KATARINA   At any rate, you force me to have sex with you, as you say you can't get an erection with any other woman.

PETER   Your need of a bad conscience is unlimited, and now that it's all over with Jan you're in rather a panic, aren't you, Katarina? You have only old Peter now to bother about you. He has the right kind of patience.

KATARINA   Oh, so you think you're the only one, do you? How touching. You think I have no one else. Let me tell you this, Peter—please excuse me, you two, if I'm rather outspoken, but Peter is asking for it and he needs a little information. I'll tell you this, Peter, you nauseate me so much, I mean physically, that I'd *buy* myself a lay anywhere at all just to wash you out of my sex organs.

PETER   *(Declaiming)*
"Abide with me; fast falls the eventide,
The darkness deepens; Lord with me abide . . ."

KATARINA   You son of a bitch—

PETER   *(Declaiming)*
"When other helpers fail, and comforts flee,
Help of the helpless, O abide with me."
(KATARINA *throws her glass of brandy at* PETER, *who bursts out laughing and dries himself with his handkerchief.* KATARINA *runs sobbing out of the room.* MARIANNE *hurries after her.* JOHAN *starts picking up the splinters of glass from the carpet)* I hope there won't be any stains on the carpet. I don't really know about brandy. If there are any, you can send me the bill. Could I

have some coffee? I'm plastered. Please excuse us, Johan. We don't usually behave like this. But you happen to be our friends. Our only friends. Forgive me. Forgive us. If you will call a cab, I'll take my maenad home and we'll go on with our little scene and finish it there. The finale isn't usually suitable for an audience.

———

Later that evening. The guests have gone.

JOHAN   What are you thinking about?

MARIANNE   Oh, lots of things.

JOHAN   Anything in particular?

MARIANNE   About Katarina and Peter, of course.

JOHAN   So am I.

MARIANNE   Do you think there is any way that two people can live together all their lives?

JOHAN   It's a damned absurd convention that we've inherited from I don't know what. People should have a five-year contract. Or one that is valid from year to year, so that they could give notice.

MARIANNE   Should *we* have one?

JOHAN   No, not us.

MARIANNE   Why not?

JOHAN   You and I are the exception that proves the rule.

We've drawn the winning ticket. In the big idiot lottery.

MARIANNE   So you think we'll live together all our lives?

JOHAN   What a funny question.

MARIANNE   Aren't you ever sorry that you won't sleep with anyone else but me?

JOHAN   Are you?

MARIANNE   Sometimes.

JOHAN   *(Astounded)*   I'll be damned.

MARIANNE   But it's a purely theoretical longing.

JOHAN   I wonder if there's something wrong with me, that I never have ideas like that. I'm content.

MARIANNE   So am I. Now I've got it!

JOHAN   What?

MARIANNE   Now I know why Katarina and Peter go through such hell.

JOHAN   Oh?

MARIANNE   They don't speak the same language. They must translate into a third language they both understand in order to get each other's meaning.

JOHAN   I think it's simpler than that.

MARIANNE   Think of us. We talk everything over and we understand each other instantly. We speak the same language. That's why we have such a good relationship.

JOHAN   I think it's the money.

MARIANNE   If they spoke the same language and trusted each other, as we do, the money wouldn't be a problem.

JOHAN   You and your languages.

MARIANNE   I'm always coming across it in my work. Sometimes it's as if husband and wife were making a long-distance call to one another on faulty telephones. Sometimes it's like hearing two tape recorders with preset programs. And sometimes it's the great silence of outer space. I don't know which is most horrible.

JOHAN   All the same, I'm not so sure.

MARIANNE   You always confuse the issue.

JOHAN   Suppose that you and I worked at a factory. Suppose we had the kids at a day nursery. That we worked in shifts, or something like that.

MARIANNE   It would make no difference.

JOHAN   I think it would.

MARIANNE   Those who speak the same language understand each other wherever they are.

JOHAN   It all sounds very romantic to me.

MARIANNE   Do you really think we'd be worse off together if we lived that kind of life? Do you mean that seriously?

JOHAN   Yes, I do. Seriously.

MARIANNE   That things would be worse between us?

JOHAN   Yes, I really mean it. Languages apart.

MARIANNE   Don't you think the danger of loneliness and estrangement is just as great in the life we live?

JOHAN   Definitely not. People doing heavy, dull work are exposed to a much greater strain. It goes without saying, Marianne!

MARIANNE   You're sillier than I thought. And it's you who are romantic.

JOHAN   We'll see.

MARIANNE *(Impatient)*   Oh? What will we see?

JOHAN   I don't know. Do you?

MARIANNE   You're teasing me.

JOHAN   Yes, I am. Aren't you hungry?

MARIANNE   Yes, terribly.

JOHAN   What about some beer and sandwiches?

MARIANNE   Sounds marvelous.

———

MARIANNE   Come and sit here on the sofa, Johan. There's something I must talk to you about. No, don't look so alarmed. It's nothing very serious.

JOHAN   I don't like the sound of this.

MARIANNE   Won't you have a brandy?

JOHAN   What about you?

MARIANNE   Yes, I think I will. You can pour me out one too.

JOHAN   Do you mind if I smoke?

MARIANNE   No, do. It doesn't matter in the least. I can stand it more now.

JOHAN   I think I'll sit down to this. Skoal.

MARIANNE   Skoal.

JOHAN   Well, what do you want to tell me?

MARIANNE   I'm pregnant.

JOHAN   That's what I said three weeks ago. And you denied it.

MARIANNE   I didn't want to worry you.

JOHAN   I'm not a bit worried.

MARIANNE   What are we going to do about it?

JOHAN   You mean you want an abortion?

MARIANNE   I want us to talk it over. Then we'll do what we've both decided.

JOHAN   I think it's for you to say.

MARIANNE   Why is it up to me?

JOHAN   Well, naturally. You'll have all the discomfort and the onus. Alternatively, the joy and the satisfaction.

MARIANNE   You mean it's all the same to you if we have another child?

JOHAN   I wouldn't put it like that.

MARIANNE   I want to know what you think. Give me a straight answer.

JOHAN   It's not so easy.

MARIANNE   Is it so hard to be honest?

JOHAN   You're being unreasonable now, Marianne.

MARIANNE   What was your first impulse?

JOHAN   It's not in my nature to have first impulses. In that respect I'm an invalid.

MARIANNE   Do you *want* another child?

JOHAN   I have no objections anyway. It might even be rather nice.

MARIANNE   But you can't pretend you're enthusiastic. Can you? Be honest now.

JOHAN   Christ, you keep harping on *my* being honest. Can't you tell me what *you* want instead? It would be much simpler.

MARIANNE   I happened to ask you.

JOHAN   I'm trying to think when we slipped up over the wretched kid. You've been on the pill the whole time. Or haven't you?

MARIANNE   I forgot to take it that time we were away.

JOHAN   Did you now. Why didn't you say so?

MARIANNE   I didn't think it mattered.

JOHAN   Did you do it on purpose?

MARIANNE   I don't know.

JOHAN   That's no answer.

MARIANNE   I suppose I thought, if I get pregnant now, then we're meant to have another child.

JOHAN   Oh my God! My God! My God!

MARIANNE   What's wrong?

JOHAN   And you're supposed to be a modern, efficient professional woman who is always going on about how important
family planning is. My God!

MARIANNE   I agree it's rather irrational.

JOHAN   Then you've made up your mind. And in that case
there's nothing to be done. Is there?

MARIANNE   I thought you might be pleased.

JOHAN   Oh yes, I'm quite pleased.

MARIANNE   It's the third month.

JOHAN   You haven't been sick at all.

MARIANNE   On the contrary. I've never felt so well.

JOHAN   Our mothers will be overjoyed, at any rate. What do
you think our daughters will say?

MARIANNE   Their tolerance is unlimited at the moment. So
one act of folly here or there on our part makes no difference. They will forgive us.

JOHAN   Well, well. Skoal, Marianne. And here's welcome to
him or her. You know, I'm quite beginning to look forward
to it. Besides, you're so pretty when you're big-bellied.
(A long silence ensues. Then MARIANNE *begins to weep.* JOHAN *looks
at her astonished)*   What's wrong now?

MARIANNE   Nothing.

JOHAN   There must be something.

MARIANNE No, nothing, really.

JOHAN Just what do you want yourself?

MARIANNE I don't know.

JOHAN What it really amounts to is that neither you nor I want any more children.

MARIANNE Do you think so?

JOHAN I think we're both appalled at the thought of a squalling brat and feedings and diapers and nursing and getting up at night and the whole damn circus. We like to think that's all behind us.

MARIANNE I have such a bad conscience.

JOHAN Why?

MARIANNE I have a bad conscience because first I go and long for a child and toy with the idea and look forward to it, and then, when it's a fact, I regret it no end. It doesn't make sense.

JOHAN Why must you be so moral about it all?

MARIANNE It's my fourth child, Johan. One died, and I take the life of another.

JOHAN Good God, you can't reason like that.

MARIANNE I do, anyway.

JOHAN It's a question of being practical.

MARIANNE No, it isn't.

JOHAN   What, then?

MARIANNE   It's a question of love.

JOHAN   Aren't you too worked up now?

MARIANNE   No.

JOHAN   Then can't you explain what you mean?

MARIANNE   No, I can't, because it's a feeling. It's as if I no longer felt I was real. You're not real either. Nor are the children. Then along comes this baby. *That*'s real.

JOHAN   You might say just the opposite.

MARIANNE   We're too comfortable, that's the trouble, and then we're left with our wretched cowardice and unreality and shame. And we have no affection either. And no love. And no joy. We could easily welcome this baby. And I think I was right in looking forward to it when I went around daydreaming about it. I had the right feeling. I'd be *ready* now to have a baby.

JOHAN   I don't know what you're talking about.

MARIANNE   No.

JOHAN   You speak as if you'd already had an abortion.

MARIANNE   In one way I have.

JOHAN   One can't blame oneself for thoughts.

MARIANNE   *(Shouting)*   This is serious, Johan. *The whole of our future's at stake.* Suppose we now do something irrevocable. Suppose it's crucial and we don't know it is.

JOHAN   What are these ridiculous, ghostly, intangible demands you're making? They're pure superstition.

MARIANNE   You don't understand.

JOHAN   No, I'm damned if I do understand a single word of what you've been saying.

MARIANNE   We're only trying to get out of it.

JOHAN   We're trying to avoid dramatic decisions and anything rash, if that's what you mean. And I think that's sensible. *(Gives* MARIANNE *a glum look)*

MARIANNE   You don't look so happy either.

JOHAN   This conversation makes me feel sick.

MARIANNE   Johan!

JOHAN   Yes?

MARIANNE   Couldn't we have this baby and look forward to it? Couldn't we spoil it a little and be fond of it just because we were careless about it?

JOHAN   I've already said it would be nice, so there's no need to harp on it. You're the one who has made it all so complicated. Not I.

MARIANNE   Let's make up our minds then.

JOHAN   About what?

MARIANNE   Let's decide to have another baby.

JOHAN   Well, that's that.

MARIANNE   I feel quite relieved.

JOHAN *(Kindly)*   There's nothing so strange about both wanting to and not wanting to.

MARIANNE   No, I suppose not.

JOHAN   If anything, it's the rule.

MARIANNE   Actually, it had nothing to do with the baby.

JOHAN   No, I suppose not.

MARIANNE   It had to do with you and me.

JOHAN   You're not still crying?

MARIANNE   I don't know what's the matter with me.

JOHAN   I think you need a brandy.

MARIANNE   Yes, I think I do.

———————

Some time later. MARIANNE *is lying in a bed.* JOHAN *comes in and sits down. He takes her hand.*

JOHAN   How do you feel?

MARIANNE   Oh, all right.

JOHAN   Was it difficult?

MARIANNE   Not particularly.

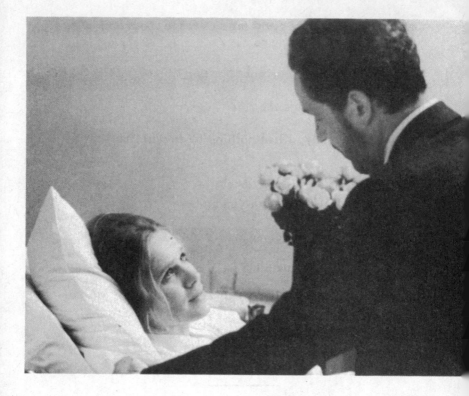

JOHAN   The doctor said you could come home tomorrow, or the day after at the latest.

MARIANNE   I'm going to sleep and sleep.

JOHAN   I thought you and I would go down to the country for a week when you're fit. I think I can take some time off after the tenth. I phoned your mother and asked if she'd mind looking after the girls and she was delighted. So that's no obstacle.

MARIANNE It *would* be rather nice.

JOHAN I had dinner with Göran and Sven yesterday. They think that Sture will be made ambassador to Pretoria of all places. I wonder what Aina will say to *that* appointment. What a blow to her pride! And imagine not being able to take tea with Princess Sibylla on Fridays. She'll never survive that.

MARIANNE When is it to be decided?

JOHAN Any day now.

MARIANNE By the way, have you phoned the Egermans at Högsätra and told them we can't come to dinner?

JOHAN No, I forgot. I'll do it right away.

MARIANNE Have you talked to our parents?

JOHAN I said that you had had a minor operation and that it was all rather sudden because the doctor was going abroad.

MARIANNE What did Mother say?

JOHAN She sniffled with sympathy and might be here any moment.

MARIANNE That's what I'm afraid of.

JOHAN If you like I'll call her up and ask her to come some other time. I can say you're asleep.

MARIANNE No, that will only make it worse.

JOHAN Is it hurting?

MARIANNE I'm just a little sore.

JOHAN   I thought we'd talk about the country house. Do you feel up to it? Or would you rather . . .

MARIANNE   Yes, of course I do.

JOHAN   What about building on a nice rustic veranda to the house? And painting it blue?

MARIANNE   Shouldn't we repaint the house too?

JOHAN   Yes, I did think of it. And sooner or later we must retile the roof. It won't last much longer.

MARIANNE   Can we afford it?

JOHAN   It won't cost an awful lot.

MARIANNE   You'd better speak to Gustav about it.

JOHAN   Yes, I'll have a word with Gustav.
(Silence)

MARIANNE   Johan.

JOHAN   Yes, darling?

MARIANNE   Hold my hand, will you?

JOHAN   Does that feel better?

MARIANNE   Yes.

JOHAN   Good.

MARIANNE   *(Whispering)*   Johan.

JOHAN   Yes?

MARIANNE   I feel such awful remorse. (JOHAN *makes no reply, holds her hand*) I can't tell you how awful.

JOHAN   You'll feel better tomorrow.

MARIANNE   *What have I done?*

JOHAN   There's no point in thinking like that.

MARIANNE   No.

JOHAN   In a few weeks you'll have forgotten all about it.

MARIANNE   Do you think so?

JOHAN   I'm quite sure you will.

MARIANNE   Johan.

JOHAN   Yes?

MARIANNE   I don't know how I shall get over it.

JOHAN   Won't you try and get some sleep?

MARIANNE   Yes.

JOHAN   I must go now anyway. Look after yourself.

MARIANNE   Bye-bye. Give my love to the girls.

JOHAN   Sleep well. If your mother comes, I'll ask the nurse to say you're asleep.

MARIANNE   Maybe it's just as well. You can try to call her. So she doesn't come all the way for nothing.

JOHAN   Yes, I will.

MARIANNE   You're so kind.

JOHAN   I'm glad you think so.

MARIANNE   We'll have a nice time in the country.

JOHAN   Eating and sleeping and watching TV. And not thinking.

MARIANNE   We'll sit and hold hands.

JOHAN   Sleep well.

MARIANNE   Don't forget to call up the Egermans.

JOHAN   No, I won't forget.
(MARIANNE *is left alone. She closes her eyes but can't get to sleep. She lies staring at the ceiling. Her eyes fill with tears. She sighs over and over again*)

SECOND SCENE

THE ART
OF SWEEPING
UNDER THE RUG

CHARACTERS

Johan
Marianne
Karin and Eva, their daughters
Mrs. Jacobi
Secretary
Eva

MARIANNE Good morning.

JOHAN Good morning.

MARIANNE Did you sleep well?

JOHAN Like a log. And you?

MARIANNE Oh, so-so. Stupidly I woke up at five o'clock and couldn't get back to sleep.

JOHAN Why not?

MARIANNE I lay there getting all worked up.

JOHAN Should I have a bad conscience?

MARIANNE For once you're not to blame, my darling. I lay fuming about that wretched Sunday dinner with my parents.

JOHAN But we always have Sunday dinner with our parents. Either yours or mine.

MARIANNE It's utterly absurd.

46

JOHAN   We do it for their sake.

MARIANNE   I'm going to call anyway and say we can't come.

JOHAN   Can't come! Whatever will your mother say?

MARIANNE   She can say what she darn well pleases. You and I are going to have a nice Sunday to ourselves together with the children.

JOHAN   Well, if you can accomplish *that!*

MARIANNE   I'm beginning to lose my temper.

JOHAN   Is it the curse?

MARIANNE   You always think it's that.

JOHAN   Well, isn't it?

MARIANNE   Even if my period *is* due on Monday, that's not necessarily why I feel like blowing my top.

JOHAN   But Marianne dear, what is it?

MARIANNE   Just think about it. Our life's mapped out into little squares—every day, every hour, every minute. And on every square it's written down what we're supposed to do. The squares are filled one by one and in good time. If there's suddenly an empty square we're dismayed and scrawl something onto it at once.

JOHAN   But we have our vacation.

MARIANNE   *(With a laugh)* Johan! You haven't a clue to what I mean. On our vacation we have more of a schedule than ever. It's all Mummy's fault, actually. And your mother's not much better.

JOHAN *(Laughing)*   What have the dear old ladies done wrong?

MARIANNE   You don't understand anyway, so there's no point talking about it.

JOHAN   Aren't you going to wake up the girls?

MARIANNE   No, they're having a late morning. Karin has the day off from school and Eva had rather a sore throat last night, so I thought I'd let her stay home. *(Angry)* So that she can come with us to dinner on Sunday. Otherwise there'll be a hell of a fuss with comments and questions. You must admit.

JOHAN   You were going to phone and say we can't come.

MARIANNE   I'd rather you did.

JOHAN   Oh no, thank you! I'm not getting tangled up in making excuses to your mother. You can do that yourself.

MARIANNE   Then I'm going to call up your sister and tell her I don't want to go with her to the fashion show on Friday. Then I'm going to send our regrets to the Bergmans about dinner on Friday. They'll be madly hurt but I don't give a damn. Then you can refuse the invitation to the Peruvian ambassador's cocktail party. And I have no intention of going to your mother's French course, nor am I going to the theater this evening. And you can take next week off and we'll go away somewhere together. *(With tears in her eyes)* Oh God, how stupid. This isn't the way to solve problems.

JOHAN *(Kindly)*   What is it you want then?

MARIANNE *(Shaking her head)*   I can't express it. We work hard, both of us. It isn't that. We're always meeting people. There's nothing wrong with that either. We spend time with our children as often as we can. That too is just as it should be. We hardly ever quarrel, and if we do we're sensible and listen to each other and make a valid compromise. Things couldn't be better.

JOHAN It sounds ideal.

MARIANNE It's troubling all the same.

JOHAN *(Smiling)* And our mothers are to blame.

MARIANNE Yes, I think so, though I can't prove it.

JOHAN   Then we can only express a pious wish that the dear ladies die as soon as possible.

MARIANNE *(Earnestly)*   Someone should have killed them long ago!

JOHAN   For that matter, doesn't the Bible say . . .

MARIANNE *(Absent-mindedly)*   Hmm? What does the Bible say?

JOHAN   "Therefore shall a man leave his father and his mother, and shall cleave unto his wife, and they shall be one flesh." Call up your mother now. She's a horribly early riser.

MARIANNE   Didn't we agree that *you* were going to make our excuses?

JOHAN   Oh no, my darling. Go on, call her. I'll hold your hand and be your moral support.

MARIANNE   All right, I will. Feel how my heart's pounding. But sooner or later we must take the first step.

JOHAN   The first faint cries of the great revolution. No answer? What a relief!

MARIANNE   Hello. Good morning, Miss Alm. Is Mother there? Oh, good. May I have a word with her? By the way, Miss Alm, how is your knee? Oh, not any better. Is it worse? Oh, I *am* sorry. What does the doctor say? Not much sympathy, eh? No, that's how it is these days. *(With a change of tone)* Good morning, Mummy. How are you? That's good to hear. Has Daddy gone yet? Oh yes, of course, he was going to the country. Can you let him go off on his own like that? Oh, Erik's with him. That's good. Er, Mummy, I have something to tell you. I'm awfully sorry, but . . . *(Long pause, while her mother speaks)* Yes, how did you guess? What are our reasons? I just want to be alone with Johan and the children

for a whole Sunday. No, we're not going anywhere. No, we just don't want to come to dinner. *(Her mother talks)* I don't think for a moment that Daddy was looking forward to Sunday dinner. *(Her mother talks)* Yes, but Mummy, it should be a pleasure, not a duty. *(Her mother talks)* Yes, I see. I see. I didn't know that. You didn't tell me. *(Her mother talks)* Bored stiff, to be quite honest. No, no, forget all about it, Mummy. No, no, please! *(Her mother talks)* We'll come as arranged. Yes, we'll manage. Yes, that's all right. Johan sends his love. Bye for now, Mummy dear.
(She puts down the phone)

JOHAN   The revolution was smothered at birth.

MARIANNE   Aunt Elsa was coming to dinner. She hasn't been up to town for over six months. And she was *particularly* looking forward to seeing us. And she was bringing a present for you. *(Angry)* Damnation!

JOHAN   And your mother had asked Mrs. Danielson to come and cook the dinner. And your father was *so* looking forward to seeing us.

MARIANNE   Hell and damnation!

JOHAN   I admire your pluck all the same. *(Kisses her)* We'll say no some other time. Don't upset yourself.

MARIANNE   Will you be home for dinner?

JOHAN   No, we'd better meet at the theater. Let's say twenty past seven at the righthand box office. I'll be there in plenty of time to pick up the tickets.

MARIANNE   It's a funny thing, you know.

JOHAN   What's funny?

MARIANNE   Do you like coming home?

JOHAN *(Kindly)*   Is everything so awfully complicated today?

MARIANNE   I'd like us to hide in bed and just hold each other tight and not get up for a whole week. And we'd both have a good cry.

JOHAN   We haven't chosen that sort of life.

MARIANNE   If only I were sure that it's we who have chosen, and not our mothers.

JOHAN   You're suffering from mother persecution mania.

MARIANNE   Did you *want* your life to be like this?

JOHAN   I think that life has the value you give it, neither more nor less. I refuse to live under the eye of eternity.

MARIANNE   Imagine if you and I started being unfaithful to each other.

JOHAN *(Embarrassed)*   Why, Marianne!

MARIANNE   I don't mean temporarily. But all the time. I mean if we seriously fell in love with someone else. What would you say?

JOHAN   I'd kill you of course.

MARIANNE *(With a sigh)*   Sometimes I wish . . .

JOHAN   What?

MARIANNE   Nothing. *(Kiss)* So long, darling!

JOHAN   So long!

MARIANNE Wait a second, Johan. I'll come with you.

JOHAN Wouldn't it be better if you took your own car?

MARIANNE No, I'm staying in town too. Then we'll drive home together after the theater this evening. It's much better.

JOHAN What about the girls?

MARIANNE Mrs. Andersson's coming to clean today. I'll phone home and ask her to give them something to eat. She makes wonderful pancakes. Wait, I'll just go in and wake up the children.

JOHAN But I'm in a hurry.

MARIANNE It won't take a minute.
(MARIANNE *hurries into the girls' room and is heard rousing two sleepy princesses on their peas.* JOHAN *picks up the phone but changes his mind and puts it down again. At the same moment* MARIANNE *is back. She has grabbed a briefcase and* JOHAN *helps her on with her coat. Then off they go. It is pouring rain*)

JOHAN I'll snatch a bite on the way to the theater.

MARIANNE Don't forget the dentist today at three o'clock. Last time—

JOHAN I forgot. I know, you've told me four times now. By the way, I have to leave the car to be serviced. One of the rear lights is broken.

MARIANNE I do enjoy driving with you. We should do it more often. Did it put you out my asking to come with you?

JOHAN I don't like improvisations, you know that.

MARIANNE   I'm just the opposite. Sometimes I'd like to take
the day just as it comes. Eat when I'm hungry, sleep when
I'm sleepy, make love when I feel desire. Perhaps even do
some work, when the mood strikes me. Sometimes I have an
irresistible urge just to drift, perhaps sink.

JOHAN   Who doesn't?

MARIANNE   *You.* You don't have that urge.

JOHAN   *(Sharply all of a sudden)*   How do you know?

MARIANNE   *(With a smile)*   No, my sweet, I think I know you
pretty well by now. You're far too methodical to get ideas
like that. You love everything neat and tidy.

JOHAN   So do you.

MARIANNE   I don't know. Do I?

JOHAN   You're as pedantic as they come.

MARIANNE   You don't say so.

JOHAN   You hate mental and physical untidiness.

MARIANNE   Oh, do I. Well, well.

JOHAN   So there.

MARIANNE   I'm not as certain as you are.

JOHAN   Of what?

MARIANNE   Who I really am.

JOHAN   Before I forget, for goodness' sake pay your parking
tickets. You have a whole sheaf of them in the car now. It's
quite unnecessary.

MARIANNE   Yes, sir. Heavens, what a downpour. I should have brought an umbrella. And I don't have the right shoes either.

JOHAN   Well, here we are.
(The lawyers' office is on a small, quiet street. MARIANNE *gives her husband a peck on the cheek and gets out of the car.* JOHAN *waves to her and drives off. It's raining heavily and* MARIANNE *hurries into the doorway and up the stairs of the dignified old house with its gleaming banisters, stained-glass staircase windows, and heavy marble walls. She nods to the secretary and the day's first client, who is already sitting waiting. Once inside her room she changes her shoes, hangs up her jacket, and puts on a sweater. She asks the client to come in)*

MARIANNE   How do you do, Mrs. Jacobi. Please sit down. At this first meeting we usually try just to pose the actual problem. Then we'll see how we can solve it.

MRS. JACOBI   I want a divorce.

MARIANNE   How long have you been married?

MRS. JACOBI   I've been married for twenty years.

MARIANNE   Have you worked outside your home?

MRS. JACOBI   No, I've been a housewife, as it's called.

MARIANNE   How many children do you have?

MRS. JACOBI   We have three children. They're grown up now. The youngest is doing his national service. The oldest, a girl, is married and the younger girl is in college and doesn't live at home.

MARIANNE   Then you're alone now?

MRS. JACOBI   I have my husband, of course.

MARIANNE *(Smiling)*   Of course. Is he at home all the time?

MRS. JACOBI   No, he's a schoolteacher.

MARIANNE   Why do you want a divorce?

MRS. JACOBI   It's a loveless marriage.

MARIANNE   Is *that* your reason?

MRS. JACOBI   Yes.

MARIANNE *(Cautiously)*   But you've been married for such a long time. Has it always been like that, or . . .

MRS. JACOBI   Yes, it has always been like that.

MARIANNE   And now that the children have left home you want to break away. Is that right?

MRS. JACOBI   My husband is very dependable. I have no fault to find with him. He is kind and conscientious. He has been an excellent father. We have never quarreled. We have a nice apartment and a pleasant old house in the country that was left to us by his mother. We're both interested in music and are members of a chamber music society—we play together ourselves.

MARIANNE   It all sounds ideal.

MRS. JACOBI   Yes, doesn't it. But there is no love in the marriage. There never has been.

MARIANNE   Forgive my asking: Have you by any chance met another man?

MRS. JACOBI   No, I haven't.

MARIANNE   And your husband?

MRS. JACOBI   As far as I know he has never been unfaithful.

MARIANNE   Won't it be rather lonely?

MRS. JACOBI   Yes, very likely. But I prefer that loneliness to living in a marriage without love.

MARIANNE   Please forgive another question. What form does this lovelessness take?

MRS. JACOBI   It doesn't take any form.

MARIANNE   Then I don't understand.

MRS. JACOBI   No, it's hard to explain.

MARIANNE   Have you told your husband that you want a divorce?

MRS. JACOBI   Naturally. Fifteen years ago I told him that I didn't want to live with him any longer, as there was no love in our marriage. He was very understanding. He merely asked me to wait for the divorce until the children were grown up. Now all three have grown up and left home. So now I can get my divorce.

MARIANNE   And what does your husband say?

MRS. JACOBI   He wants me to think it over carefully. He has asked me hundreds of times what is wrong with our marriage, that I want to leave him. I've told him it's impossible to continue a relationship in which there is no love. Then he asks me what this love is supposed to consist of. And I've answered him a hundred times that I don't know, for it's impossible to describe something that doesn't exist.

MARIANNE   Have you been on good terms with your children?
I mean emotionally.

MRS. JACOBI   I have never loved my children. I know that for
sure. But I've been quite a good mother all the same. I've
done all I could, although I've never actually felt anything
for them. *(Smiles)* I know just what you're thinking.

MARIANNE *(Caught)*   Oh, really? Are you a mind reader?

MRS. JACOBI   You're thinking: That Mrs. Jacobi is a spoiled
woman if ever I saw one. She has everything one could wish
for in this world but never stops feeling sorry for herself and
fussing about something vague and remote which she calls
love. There are other things, after all: comradeship, loyalty,
affection, friendship, wellbeing, security.

MARIANNE   I *was* perhaps thinking something of the kind.

MRS. JACOBI   Let me tell you something. I go around with a
mental picture of myself. And it doesn't tally on a single
point with reality.

MARIANNE   May I ask a personal question, Mrs. Jacobi? Isn't
it true of love that . . .

MRS. JACOBI   What were you going to say?

MARIANNE   I don't know.

MRS. JACOBI   I tell myself that I have the capacity for love, but
it's all bottled up inside me. The trouble is that the life I have
lived up to now has just stifled my potentialities more and
more. At last I must do something about it. So my first step
must be to get a divorce. I think my husband and I are
hindering each other in a—fatal way.

MARIANNE   It sounds frightening.

MRS. JACOBI   It *is* frightening. Something most peculiar is happening: my senses—I mean feeling, sight, hearing—are starting to fail me. For instance, I can say that this table is a table, I can see it, I can touch it. But the sensation is thin and dry, if you can understand.

MARIANNE *(Suddenly)*   I think I do.

MRS. JACOBI   It's the same with everything else. Music, scents, people's faces and voices. Everything's getting meaner and grayer, with no dignity.

MARIANNE   Do you think now that you will meet some other man?

MRS. JACOBI *(With a smile)*   No, I don't. I have no illusions.

MARIANNE   Can you make your husband understand this breaking away?

MRS. JACOBI   He only gets bitter and bad-tempered and says I'm romantic and silly and suffering from change of life.

MARIANNE   The best thing would be if you could get your husband to agree willingly to a divorce.

MRS. JACOBI   He says he's refusing for my sake. I'll regret it, he says.

MARIANNE   But you've made up your mind?

MRS. JACOBI   I have no choice. Do you understand what I mean?

MARIANNE *(Evasively)*   I think so. *(Suddenly Marianne remembers something and asks Mrs. Jacobi to excuse her for a moment. She goes into the outer office and makes a call on the secretary's phone. Johan answers)* Hello. Sorry to disturb you.

JOHAN   It doesn't matter.

MARIANNE   I wondered if we could have lunch together.

JOHAN   Yes, if you like. I'm going to just grab a sandwich at twelve thirty.

MARIANNE   Where is it you usually go? The grill bar, isn't it? I'll see you there just after twelve thirty. Bye!

———

JOHAN *in the laboratory. He is standing on a small metal stepladder, photographing hit values on square white cardboard targets. The telephone rings. He mutters an oath, gets down reluctantly, and answers.*

JOHAN   Hello. Yes, speaking. Why, hello, Mother, I didn't hear it was you at first, the phone's crackling. Oh, I'm fine. How are you? You're worried? What do you mean by that? Has Marianne's mother called? Now what's all this. Is she worried too? Good heavens! No, no, no, I assure you. Everything's just fine with Marianne and me. We're strong and healthy and cheerful and optimistic and madly happy together. Nothing whatever has happened. I swear. Mother dear, don't *worry*. Your intuition? Well, it has led you astray this time, I can assure you. Everything is just fine between Marianne and me. I think you ought to call up Marianne's mother and tell her she ought to know better than to gossip with you on the phone. Look, Mother, I'm in rather a hurry just now. Yes, yes, I'll see you soon. We'll drop by on Friday as agreed. Give my love to Father. *(Hangs up)* Phew! Hell and damnation! *(He climbs up the ladder and resumes work. There is a knock at the door)* Come in.

EVA   Hello.

JOHAN   Hello.

EVA   Am I disturbing you?

JOHAN   Yes, but I'm glad of it.

EVA   I just wanted to see what you're up to. I've heard the most extraordinary rumors about your doings. *(Looks about her)* Whatever is all this? It does look mysterious.

JOHAN   Shouldn't you be in Lund?

EVA   Yes, by rights. But the students are demonstrating for some deserving cause or other, so the lectures were canceled.

JOHAN   How nice.

EVA   Yes, so here I am. Just what are you up to? Do tell me.

JOHAN   Look for yourself.

EVA   What do I do?

JOHAN   Take this pen in your right hand. When I put the light out you'll see a brightly shining fixed dot on the wall in front of you. Try to touch it with the point of the pen. If you miss it you must draw a line until you reach it. This TV camera will register your efforts on a monitor. Off you go. *(The experiment is carried out. Toward the end* EVA *is quite annoyed at not hitting the dot)*

EVA   I've had enough of this. Please put the light on.

JOHAN   Aren't you cross!

EVA   Well, it was a bit nerve-racking.

JOHAN   Yes, it does get on your nerves. Funny, isn't it? Look at this—you've wandered all over the place, getting more and more irritated.

EVA   Hmm. And what do we learn from all this?

JOHAN   That remains to be seen. This is only the beginning.

EVA   Oh. I'd like a cigarette.

JOHAN   Sit down.

EVA   I've stopped smoking for six days now. It's awful.

JOHAN   Having abstinence trouble, eh?

EVA   Stefan's away, my friends shun me. I suspect I'll start again but I'll try to stick it out a bit longer.

JOHAN   Go on, have one now. Broméus forgot these when he was in here spying yesterday. There now.

EVA   *(Sighs, takes a cigarette, lights it, inhales luxuriously)* Oh, that's heaven. God, what bliss! Now I feel better.

JOHAN   Now you'll have a bad conscience and that's nice too. One must seize every chance of enjoyment these days. *(With a smile)* Well?

EVA   Actually, that's why I came.

JOHAN   That's good of you.

EVA   I sat down yesterday afternoon and read your poems very carefully twice.

JOHAN   And?

EVA   I couldn't make head or tail of them.

JOHAN   Was that so strange?

EVA   On the contrary.

JOHAN   It wasn't strange?
(*Smiles ruefully*)

EVA   I don't know, maybe I'm wrong. Has Marianne read the poems?

JOHAN   No, you're the only one I've shown them to. Marianne's not interested in poetry.

EVA   But she ought to be interested in you.

JOHAN   (*Crossly*)   Oh, she is, but not quite in that way.

EVA   (*Looks at him with a smile*)   Oh, I see. No.

JOHAN   Well, what's so odd about it? You and I have known each other since we were students. We're not lovers. From you I can get an objective opinion before going to a publisher and trying to get the poems printed.

EVA   I wouldn't if I were you.

JOHAN   Wouldn't what?

EVA   Go to a publisher.

JOHAN   Are they as bad as that?

EVA   It's not that they're bad, Johan. If only they *were*, I was going to say.

JOHAN   You mean they're mediocre? (EVA *sighs*) You mean that they're insipid and neat and puerile. You mean that it's just a private gripe. A little mental masturbation.

EVA   I'll tell you something.

JOHAN   Well?

EVA   There were several of us in our set who thought you were going to make a name for yourself. We thought you were phenomenal. You left us all behind and we admired you, even envied you.

JOHAN   What does that have to do with the poems?

EVA   I don't know. It was just a thought.

JOHAN   I have no cause for complaint.

EVA   Well, that's just fine then.

JOHAN   Are you sure you didn't read the poems under the influence of your nicotine craving? You're pretty nervy just now.

EVA   It's quite possible. ·

JOHAN   Don't you think that the whole of this unpleasant situation is caused by your not having smoked for six days?

EVA   Yes, I suppose so.
    (Gives a friendly smile)

JOHAN   I'm going to let others read my poems before I scrap them.

EVA   Why, Johan my dear, of course!

JOHAN   I'm going to send them to several different publishers, to make quite sure of their mediocrity.

EVA   You've really taken offence, haven't you?

JOHAN   You bet I have!

EVA   I'm sorry.

JOHAN   Anyway, there's *one* person who likes my poems.

EVA   Oh, who's that?

JOHAN   That made you curious, eh?

EVA   Well then, Johan. One for, one against. Don't take any notice of what I said. Let's say it's just nicotine craving. Bye-bye, my dear. I'll leave the manuscript with the door-man. My regards to Marianne. *(Turns)* Remember, I'll stick by you through thick and thin. Bye!

JOHAN   Bye-bye.
(EVA *goes out, leaving* JOHAN *alone in his laboratory. He reaches for the telephone but checks himself. Resumes his photographing)*

The grill bar is poky and crowded. JOHAN *and* MARIANNE *have found an apology for a table by a window.*

MARIANNE   It's ages since we had lunch together. How nice.

JOHAN   And what brings you?

MARIANNE   I think you and I ought to go away together next summer. We've arranged to take our vacation at the same time, so it would be a good idea to go abroad. I popped into one or two travel agents and got all these brochures—look. As long as you book early you can join a cheap package tour. Then once you get there you can do just as you like. It's just that the actual trip is much cheaper.

JOHAN   You mean, we wouldn't be down in the country at all?

MARIANNE   We can be there all the spring and fall.

JOHAN   Where did you think of going?

MARIANNE   Anywhere. We've never been to Florence, for instance. Or what about the Black Sea? That's an idea. Or Africa? There are some fantastically cheap trips to Morocco. Or Japan. Suppose we went to Japan!

JOHAN   Why this sudden urge to travel?

MARIANNE *(Pause)*   Don't *you* think it would be fun? Just to go off like that?

JOHAN   I don't know.

MARIANNE   Then let's forget it.
    (Gathers up the brochures)

JOHAN   Are you disappointed?

MARIANNE   When you're in a bad mood you always come out with a very funny accusation: You say I couldn't care less about our marriage. Isn't that what you say? Well, now I *am* caring about it.

JOHAN   How thoughtful of you.

MARIANNE   Why the sarcasm?

JOHAN   It's not sarcasm at all. I do think it's thoughtful. It's just that I don't think I want to trail around foreign parts in the blazing heat. When I could be sitting in a boat fishing.

MARIANNE   It'll all be the same as usual then.

JOHAN   Why not send the children to your sister? That would be a big relief.

MARIANNE   Not if we stay at home.

JOHAN   Why not?

MARIANNE   It would look awfully funny.

JOHAN   So what?

MARIANNE   It won't do. And what do you think Mother would say? She'd grumble and fuss and we'd never hear the end of it. Besides, the children would also think it was funny. Of course, we could ask Valborg to look after them for a week, or ten days at the most, but certainly no more.

JOHAN   Must we be so dependent on what everyone thinks?

MARIANNE   I don't understand what you're getting at.

JOHAN   Marianne . . .

MARIANNE *(Serious suddenly)*   Yes, Johan.

JOHAN   Do you think life is dull?

MARIANNE   No. What a question! Do you?

JOHAN   I don't know. I've never thought in those terms.

MARIANNE   I still think life's exciting.

JOHAN *(Looking at her)*   You *are* pretty, you know.

MARIANNE   With my hair in a mess, and this awful old jumper, and no make-up . . .

JOHAN   Marianne!

MARIANNE   Is there something you want to tell me?

JOHAN   Can the scheme of things be so treacherous that life suddenly goes wrong? Without your knowing how it happens. Almost imperceptibly.

MARIANNE *(Softly)*   Do you mean us?

JOHAN   Is it a matter of choosing, and making the wrong choice? Or of jogging along in the same old rut without thinking. Until you lie there on the garbage dump.

MARIANNE *(Searchingly)*   Has something happened, Johan?

JOHAN   Nothing. Absolutely nothing. I swear.

MARIANNE   We're pretty honest with each other, you and I. Aren't we?

JOHAN   I think so.

MARIANNE   It's awful to go around bottling things up. One must speak out, however painful it is. Don't you think?

JOHAN *(Irritably)*   Hell, yes. What time is it?

MARIANNE   One fifteen.

JOHAN   My watch is always stopping. What were you saying? Oh yes, honesty. I suppose you mean over sex, to put it bluntly.

MARIANNE   Sometimes I think we . . .

JOHAN   People can't always live cheek by jowl. It would be too tiring.

MARIANNE   Yes, *that* is the big question.

JOHAN   Anyway, I must go now.

MARIANNE   I'll take a little walk. I have to buy some new slacks for Karin, too.

JOHAN   Good Lord, you bought a pair last week.

MARIANNE   Those were for Eva.

JOHAN   Can't their clothes be handed down? It certainly had to be done in my childhood.

MARIANNE   Well, it's not done nowadays, you see, my poor darling. Bye-bye, see you at the theater.

JOHAN   Yes.

MARIANNE   *(Suddenly)*   I'm so fond of you, do you know that? Do you know that I'm dead scared of losing you? I ought to say nice things to you much more often, I know they mean a lot to you. I'm not very good at it, I'm afraid. I'll try to improve. You're so kind. And I'm very, very fond of you.

JOHAN   I'll try to remember that.

MARIANNE   So long, and drive carefully.

MARIANNE *and* JOHAN *are on their way home in the car after having been to a performance of Ibsen's* A Doll's House.

JOHAN   Now for a sandwich and some beer. Having to skip

dinner like that and bolt a hot dog before struggling through a whole evening of Ibsen is enough to kill anyone.

MARIANNE I thought Nora was good.

JOHAN Yes, but the play damn well creaks. Even Strindberg thought so.

MARIANNE He was just jealous.

JOHAN A few things have happened during the last hundred years, after all. Though not in the way Ibsen hoped.

MARIANNE Have they?

JOHAN *(Laughs and yawns)* Feminism is a worn-out subject, Marianne. Women nowadays can do whatever they like. The trouble is they can't be bothered.

MARIANNE *(Smiles)* Oh, that's interesting!

JOHAN Women pose as martyrs. It's much more convenient. And above all it involves no responsibility when things get hot. I always thought there was something absurd and pathetic about suffragettes, and now Women's Lib. Especially when they try to put some life into their sisters. A parochial, ineffectual, moronic mob who brainwash themselves from birth. It's too damn heartbreaking for words.

MARIANNE We're only starting. Just you wait and see.

JOHAN I'll never see anything. There are a couple of middle-aged women at my office who have been sharing the same room for donkey's years. They still address each other as Miss Schoultz and Mrs. Palmgren, and they seize every opportunity of sabotaging each other or running one another down.

MARIANNE   That was a telling argument.

JOHAN   Have you ever heard of a female symphony orchestra? Imagine a hundred and ten women with menstrual
trouble trying to play Rossini's overture to *The Thieving
Magpie.*

MARIANNE   Lucky no one can hear you.

JOHAN   Women are crazy. Imagine a regular goddamn carcass
of a man, an alcoholic, rotten to the core and ready to end
it all. I bet you anything that around the remains of this
swine a lot of fantastic women will hover like big white
birds. The carcass stinks, he ill-treats them—it makes no
difference. It's one glorious combination of greedily spar-
kling eyes, rosy cheeks, and a general air of martyrdom.
Some idiot of a man who was champion of women's rights
—I think it was a progressive bishop, at that—made out that
women have been tyrannized for so long that they have at
last accepted their degradation.

MARIANNE   *(With a smile)*   Yes, that was very stupid.

JOHAN   Women pinched the best part at the outset. You bet
your sweet life they're not giving it up now that they've
learned to play it to perfection. Besides, they've achieved
what they've always been after: man's collective bad conscience, which gives them unbelievable advantages without their having to lift a finger. What do women want in
parliament or in the government? It would only force
them to share a responsibility. They would lose their
comfortable role of opposition. They would have to get
rid of their pet vices: bringing up children and letting
themselves be supported and oppressed. I heard one
woman say, "But don't we women have a very special
talent for affection?" I was too polite to laugh. But those
are the kind of propaganda slogans you women use when

you want to wriggle out of a tricky situation. What I'd
like to ask is this: Don't women have a very special talent
for cruelty, brutality, vulgarity, and ruthlessness? *(Laughs)*
I don't mean a word of what I say, and anyway I
couldn't care less about it.

———————

Beer and sandwiches are on the kitchen table. MARIANNE *has taken off
her best black dress and put on a white dressing gown made of Turkish
toweling.* JOHAN *is sitting in his shirtsleeves.*

MARIANNE   When I got back to the office this afternoon, Elsa
—you know, our secretary—was crying on a sofa. Her nose
was bleeding and she had a nasty bruise over one eye. She
had been attacked in the street by three teen-age louts. In
broad daylight. People had stood around watching and
never lifted a finger to help. Then a couple of bored-looking
police came along and asked questions and told Elsa off for
going around with her salary in her pocketbook. They more
or less implied that it was her own fault.

JOHAN   Sometimes you feel that the whole community is going to the dogs.

MARIANNE   When we were younger we were so hopeful.

JOHAN   Do you remember when our parents practically
turned us out because we joined the May Day procession?

MARIANNE   And we used to go in for amateur dramatics.

JOHAN   You were more religious than I was.

MARIANNE   And you accused me of neglecting my home.

JOHAN   That was the winter when we all had the Asian flu.

And you tried to crawl off to your political meetings, and on top of that insisted you could manage the kids without help *and* run the house *and* hold down a job. *That* was a quarrel.

MARIANNE Then we gave it up. *(Pause)* It was fun while it lasted.

JOHAN Yes, I suppose it was.

MARIANNE We believed in humanity's future, anyway.

JOHAN It's always nice to have a belief, I grant you. Besides, we had the pleasure of annoying our parents, and that meant a lot. You weren't even-tempered in those days. Cute and hot-tempered. In fact, you were damned attractive as a socialist.

MARIANNE Aren't I now?

JOHAN What?

MARIANNE Damned attractive.

JOHAN Yes, of course you're attractive. Why?

MARIANNE I've also been thinking about it.

JOHAN Must it always be that two people who live together for a long time begin to tire of each other?

MARIANNE We haven't tired.

JOHAN Almost.

MARIANNE *(Indulgently)* We work too hard—that's what's so banal. And in the evenings we're too tired.

JOHAN   Marianne, that wasn't a reproach.

MARIANNE   I'm not so sure.

JOHAN   Word of honor.

MARIANNE   But we like each other in every way.

JOHAN   Not in that way. Not very much anyhow.

MARIANNE   Oh yes, we do.

JOHAN   It's just that our life together has become full of evasions and restrictions and refusals.

MARIANNE *(Hurt)*   I can't help it if I don't enjoy it as much as I used to. I can't help it. There's a perfectly natural explanation. You're not to accuse me and give me a bad conscience about this.

JOHAN *(Kind)*   You needn't get so upset!

MARIANNE   I think it's all right as it is. God knows it isn't passionate, but you can't expect everything. There are those who are much worse off than we are.

JOHAN   Without a doubt.

MARIANNE   Sex isn't everything. As a matter of fact.

JOHAN *(Laughing)*   Why, Marianne!

MARIANNE *(On the verge of tears)*   If you're not satisfied with my performance you'd better get yourself a mistress who is more imaginative and sexually exciting. I do my best, I'm sure.

JOHAN *(Sourly)*   There we have it.

MARIANNE   You've got that look again.

JOHAN   I haven't got any look.

MARIANNE   That look and that tone of voice. Whatever it is you're brooding about, come out with it.

JOHAN   It's no use. You lose your temper at whatever I say on this subject.

MARIANNE   No, I promise. I'm listening. Quite objectively.

JOHAN   Sometimes I wonder why we complicate this problem so frightfully. This business of lovemaking is pretty elementary, after all. It was surely never meant to be a huge problem overshadowing everything else. It's all your mother's fault, if you ask me. Though you don't like my saying so.

MARIANNE   I just think it's so damn superficial of you to talk like that.

JOHAN   Don't be so sour, Marianne. I'm being kind.

MARIANNE   All the same, you think it's my fault that we don't enjoy it any more.

JOHAN   You said just now that you do your best.

MARIANNE   Yes, indeed I do. I do, Johan.

JOHAN   Can't you hear yourself how awful that sounds?

MARIANNE   So you think I'm lying?

JOHAN   No, for Christ's sake! No! No!

MARIANNE   Then I don't understand.

JOHAN   Let's drop this subject now and go to bed. It's late anyway.

MARIANNE   Isn't that just like you. First you start a huge discussion and then, having got me all worked up, you yawn and say you're sleepy and want to go to bed.

JOHAN   Marianne! (Pause) You suffer from devastatingly high standards. We've often joked about it. Sometimes we've quarreled about it too. But can't our poor sex life be spared your ambitions.

MARIANNE *(In tears)*   Why must you always wrangle with me on this particular point? First you abuse me for not trying, and then you abuse me because I exert myself.

JOHAN *(Gently)*   Now look what I've gone and done.

MARIANNE   Yes, haven't you. Can't you be nice and kind instead. It would help a lot more.

JOHAN   Yes. *(Giving in)* There, there, sweetheart, don't be upset. It was silly of me to bring all this up.

MARIANNE   Let me tell you this. You can talk too much about these things.

JOHAN *(Giving in)*   I suspect you're right.

MARIANNE   I know you're supposed to tell everything and not keep anything secret, but in this particular matter I think it's wrong.

JOHAN *(Who has heard this before)*   Yes, you're probably right.

MARIANNE *(Following up her advantage)*   There are things which must be allowed to live their life in a half-light, away from prying eyes.

JOHAN *(Total retreat)*   You think so?

MARIANNE   I'm quite convinced of it. We upset and hurt each other all to no purpose when we carry on like this. And all the barbs are still there when we get into bed. My God, it's like lying on a bed of nails.

JOHAN *(Laughing)*   Ha . . .

MARIANNE *(Suspicious)*   What are you laughing at?

JOHAN   The bed of nails.

MARIANNE *(More graciously)*   It's all very well for you to laugh.

JOHAN   Can't we go to bed now?

MARIANNE   You must admit you've been unusually stupid and cocky and tactless.

JOHAN   I apologize.

MARIANNE   Do you think I don't give you enough affection?

JOHAN   Affection takes time.

MARIANNE   Then you *don't* get enough.

JOHAN   *We* don't get enough. And don't give enough.

MARIANNE   That's why I wanted us to go away together this summer.

JOHAN   I don't think affection should be kept only for vacations.

MARIANNE *(Kissing him)*   You're kind anyway, even if you *are* an idiot.

JOHAN   Then it's lucky I'm married to you.

MARIANNE *(Kissing him)*   You have your great moments, but in-between you're horribly mediocre.

JOHAN   At our age tens of thousands of brain cells snuff out every day. And they're never replaced.

MARIANNE *(Kissing him)*   With you it must be ten times as many, you're so silly.

JOHAN   You're sweet even if you do scold and make a fuss. *(He kisses her and touches her breasts. She moves his hand gently away. He gives a short laugh, stands up, and yawns. MARIANNE smiles a little guiltily)* I'm nearly asleep.

MARIANNE   I'll just look in on the children.
(When she goes into the girls' room she sees that KARIN is lying awake, silent and unmoving) Why, Kajsa! Aren't you asleep?

KARIN   No.

MARIANNE   Why not?

KARIN   I'm afraid to sleep, I have such nasty dreams.

MARIANNE   What sort of dreams?

KARIN   Every time I go to sleep I dream there's a war.

MARIANNE   Would you like a glass of milk?

KARIN   Yes, please.
(MARIANNE goes out into the kitchen and gets a glass of milk. When she comes back KARIN has fallen asleep. She puts the glass on the bedside table and tiptoes out of the room, leaving the door ajar. JOHAN is already lying in their big double bed. He is wearing glasses and reading. She too picks up a book, puts on her glasses, takes a sip of water, swallows a little pill, and snuggles down. Soon afterward JOHAN puts his light out. MARIANNE switches hers off too)

JOHAN   Good night.

MARIANNE   Good night, darling.

JOHAN   Have you set the alarm?

MARIANNE   Yes, I actually remembered. *(Pause)* Johan! If you'd like to make love I . . .

JOHAN   Thanks for the offer, but I'm nearly asleep. Good night, darling.

MARIANNE   Good night. Sleep well.

THIRD SCENE

PAULA

CHARACTERS

Marianne
Johan
Karin and Eva, their daughters

The house in the country. Late evening.

MARIANNE *has gone to bed and is almost asleep. When she hears the car drive up she is wide awake and immediately gay. She leaps out of bed and rushes downstairs in nothing but her nightie.* JOHAN *enters from the veranda and puts down his little bag.*

Before he has time to take his coat off, she flings her arms around his neck, hugs him, and gives him four loud kisses.

MARIANNE Here already! You weren't coming until tomorrow. What a lovely surprise. Are you hungry? And me with my hair in curlers. How good of you to come this evening. The children are asleep, we went to bed early. There was nothing on TV and we thought it would be nice to have an early night. The girls and I have been dieting today. Would you like an omelet or a sandwich and some beer?

JOHAN That sounds good.

MARIANNE Or would you like a real meal? Shall I fry some eggs and bacon? Or heat some soup?

JOHAN Sandwiches and beer are fine. While I think of it, I have a message from Peter and Katarina. They're going to call you up on Monday at the office.

MARIANNE That's a long and nerve-racking business, poor things.

JOHAN   *Are* they getting divorced? It seems to me as if they don't know what they want to do.

MARIANNE   Do you think that's so strange? I've asked them to each get a lawyer, but they won't. Why not get undressed and I'll bring the tray up to the bedroom.

JOHAN   No, I'd rather sit in the kitchen.

MARIANNE   And here I've been worrying that you were angry with me.

JOHAN   Why should I be angry with you?

MARIANNE   You know quite well! I was beastly on the phone last night.

JOHAN   Oh, that! That was nothing.

MARIANNE   I called you right back, but you must have pulled the plug out.

JOHAN   I was pretty tired last night. I'd been out all day at the institute with that zombie from the ministry. You wonder sometimes who these idiots are who sit on the state money-bags and determine our weal and woe.

MARIANNE   I still think I was nasty to you last night. I really do.

JOHAN   Can't we just forget it?

MARIANNE   You *are* funny, you never finish talking about anything. I won't be long-winded, darling. All I want to say is that I think you're right. And I'm right too. In a different way. If you don't want to go out to dinner in a tuxedo, then that's your business. You're right there. On the other hand, I do think you could get yourself a new tuxedo.

JOHAN   I don't like tuxedos. I hate wearing a tuxedo. I think it's an idiotic get-up. I feel like a dressed-up chimpanzee in a tuxedo.

MARIANNE   Yes, I remember you said that. *(Laughs)* Well, let's not start quarreling again. I love you, even if you won't dress up in a tuxedo. It's not absolutely essential to our marriage.

JOHAN   It seemed like it last night.

MARIANNE   I told you I was wrong. God, I am getting hungry watching you eat. I'll simply have to have a sandwich. It can't be helped. I'm dizzy with hunger. I've lost over four pounds this last week. Does it show?

JOHAN   No.

MARIANNE   I feel it anyway, let me tell you. Sometimes everything seems utterly pointless. Why should we grudge ourselves all the good things in the world? Why can't we be big and fat and good-tempered? Just think how nice it would make us. Do you remember Aunt Miriam and Uncle David? They were perfect dears and got along so well together, and they were so *fat!* And every night they lay there in the big creaky double bed, holding hands and content with each other just as they were, fat and cheerful. Couldn't you and I be like Aunt Miriam and Uncle David and go around looking comfortable and safe? Shall I take my curlers out?

JOHAN   Don't mind me.

MARIANNE   Yes, I will. I know you don't like them. No, let's leave the washing up. Come on, darling, let's go to bed. You must be awfully tired and I'm a bit drowsy too, though I slept for a while before you came. What is it, Johan? Are you worried about something? Has something happened? What's wrong? Tell me what it is.

JOHAN   I came here this evening to tell you something. I've gone and fallen in love, you see. It's quite absurd and maybe it's all a goddamn mistake. It probably is a goddamn mistake. I met her during the convention in June. She was the interpreter and secretary. Actually, she's studying for her degree. She's going to teach Slavic languages. She's nothing much to look at. In fact, you'd undoubtedly think she was ugly. I have no idea what this will lead to. I have no idea about anything. I'm completely bewildered. Of course I'm pleased in one way. Though I have a hell of a bad conscience about you and the children. We've always got along well, haven't we? I mean, things haven't been any better or worse for us than for the average family. Say something, for Christ's sake.

MARIANNE   I don't know what to say.

JOHAN   I suppose you think it was wrong of me not to tell you about this before. But I didn't know how it would turn out. I thought: I'll soon get over it. It's just a passing phase. So I didn't want to worry you.

MARIANNE   It's so funny.

JOHAN   What's funny?

MARIANNE   That I haven't realized anything. That I haven't been suspicious or noticed anything. Everything has been as usual, better in fact. You've been so kind. And I've just gone around like a silly fool, blind and unsuspecting. God in heaven!

JOHAN   No, you haven't noticed anything. But then you never were very clear-sighted. Especially where our personal relations were concerned.

MARIANNE   What are we to do now then?

JOHAN   I don't know.

MARIANNE   Do you want a divorce? Are you going to marry
her? Anyway, why do you have to tell me about this tonight
of all times? Why the sudden hurry?

JOHAN   We're going to Paris tomorrow afternoon.
(MARIANNE *looks at him in silence*) I want to get away from all
this. At any rate for a time. I was going down anyway in the
fall to see Grandin and his assistant. And Paula has a study
grant and was going to use it up this fall. I want to be with
her. I can't be without her. So we're leaving together tomorrow afternoon. (MARIANNE *looks at him in silence*) Now that
I'm talking to you, now that I'm at home, I'd prefer to scrap
the whole damn thing. I feel tired and scared. (MARIANNE
looks at him in silence) Nothing could be sillier or more com-
monplace and absurd than this. I know just what you're
thinking and I have no excuses to offer.

MARIANNE   How can you know what I'm thinking?

JOHAN   I'm trying not to have a bad conscience, but it's only
affectation. This is the way it *is*, Marianne. There's nothing
to be done about it. (MARIANNE *looks at him in silence*) We'd
better not talk. There's nothing sensible to say in any case.
You know the truth now and that's the main thing.

MARIANNE   I know nothing. Let's go to bed. It's late. And I
suppose you're off early.

JOHAN   I have a meeting at nine.

MARIANNE   Then I suggest we go to bed. (*They go upstairs to the
bedroom.* MARIANNE *sits on the bed and watches* JOHAN *undress. He
is embarrassed by her gaze, and to make matters worse he has some
incriminating marks on his chest*) You have marks on your
chest.

JOHAN   I know.

MARIANNE *(Smiling)*   How indiscreet of you both.

JOHAN   Do you know if my gray suit is here or in town? I've been hunting for it.

MARIANNE   It's at the dry cleaners.

JOHAN   What a nuisance.

MARIANNE   I have the receipt if you'd like to call for it tomorrow.

JOHAN   I won't have time. I'll be busy all day until three o'clock, and then we're off.

MARIANNE   If you like, I'll drive in and pick it up for you. And I'll gladly do your packing. You're not very good at it.

JOHAN   No thank you.

MARIANNE *(Smiling)*   You're being silly.

JOHAN   Yes, I am in fact rather conventional.

MARIANNE   Otherwise I think you have all you need. There are clean shirts and underclothes here, so you can take those with you. Can't you travel in your jacket and flannel pants? They give you a nice youthful air.

JOHAN   Yes, I suppose so.

MARIANNE   How long will you be away?

JOHAN   I don't know. It all depends.

MARIANNE   What do you mean?

JOHAN   I have requested and been given six months' leave of absence. Before then I have about a month's work which I'm taking with me. So it will be seven or eight months at least.

MARIANNE *(Thunderstruck)*   Oh.

JOHAN   It's just as well to make a clean break.

MARIANNE   Do you suppose I'll still be here when you come back?

JOHAN   I don't give a damn.

MARIANNE   I see.

JOHAN   Do you know how long I've had this in mind? Can you guess? I don't mean about Paula, but about leaving you and the children and our home. Can you guess?

MARIANNE *(Looks at him in alarm)*   Don't tell me.

JOHAN   For four years I've wanted to get rid of you. Not that I didn't like you. You mustn't think that.

MARIANNE *(Drawing the sheet up to her face)*   No more now.

JOHAN   No, you're right. It's just empty words.

MARIANNE   What are you going to live on? I mean now, during your leave of absence. You'll have to pay an allowance to the children in any case.

JOHAN   Don't worry. I have enough to get by on.

MARIANNE   Then you must have income that I don't know of.

JOHAN   How right you are.

MARIANNE   How is that possible?

JOHAN *(Beside himself)*   Listen now, for Christ's sake, though it's no goddamn business of yours. For one thing I've sold the boat, and for another I've taken a loan, which Frid has been kind enough to put his name to. From the first of September the bank will pay one thousand six hundred kronor a month to you and the girls. For the time being. Then we'll make some other arrangement when I come home. You'd better talk to one of your lawyer colleagues at the office. I don't give a damn. Name your price. I'm not taking anything with me, except perhaps my books, if you have no objection. I'll just vanish, do you hear? Into thin air. I will pay all I reasonably can to support you and the children. My needs are nil. All that interests me is to take the step out of all this. Do you know what I'm most fed up with? All this fucking harping on what we're supposed to do, what we must do, what we must take into consideration. What your mother will think. What the children will say. How we had best arrange that dinner party and shouldn't we invite my father after all. We must go to the west coast. We must go to the mountains. We must go to St. Moritz. We must celebrate Christmas, Easter, Whitsun, birthdays, namedays, the whole fucking lot. I know I'm being unfair. I know that what I'm saying now is all goddamn nonsense. I know that we've had a good life. And actually I think I still love you. In fact, in one way I love you *more* now since I met Paula. But can you understand this bitterness? I don't know what to call it. This bitterness, I can't hit on any better word. No one can explain it to me for the simple reason that I have no one to talk to except Erik Broméus and he's intellectually illiterate, so he hasn't much to offer except his money, and there are worse things than that in this situation. No, I don't understand. I don't understand this thing I call bitterness, which has kept getting worse and worse.

MARIANNE   Why haven't you said anything?

JOHAN   How can one talk about something which hasn't any words? How can one say that it's boring to make love although technically everything is perfect? How can I say that it's all I can do not to strike you when you sit there at the breakfast table all neat and tidy eating your boiled eggs? And the girls giving themselves airs in that silly spoiled way. Why have we indulged them so hysterically? Can you tell me that? I'm not blaming you, Marianne. Everything has just gone to pot. And no one knows why.

MARIANNE   I must have been doing wrong the whole time.

JOHAN   Stop that. It's an easy way out always to take the blame. It makes you feel strong and noble and generous and humble. You haven't done wrong and I haven't done wrong. It's no use trotting out guilty feelings and a bad conscience, though God knows my conscience is so bad it's nearly choking me. It's all sheer chance, a cruel coincidence. Why should you and I of all people be able to dodge the humiliations and the disasters? It's all perfectly logical. So why start talking about guilt and doing wrong.

MARIANNE   My poor darling.

JOHAN   I don't want your sympathy. Don't paw me. I think it's only affectation on my part. I mean this empty talk. I don't think for one minute I'm getting at the truth about us. As a matter of fact, I don't think there *is* any plain truth. It's just a lot of sores everywhere. And whichever way we turn and whatever we say, it hurts.

MARIANNE   Won't you change your mind and not go?

JOHAN   That's impossible.

MARIANNE   But if I plead with you.

JOHAN   It's no use, and it's only distressing.

MARIANNE   Can't you at least postpone the trip for a month or two? You're not giving me a chance. I think we could repair our marriage. I think we could find a new form for our life together. Perhaps Paula would understand me better than you do. I ought to meet her and talk to her. It's a mistake to cut everything off just when we're starting to be honest with each other. Can't we let the disaster sweep over us together? I mean, we're destroying so much by tearing down all we've built up. You must give me a chance, Johan. It's unkind of you just to present me with a *fait accompli*. You're putting me in a ridiculous and intolerable position. Surely you can see that.

JOHAN   I know just what you mean: What are our parents going to say? What will my sister think, what will our friends think? Jesus Christ, how tongues are going to wag! How will it affect the girls, and what will their school friends' mothers think? And what about the dinner parties we're invited to in September and October. And what are you going to say to Katarina and Peter? To hell with all that! I intend to behave like a cad, and what a relief!

MARIANNE   That wasn't what I meant.

JOHAN   Oh, what did you mean?

MARIANNE   *(Softly)*   Nothing. *(They've gotten into the big double bed and put out the light. Neither can get to sleep. They lie for a long time silent and unmoving, deeply distressed. There is complete silence around them)* I forgot to set the alarm. What time do you have to get up?

JOHAN   Set it for five thirty, will you. I must do some packing too. I have to be at the institute at nine for a conference.

MARIANNE   I've been meaning to get another alarm clock. This one is loud enough to wake the dead. It's not terribly reliable either. There, it's set for five thirty. Anyway, I usually wake up without an alarm. Don't worry. *(Suddenly)* I want you to tell me about Paula.

JOHAN   What's the point of that?

MARIANNE   Please.

JOHAN   Why do you want to torment yourself?

MARIANNE   It's not self-torment. I want to know what she's like. It's much worse to go around trying to picture someone who has no outlines. Do you have a photo of her? You must.

JOHAN   Please, Marianne, can't we be spared?

MARIANNE   Do, I beg you. Can't you help me with this?

JOHAN   Well, let it be on your own head. Where's my wallet? Oh yes, in my coat pocket. Here are two photos. One was taken two years ago, when she was on vacation down by the Black Sea. The other's a passport photo taken a couple of weeks ago. It's a good likeness, I think.

MARIANNE   She has a nice figure. Lovely breasts, it seems. Are they?

JOHAN   Yes, she has lovely breasts.

MARIANNE   Does she dye her hair? It looks like it, I mean.

JOHAN   It hadn't occurred to me, but it's possible.

MARIANNE   She has a nice smile. How old is she?

JOHAN   Twenty-three. She hasn't been very lucky in love. She's been engaged twice and I think in that particular respect she's made a muddle of her life with all kinds of men.

MARIANNE   Does that upset you?

JOHAN   I'll say it does. Her outspokenness can sometimes be rather unpleasant. I would prefer not to know anything, but she insists on giving me the details of her erotic past. It's rather trying, since I suffer from retrospective jealousy. She has no illusions. She says that she has no great hopes for the two of us. She says she knows that I'll go back to you, that she doesn't have a chance against you. Sometimes it sounds like lines from a badly written old play that one has seen far too often. She has a compulsion to safeguard herself against every form of failure. It makes her rather sympathetic. There's something childish about her altogether, despite her twenty-three years and her intelligence and general capability. She's horribly jealous, but then so am I, so in that we're alike. She's terribly afraid of you, and that I can understand. But she's also afraid of my secretary and of other women whom she knows I associate with. She's unsure of herself in many ways. I try to help her all I can. It's all pretty strange and bewildering.

MARIANNE   Are you good together in bed?

JOHAN   At first it was dreadful. I suppose it was my fault too. I'm not really used to it. I mean with other women, and you and I have spoiled each other. I couldn't do a thing. But she said that no one had ever been so kind and tender toward her. I wanted to break the whole thing off, although I was in love with her. You see, I realized that if I couldn't have sex with her, the whole affair was doomed. But she got in an awful state when I wanted to end it all. I was afraid she would hurt herself. Then we were out of town for a week.

MARIANNE   Did you go away together?

JOHAN   Yes. You remember I gave some lectures in Copenhagen in April.

MARIANNE   Oh, it was then. In April.

JOHAN   We lived it up in the evenings and behaved like pigs. We got mixed up in drunken brawls and were kicked out of the hotel. You remember I told you I had changed my hotel because the traffic was so noisy. We ended up in a squalid little place on a back street, and suddenly we clicked and made love day and night. She said that it had never been so good for her before. I felt terrifically high, of course. I know what you're thinking, Marianne, and it's true. You and I also had much better times together after that Copenhagen trip.

MARIANNE   Did you tell Paula that?

JOHAN   No, I didn't dare. I told her that you and I stopped sleeping together long ago. I said I was impotent. It wasn't exactly true, but I had been impotent with her, so I might just as well pretend I was impotent with you too. But the trouble with Paula is that she has the devil of an intuition. Or else I'm a bad liar. She always looks right at me when I'm not telling the truth. She has an alarming gift for seeing through me. Which is good for me, to be sure. It teaches me a lesson.

MARIANNE   Yes, I've always been so unsuspecting.

JOHAN   Not *only* unsuspecting. Both you and I have escaped into a state of existence that has been hermetically sealed. Everything has been neatly arranged, all cracks have been stopped up, it has all gone like clockwork. We have died from lack of oxygen.

MARIANNE   *(Smiling)*   And now you mean that along comes your little Paula and awakens you to a new life.

JOHAN   I don't have much self-knowledge and I understand very little of reality in spite of having read a lot of books. But something tells me that this catastrophe is a chance in a million for both you and me.

MARIANNE   Is it Paula who has put such nonsense into your head? Just how naïve can you get?

JOHAN   We can do without taunts and sarcastic remarks in this conversation.

MARIANNE   You're right. I'm sorry.

JOHAN   I'm trying, do you hear? I'm trying to be as honest as I can. It isn't easy. We've never talked about these things. Is it any wonder we're naïve and silly and uncertain? How else could it be? This affair with Paula is a catastrophe. Both for you and me. I've tried to break free time and again, but it's been impossible. She won't let me go, and in one way I'm —obsessed by her. It sounds so damn melodramatic to say you're "obsessed" by anyone, but it's the only adequate word. At first I resisted but now I let everything go to hell. And I'm quite content to have it that way.

MARIANNE   All I ask is that you postpone the trip.

JOHAN   Paula would never agree to put it off and I feel the same way. I've made up my mind.

MARIANNE   Can't I meet her?

JOHAN   What's the use? Besides, she won't hear you spoken of. I hardly dare to mention your name.

MARIANNE   You *are* in a spot.

JOHAN   It depends how you look at it. Paula and I get along well together. She's cheerful and kind and tender. We always have lots to talk about. In-between we have the most awful fights. But I'm beginning to wonder if it isn't pretty salutary. All my life I've been so goddamn well-behaved and sensible and balanced and cautious. I don't know. I don't know anything.

MARIANNE   Come and lie beside me. I want you to make love to me. You can do that anyway. I mean for old times' sake. *(She switches off the bedside lamp. At the window it is already dawn. They have sex. Very soon she has a violent orgasm. Then she begins to weep. She turns on her side, hides her face in her hands, and sobs. After a little while she calms down, embraces her husband ardently but gently, and kisses him several times. They look at each other tenderly and in despair)* Lie here now in my arms and let's sleep. We're both awfully tired.

JOHAN   I don't think I can sleep. The best thing would be to have some coffee and pack and leave at once.

MARIANNE   No, lie down and close your eyes. You'll go to sleep, you'll see. We need some sleep both of us. It will be a strenuous day tomorrow.

JOHAN   I'm so goddamn ashamed.

MARIANNE   Let's wait with all that. It's only you and me now. We have these few hours to ourselves. Just you and me. *(They fall asleep at last in each other's arms.* MARIANNE *wakes up with a start. Knowledge floods over her. At first she lies quite still in order to withstand the attack better, but it just increases in violence. It is easier if she moves. She turns carefully, frees herself from her husband's embrace, and reaches out her hand to shut off the alarm clock. There are still a few minutes to go before five thirty.* JOHAN *is sound asleep but has a worried expression. She props her head in her hand and regards him for a long time while the alarm clock ticks the seconds away behind her ear.*

Then the time is up and she touches him gently. He awakes instantly. Reaching out his arm he draws her to him in a gesture of helpless despair. She submits but is stiff and unwilling. They lie like this for a moment or two, then he releases her and sits up resolutely. He gets out of bed, goes into the bathroom, and begins to shave with the electric razor. MARIANNE *goes first to the toilet and has a pee, sits for a few moments as though paralyzed, feeling that she weighs about two tons, then goes to the sink and begins to wash.* JOHAN *has a long, thorough shower, then they stand there together, two mute naked strangers, drying themselves with their luxurious colored bathtowels.* MARIANNE *combs and brushes her long hair.* JOHAN *goes back to the bedroom and begins to get dressed)*

MARIANNE   Shall we pack now or have breakfast first? Would you like tea or coffee, by the way?

JOHAN   Oh, you decide. Tea, please. *(*MARIANNE *gets a suitcase down from a closet.* JOHAN *takes his traveling clothes—jacket and flannel pants—out of another and finishes dressing.* MARIANNE *begins to pack fussily.* JOHAN *goes into the bathroom, combs his hair and brushes his teeth, and comes back with the nail scissors)* Help me, please. I've a split nail and can't manage it.
*(*MARIANNE *gets her glasses and leads him over to the window. She starts clipping carefully)*

MARIANNE   You're biting your cuticles again.

JOHAN   Do you know what has become of Speer's memoirs? I'm sure I left the book on the bedside table.

MARIANNE   I thought you'd finished it, so I lent it to Mother.

JOHAN   Oh. Decent of you. Ow! Christ!

MARIANNE   I must cut down here. You've broken the nail. It's bleeding slightly, I'll have to put on a bandaid. What do you *do* to your nails?

JOHAN   Thank you, that's fine.

MARIANNE   Shall I pack the shaver, or will you take the one you have in town?

JOHAN   I have to go up to the apartment anyway to fetch some things, so you can leave it.

MARIANNE   Do you want the receipt for the dry cleaners?

JOHAN   I might as well take it, in case I have time. Which cleaners is it?

MARIANNE   The one in Storgatan, almost opposite the church.

JOHAN   Oh, I know. I'm not lugging those heavy shoes with me, if that's what you think.

MARIANNE   They might come in handy in the winter. Which pajamas are you taking?

JOHAN   Look, get out of here and make breakfast, while I finish packing.

MARIANNE   Does it bother you my helping you to pack?

JOHAN   I can't deny that I think it's indecent, though I don't know why. (*They both laugh helplessly.* MARIANNE *pulls on a shabby old pair of slacks and a large sweater.* JOHAN *goes on stubbornly packing.* MARIANNE *stands watching him with her arms crossed. After a strained silence* JOHAN *loses his temper*) What are you gaping at?

MARIANNE   Nothing. I'm sorry. (*She turns on her heel and goes out, leaving* JOHAN *to his packing. His irritation grows. When he tries to shut the suitcase and fails, he snatches out the winter shoes and hurls them across the floor.* MARIANNE *is busy with the breakfast, laying the kitchen table, boiling eggs, making tea and toast.* JOHAN *goes past with the suitcase on his way out to the car. He opens the trunk and tosses it in. Before* MARIANNE *can stop them, the tears are running down her cheeks, but she sniffles and blows her nose and pulls herself together. They sit down to breakfast, passing things to each other with ingrained routine.* MARIANNE *has forgotten to salt the eggs)* What shall I do with your mail?

JOHAN   I'll write and tell you my address. Then you can send important letters on, if you don't mind. And if you'd be good enough to pay bills and so on in the usual way.

MARIANNE   Another thing. The plumber was supposed to come and repair the bathroom before we move back to town. Have you spoken to him, or shall I call him up? You said you'd get in touch with him. I mean, if you've forgotten it in all the muddle, I could see to it that he comes and gets those jobs done at last.

JOHAN   I've phoned him dozens of times, but he's never there. So I have *not* forgotten, as you seem to think.

MARIANNE   What are you going to do with your car while you're away? Will you keep it in the garage?

JOHAN   I've asked Paula's sister to look after it. There's no point in its standing idle, and she has just moved out of town.

MARIANNE   I see.

JOHAN   But if you wouldn't mind canceling my appointment with the dentist. I'm sure to forget.

MARIANNE   One thing that's rather a problem: What are we going to do about your father's birthday on Friday? He asked us to dinner, you know. I'd be very grateful if you'd call him and explain things. Will you do that, please?

JOHAN   That's about the worst thing of all. Perhaps I can write to him.

MARIANNE   As long as you don't forget.

JOHAN   It's damned awkward about our parents. It feels so humiliating in some way. What can one say?

MARIANNE   Another thing. What do you want me to say to Mrs. Andersson?

JOHAN   Oh, shit! I couldn't care less what the cleaning woman thinks.

MARIANNE   Why are you so angry? (JOHAN *mutters something inaudible*) She has cleaned for us for ten years and knows us well and is indispensable and awfully loyal.

JOHAN   Uh. *(Pause)* Oh, you might just as well know. She caught Paula and me red-handed one morning. I didn't know you and she had changed the day, and there she was suddenly in the bedroom. A *very* awkward moment. *(Pause)* That was about a month ago. My car had broken down and we'd had dinner at a place not far away, and I thought it wouldn't matter so much if we spent the night at the apartment. I went out to the old girl in the kitchen and told her to keep her trap shut. She was practically drooling with excitement and moral indignation and loyalty to you. Then she fussed around and got breakfast for us, treating Paula more or less like the innocent victim of my brutal lusts. In the end I found myself bribing her with an extra thirty kronor. Why don't you say something?

MARIANNE   Then I needn't mention the matter to Mrs. Andersson. That's a relief.
(She gets up from the table and begins to clear. There is a clatter of dishes. Then she stands stock-still over by the sink, her head drooping and her breath coming in long, painful gasps)

JOHAN *(Kindly)*   What is it, Marianne?

MARIANNE   Oh, it will pass. *(Then it's time for him to go. They stand facing each other in the hall. He puts on his overcoat)*

What do you want me to tell the children?

JOHAN   Tell them anything you like.

MARIANNE   Shall I tell them you've fallen in love with another woman and have cleared out and left us?

JOHAN   I don't think you could put it better. It also has the advantage of being true. I don't look for understanding from that quarter.

MARIANNE   Karin is going to take it badly. She's so attached to you right now. She never stops talking about you.

JOHAN   Don't paw me. It hurts enough as it is. I must go now. I want to try to get into town before the morning traffic jam. So long, Marianne, take care of yourself.

MARIANNE   So long.

(They stand there stiff, scared, and uncertain. He bends down to kiss her on the lips but she turns her face away. He gives a laugh)

JOHAN   I may be home in a week.

MARIANNE   If only you were. We'd make a fresh start in every way. We'd dig up all routine and negligence. We'd talk over the past. We'd try to find where we've gone wrong. You'd never hear any accusations. I promise you. It's all so unreal. I don't know what to do about it. You're shutting me out. I think any solution at all would be better than this. Can't you promise to come back? Then I'd know *something*. I mean, you can't just leave me without any hope. It's not fair. Even if you have no intention of returning, you could at least *say* you're coming home again.

JOHAN   I must go now, Marianne.

(He shakes his head and looks at her unseeing. Then he walks out the door. She stands still, the door closes. Through the window she sees him get into the car. After a couple of attempts it starts reluctantly and glides out of the gate and down the hill, turning to the right and disappearing behind the rise. MARIANNE *stands for a long time rooted to the ground, as if every movement from now on were going to cost her the most terrible effort. At last she drags herself out to the kitchen and starts to do the washing-up. She turns the radio on. Suddenly she breaks off and goes into the girls' bedroom. Silence and deep sleep prevail. She sits down for a moment and looks at their sleeping faces)*

MARIANNE   *(To herself)*   I don't understand. No, I don't understand. *(Then she gets an idea. She goes to the telephone and dials a number. After a time someone answers)* Hello, Fredrik, it's Marianne. Sorry to wake you. Is Birgit there? No, it doesn't matter. Let her sleep. How are things? Oh, you like puttering around alone at this hour. No, I won't keep you long. No, it's cloudy here. Oh, how nice for you. Well, I wanted to talk to you about something. No, I just wanted someone

to talk to. You and Birgit *are* our friends. I must have . . .
I must . . . it's all so unreal, Fredrik. You see—*(Pause)*—You
see, it's like this. I'm about to burst into tears any moment
and then I'll just go on crying, and I don't *want* to cry
because that will only make it worse. You see, Johan has
fallen in love with another woman. Her name's Paula, and
they're going off to Paris today. Can't you talk to Johan and
ask him to wait a bit? He needn't rush off headlong like that.
What? You've already talked to him? Oh, I see. I see. So you
and Birgit have known all along. *You've known the whole time
and not said a word to me?* What a filthy, rotten way to behave.
How could you be so goddamn disloyal to me? I don't care
what you say. And all the times we've met and talked and

you have known and never said anything. *(In a fury) Christ!*
Jesus Christ! Fucking nice friends you are! You can go to
hell with your explanations. Just how many people have
known of this? Oh, quite a number. I'm glad to know.
(She flings the phone down. When it rings she doesn't answer. She
bites her hand to stop herself from screaming)

FOURTH SCENE

THE VALE OF TEARS

CHARACTERS

Marianne
Johan

An evening in September a year later. The doorbell rings. MARIANNE, *who has been busy in the kitchen preparing a dinner for two, goes to open the door after a quick check-up in front of the mirror.*

JOHAN   Hello.

MARIANNE   Hello. Come in!

JOHAN   Sorry if I'm late. I had trouble with the car. It wouldn't start. *(Kisses her on the cheek)* How pretty you are. And what a nice dress.

MARIANNE   I'm glad you like it. I bought it a couple of days ago but regretted it afterwards. I didn't think it suited me. And it suddenly seemed much too red.

JOHAN   It suits you admirably, I must say.

MARIANNE   Do come in, Johan. I feel nervous standing here in the hall, making polite conversation.

JOHAN   I'm nervous too. I haven't been able to settle down to anything all day. It's ridiculous, really. But I haven't seen you for quite a long time. Over six months.

MARIANNE   How was it that you suddenly . . . ?

JOHAN   Paula's in London for a week.

MARIANNE   Oh, I see. Oh. Would you like a drink?

JOHAN   Yes, please, I'd love a whisky. Straight. It settles the stomach. I mean, it calms you down.

MARIANNE   Have you taken to drinking whisky?

JOHAN   Yes, just imagine.

MARIANNE   I asked Aunt Berit to take charge of the girls for tonight. So they're staying with her until the day after tomorrow. The delight is mutual. They're going to the theater this evening, and tomorrow they have a holiday from school and are going to the country.

JOHAN   How practical. I mean, it would have been pretty rough going to meet the children too. How are they?

MARIANNE   You needn't ask after them out of politeness. But we'll write down their birthdays in your diary, so that you don't forget them again as you did this year. I bought them each a present from you, but they saw through me. And that wasn't very nice. Couldn't you take them out to dinner sometimes? Or to the movies? It's pretty awful the way you never get in touch with them. They hardly ever mention you nowadays.

JOHAN   That's understandable.

MARIANNE   Why can't Paula let you see us without raising Cain for days on end . . . ?

JOHAN   If we're meeting just to give you the chance of moralizing, I'd better go at once.

MARIANNE   You've said yourself that Paula is so jealous that you can't see either me or the children without there being a godawful fight.

JOHAN   What do you expect me to do about it?

MARIANNE   Are you so darn yellow that you can't tell her what *you* want to do? Are you so afraid of her making a scene that you let her boss you around?

JOHAN *(Wearily)*   Yes.

MARIANNE   I'm sorry.

JOHAN   It doesn't matter. I realize you think the situation is absurd. But don't scold me. It's no use.

MARIANNE   Would you like some more whisky?

JOHAN   Yes, please.

MARIANNE   How are things otherwise?

JOHAN   Oh, much the same. What about you?

MARIANNE   I can't complain. It might be worse.

JOHAN   I suppose it was silly of me to call up and suggest we meet. There's nothing we can talk about without hurting each other.

MARIANNE   Then I have an excellent suggestion. Let's have dinner. Undoubtedly we're both ravenous and that's why we're so touchy. Don't you think so?

JOHAN   A good idea.
(As they stand up he puts his arms round her and kisses her on the lips. She submits with a slight protest. Then they look at each other and smile suddenly)

MARIANNE You look a fright with that haircut. And you've put on weight, I think.

JOHAN I must admit you really turn me on when we're close together like this. What are we going to do about it?

MARIANNE Let's have dinner first. Then we'll see.

JOHAN Have you bought a new dinner service?

MARIANNE It's family stuff. Dear old Aunt Elsa died six months ago and left me a lot of household things for some obscure reason. She was always under the impression that I was so domestic. Most of it is unusable, but the china is nice. You're only getting a casserole, and wine and cheese. I haven't had time to produce anything fancier. But you usually like my cooking.

JOHAN   It smells wonderful. *(Helping himself)* Have you heard that Martin is going to marry again?

MARIANNE   My dear, I ran into them in town. They were terribly embarrassed and began to stammer and make excuses for not having called me up or anything the whole year. I felt quite sorry for them.

JOHAN   Anyway, this new one he's got hold of is a flighty little piece. Though she's said to have money.

MARIANNE   As a matter of fact I've heard just the opposite. Her father's firm went bankrupt not long ago.

JOHAN Then poor old Martin has slipped up again.

MARIANNE Isn't he one of your closest friends?

JOHAN Not exactly. Why?

MARIANNE You sound so smug.

JOHAN A wise man has said that in our friends' misfortunes there is always something that doesn't entirely displease us. Skoal, Marianne. This is a very good wine.

MARIANNE My dear, it's nothing very special. Just a rather cheap claret. But it *is* good.

JOHAN I don't mind telling you that things are going pretty well for me just now. I've been offered a chair at a university in Cleveland for three years. It's a splendid chance, both career-wise and financially. After all, it's over there that things happen in our field. And I'd be more than glad to emigrate, either temporarily or for good. There's nothing to keep me here. I'm fed up with the academic duck-pond. Besides, I have no desire to let myself be fleeced to the bone. So I leave in the spring, if all goes well.

MARIANNE Congratulations.

JOHAN And now for the unspoken question: Are you taking Paula with you to America? And the answer is no. Call it running away, if you like. Okay, I'm decamping. I've had just about enough. Paula has been good for me. She has taught me a few things about myself which I'm glad to know. But there's a limit. To be quite frank, I'm pretty tired of her. I suppose you think it's disloyal of me to sit here running Paula down. But she forfeited my loyalty long ago. I'm fed up with her. With her emotional storms and scenes and tears and hysterics, then making it all up and saying how much she loves me. *(Checking himself)* I'll tell you this,

Marianne. The best thing about Paula was that she taught me to shout and brawl. It was even permissible to strike her. I wasn't aware that I had any feelings at all. If I were to tell you . . . you'd think I was lying. Sometimes I thought I was mixed up in a grotesque play, in which I was both actor and audience. Our fights used to go on for days and nights on end, until we collapsed from sheer exhaustion.

MARIANNE   Would you like another helping?

JOHAN   Thanks, I haven't quite finished this. It's simply delicious. And I'm talking your ear off. But it puts you in such a terribly good mood. I've felt on top of the world ever since I was offered that professorship.

MARIANNE *(Quietly)*   In that case perhaps we could discuss the divorce. I mean, if you're going to be away for several years it would be better to clinch the matter before you go. Don't you think?

JOHAN   You should do as you see fit.

MARIANNE   Then I suggest that we do get a divorce. One never knows what may happen. I might want to remarry. And it would be awfully complicated if you're in America.

JOHAN   Is something up?

MARIANNE   That made you curious, didn't it?

JOHAN   Look here, Marianne! Suppose you tell me something about yourself. And not just let me rattle on.

MARIANNE   Would you like some more wine?

JOHAN   No thanks. It has already gone to my head. No more of anything. Well, perhaps a little cheese. No, no, we don't need fresh plates. What sort of cheese is this? It looks tasty.

MARIANNE   It's a Bel Paese. Try it.

JOHAN   Delicious. But don't think you're wriggling out of it.
How are things, Marianne? Judging by your appearance,
your hairdo, your dress, your figure, and your general amia-
bility, they must be pretty good. What I'm most anxious to
know, of course, is whether you have a lover.

MARIANNE   I'll make the coffee. You'd like some, wouldn't
you?
*(She goes around the table and, taking his head in both hands, bends
down and kisses him on the lips. He lends a hand clearing the table.
While* MARIANNE *is making the coffee* JOHAN *wanders about rather
restlessly. He stops in a doorway and looks in)*

JOHAN   You've changed things around, I see.

MARIANNE   Any objections?

JOHAN   Oh, none at all.

MARIANNE   I've moved into your study.

JOHAN   And what have you done with my things?

MARIANNE *(Gaily)*   They're in storage and I'm paying for
it. I decided finally that I had a right to a workroom of my
own. So I bought some furniture and put up new curtains
and my own pictures which there wasn't room for here in
the old days and which you didn't like. Was that tactless,
perhaps? Do you think I should have waited until the divorce was over? Should I have observed a year of mourning?
Oh, and I've also changed the telephone, so it's in my name
now.

JOHAN   Oh, that's good.

MARIANNE   You're a tiny bit bitter about something all the
same.

JOHAN   By no means. I think you did right.

MARIANNE   Thank you. Before, I always had to sit and work at the writing desk in the bedroom when I brought work home. It was rather inconvenient. But all that mattered then was that you had a proper study where you were not disturbed by the children. Oh, and I've taken away the double bed.

JOHAN   What was the point of that?

MARIANNE   I nearly went crazy sleeping in one corner of a huge bed. So it's now a little more chaste here, as you see.

JOHAN   And what about your lover? Where do you house him?

MARIANNE   For the time being I think it's better for us to meet at his place.

JOHAN   You mean because of the girls?

MARIANNE   *(With a smile)*   No, silly. They're always after me to get married again.

JOHAN   Well, I'll be damned.

MARIANNE   Would you like a brandy or something?

JOHAN   No thanks. This is a place fit for human beings to live in anyway.

MARIANNE *(Smiling)*   You live out of town, don't you?

JOHAN   We live in a concrete hutch consisting of three rooms. On the tenth floor. With a view of another concrete hut. At the downstairs entrance drunken thirteen-year-olds stagger about. They amuse themselves by knocking down the old people. The building has cracks everywhere. The windows fit so badly that the curtains flutter in the draught. For two whole weeks not long ago I had to get every drop of water from a hydrant. None of the toilets worked. If possible, people avoid the subway after eight in the evening. In the middle of it all is something which a demented architect has called the piazza. Not that I'm complaining. In fact I think it's interesting, since what it most resembles is my idea of hell.

MARIANNE   I didn't know you believed in hell.

JOHAN   Hell is a place where no one believes in solutions any more. But Paula likes it out there. She says it all fits in with her picture of the world. And that it feels safe. I don't really care where I live. To me every domicile is only temporary. You must have your security inside yourself.

MARIANNE   Do *you?*

JOHAN   I didn't, as long as I was living here at home. Everything around us then was so confoundedly important. We were forced to make a ritual of security.

MARIANNE   I don't know what you mean.

JOHAN   All security was anchored in the things outside ourselves. Our possessions, our country house, the apartment, our friends, our income, food, holidays, parents.

MARIANNE   *(Anxiously)*   Why did we stop showing each other affection, Johan? Why did we hardly ever kiss? Why did we only caress one another when we had sex? Why did we cuddle the children so little?

JOHAN   Do you know what my security looks like? I'll tell you. I think this way: Loneliness is absolute. It's an illusion to imagine anything else. Be aware of it. And try to act accord-

ingly. Don't expect anything but trouble. If something nice
happens, all the better. Don't think you can ever do away
with loneliness. It is absolute. You can invent fellowship on
different levels, but it will still only be a fiction about reli-
gion, politics, love, art, and so on. The loneliness is nonethe-
less complete. What's so treacherous is that sometime you
may be struck by an idea of fellowship. Bear in mind that
it's an illusion. Then you won't be so disappointed afterwards, when everything goes back to normal. You must live
with the realization of absolute loneliness. Then you will
stop complaining, then you will stop moaning. In fact, then
you're pretty safe and are learning to accept with a certain
satisfaction how pointless it all is. By that I don't mean that
you should settle down resignedly. I think you should carry
on as long as you can. If only because it's better for you to
do your best than to give up.

MARIANNE   I wish I were as certain as you.

JOHAN   It's nothing but words. You put it into words so as to
placate the great emptiness. It's funny, come to think of it.
Has it ever struck you that emptiness hurts? You'd think it
might make you dizzy or give you mental nausea. But my
emptiness hurts physically. It stings like a burn. Or like
when you were little and had been crying and the whole
inside of your body ached. I'm astonished sometimes at Paula's tremendous political faith. It's both true and sincere and
she's incessantly active within her group. Her conviction
answers her questions and fills the emptiness. I wish I could
live as she does. I really mean that, without any sarcasm.
(*Leaning forward*) Why are you sneering? Do you think I'm
talking rubbish? I think so too as a matter of fact. But I don't
care.

MARIANNE   I don't know what you're talking about. It seems
so theoretical. I don't know why. Perhaps because I never
talk about such big matters. I think I move on another plane.

JOHAN *(Roughly)* A more select plane, oh. A special plane reserved for women with a privileged emotional life and a happier, more mundane adjustment to the mysteries of life. Paula too likes to change herself into a priestess of life. It's always when she has read a new book by some fancy preacher of the new women's gospel.

MARIANNE I remember you always talked and talked. I used to like it, though I hardly ever took any notice of what you said when you held forth at your worst. It sounds as if somewhere you were disappointed.

JOHAN *(Quietly)* That's what you think.

MARIANNE *(Gently)* I want you to know that I'm nearly always thinking of you and wondering if you're all right or whether you're lonely and afraid. Every day, several times a day, I wonder where I went wrong. What I did to cause the breach between us. I know it's a childish way of thinking, but there you are. Sometimes I seem to have got hold of the solution, then it slips through my fingers.

JOHAN *(Sarcastically)* Why don't you go to a psychiatrist?

MARIANNE I do go to a doctor who has also had psychiatric training, and we have a couple of talks a week. Sometimes we meet privately.

JOHAN Is *he* your lover?

MARIANNE We've gone to bed together a couple of times but it was a dead loss. So we gave up the attempt and devoted ourselves to my interesting mental life instead.

JOHAN And where has that got you?

MARIANNE Nowhere. I'm trying hard to learn to talk. Oh yes, and I got rid of your furniture and moved into your study.

If you only knew what a bad conscience I had!—while at the same time feeling awfully daring.

JOHAN   That was one result anyway. *(Yawns)*

MARIANNE   What a huge yawn. Are you tired?

JOHAN   It's just the wine. I'm sorry. And I don't sleep terribly well. That added to the tension, I suppose.

MARIANNE   If you'd like to go home, don't mind me.

JOHAN   Oh, don't make such a thing of it.

MARIANNE   You can lie down and have a nap if you like. I'll wake you in an hour.

JOHAN *(Smiling)*   What a fuss about that one wretched yawn. I don't *want* to lie down. Please tell me about your explorations inside yourself instead. That's much more interesting. I promise you.

MARIANNE   There's not really very much to tell. Though something funny did strike me. But I haven't spoken to the doctor about it because it only occurred to me last night.

JOHAN *(Not very interested)*   Oh, that sounds exciting.

MARIANNE   The doctor said I should write down whatever came into my head. It didn't matter how irrelevant. Anything at all. Dreams, memories, thoughts. There's nothing much so far. It's hard to write when you're not used to it. It sounds so stilted and you can't find the right words and you think how silly it all is.

JOHAN *(Politely)*   Won't you read me what you wrote last night? I'd like very much to hear it.

MARIANNE   Would you really? Are you sure? I'll go and get the
book. I wrote for several hours and didn't get to sleep till
about three o'clock. I looked a fright this morning and
thought it *would* be today, just when I was going to see you
after so long.
(During the foregoing she has been into her workroom and found the
notebook, thick, with black oilcloth covers. She comes back, cheerfully
excited and smiling. She sits down and lights a reading lamp)

JOHAN   You really are fabulously pretty.

MARIANNE   Now don't start paying compliments. You must
take an interest in my soul instead. Sit down, please. *(But*
JOHAN *has gone up to her and embraced her. He gives her a long*
ardent kiss on the lips. She sits quite still, her face turned up and
her eyes closed, and lets him kiss her. When he puts his hand on her
breast she twists aside and pushes it away) No, don't. Sit down
and be good and I'll read to you instead.

JOHAN *(With a smile)*   One good thing needn't exclude another.

MARIANNE   I've been thinking about that the whole time. What would it matter if we made love this evening? I've been longing for it and have worked myself up. But then I thought—what about afterwards? I mean after you've gone. I'd be left longing for you again. And I don't want that. I'm in love with you, Johan. Don't you see? Sometimes I hate you for what you've done to me. And sometimes I don't think of you for several hours at a stretch. It's lovely. Oh no. I have everything I could want. I have friends and even lovers. I have my children and I hold down a good job and like my work. No one need feel sorry for me. But I'm bound to you. I can't think why. Maybe I'm a perverted masochist or else I'm just the faithful type who forms only one attachment in life. I don't know. It's so difficult, Johan. I don't want to live with anyone else. Other men bore me. I'm not saying this to give you a bad conscience or to blackmail you emotionally. I'm only telling you how it is. That's why I just can't bear it if you start kissing me and making love to me. Because then all my defenses break down. I can't explain it in any other way. And then it's so lonely again after you've gone. When I keep you at a distance like this it's all right. In fact, it's awfully nice. But don't let's fondle each other. Because then it's hopeless after you've gone.

JOHAN   I'm still in love with you. You know that.

MARIANNE   Why do you say that when it's not true?

JOHAN   Why should my feelings for you have changed? Do you imagine I haven't longed to come back to you nearly every day during this time? We had a good life together. We were always friends, we had fun together. If we feel like making love now, why shouldn't we? It only shows we still long for one another. Marianne! Why the mental reservations? Why think about how it's going to feel tomorrow? Isn't that being very silly?

(MARIANNE *lets him kiss her several times. He fondles her more and more passionately. The diary falls to the floor. He draws her down to him and starts unbuttoning her blouse. Then she breaks free and sits up, smoothing her hair and buttoning up her blouse. She shakes her head*)

MARIANNE No, I don't want to. No! No, I don't *want* to. I don't want to moon about here, pining and weeping and longing. Please understand. Things really are the way I say. There's nothing sillier than this. If you persist, you might just as well go. I mean it, Johan. I don't want us to make love. I really don't. Please try to understand!

JOHAN I'll try to understand although I don't. So I'll sit down here and you can give me a brandy and some more coffee. Then we'll devote ourselves to reading aloud instead and then I'll go home at a respectable hour and call Paula in London and tell her I've been to the theater.
(MARIANNE, *distressed, pats his cheek. They are embarrassed and upset. She gets the brandy and he pours himself more coffee. He takes out his pipe and fills it.* MARIANNE *puts on her reading glasses. They toast each other jokingly.* MARIANNE *has a lump in her throat but manages to control herself.* JOHAN *lights his pipe with several matches.* MARIANNE *turns the pages of the notebook*)

MARIANNE I feel like an awful fool now. I want to run away and hide. I want to have a good cry.

JOHAN I'll go now if you like. We can meet tomorrow instead and go out and have dinner or something.

MARIANNE Perhaps it would be better. No, stay after all. Besides, I don't have time tomorrow.

JOHAN (*Gently*) Hey! I'm awfully fond of you.

MARIANNE (*Gently*) Hey! I'm behaving like a child.

JOHAN *(Gently)*   It's all right again now. The situation is under control. We've pulled through the crisis.

MARIANNE   It's such a scrawl that I can hardly read my own writing. All this first part is nothing important . . . *(Reads aloud)* "Yesterday I was suddenly seized by an almost reckless gaiety and for the first time all this year I felt the old lust for life, the eagerness to know what the day would bring . . ." *(Skipping)* and so on and so on. *(Goes on reading)* "Suddenly I turned around and looked at the old picture of my school class, when I was ten. I seemed to be aware of something that had been lying in readiness for a long time but beyond my grasp. To my surprise I have to admit that *I don't know who I am*. I haven't the vaguest idea. I have always done what people told me. As far back as I can remember I've been obedient, adaptable, almost meek. Now that I think about it, I had one or two violent outbursts of self-assertion as a little girl. But I remember also that Mother punished all such lapses from convention with exemplary severity. For my sisters and me our entire upbringing was aimed at our being *agreeable*. I was rather ugly and clumsy and was constantly informed of the fact. By degrees I found that if I kept my thoughts to myself and was ingratiating and farsighted, such behavior brought its rewards. The really big deception, however, occurred during puberty. All my thoughts, feelings, and actions revolved round sex. I didn't let on about this to my parents, or to anyone at all for that matter. Then it became second nature to be deceitful, surreptitious, and secretive. My father wanted me to be a lawyer like himself. I once hinted that I'd prefer to be an actress. Or at any rate to have *something* to do with the theater. I remember they just laughed at me. So it has gone on and on. In my relations with other people. In my relations with men. The same perpetual dissimulation. The same desperate attempts to please everybody. I have never thought: What do *I* want? But always: What does *he* want me to want? It's not unselfishness as I used to think, but sheer cowardice, and what's worse—utter ignorance of

who I am. I have never lived a dramatic life, I have no gift
for that sort of thing. But for the first time I feel intensely
excited at the thought of finding out what exactly I want to
do with myself. In the snug little world where both Johan
and I have lived so unconsciously, taking everything for
granted, there is a cruelty and brutality implied which
frightens me more and more when I think back on it. Outward security demands a high price: the acceptance of a
continuous destruction of the personality. (I think this ap-
plies especially to women; men have somewhat wider mar-
gins.) It is easy right at the outset to deform a little child's
cautious attempts at self-assertion. It was done in my case
with injections of a poison which is one hundred percent
effective: *bad conscience.* First toward Mother, then toward
those around me, and, last but not least, toward Jesus and
God. I see in a flash what kind of person I would have been
had I not allowed myself to be brainwashed. And I wonder
now whether I am hopelessly lost. Whether all the potential
for joy—joy for myself and others—that was innate in me
is dead or whether it's just asleep and can be awakened. I
wonder what kind of wife and woman I would have become
if I'd been able to use my resources as they were intended.
Would Johan and I have got married at all in that case? Yes,
I'm sure we would, because now that I think about it, we
were genuinely in love with each other in a devoted and
passionate way. Our mistake was that we didn't break out
of the family circle and escape far away and create something worthwhile on our own terms."

(MARIANNE *finishes reading and looks up from the notebook.* JOHAN
*is sitting with his head sunk on his chest and breathing deeply. He
is asleep. She gives a sad little smile and puts the notebook down
carefully. Then she finishes her brandy and, without waking him,
tiptoes out into the kitchen and starts putting the dishes in the
dishwasher. The phone rings. She hurries into the study and answers
in a whisper)*

MARIANNE   Hello. Oh, it's you. You weren't going to call this
evening. Are you jealous? You needn't be, I assure you. Do

I sound funny? No, I don't want to wake Johan. What? No, he's sitting. Sitting in the living room and sleeping like a little child. He is, really. My conversation bored him so much. No, don't come over, there's a dear. Don't be silly now, David. I'll see you tomorrow evening. Let's have dinner out and then go to a movie. It's been ages. Good. Will you call me up tomorrow morning as usual? If I sound a bit funny it's not really so strange. You can't expect me to stand here cooing into the phone. I don't know whether Johan has woken up. No, don't be idiotic, David. *(Laughs)* Precisely. I'll go in and wake my beau now and thank him for a nice evening, and then I'll pack him off home. You can call again in an hour. All right? Good. So long. What did you say? No, he hasn't even tried to kiss me, you needn't worry. It has been a very chaste evening. Bye!
(MARIANNE *goes back and wakes* JOHAN *gently. He is very ashamed and passes his hand time and again over his face*)

JOHAN   To think I damn well fell asleep. And what you were reading was so interesting too. Please forgive me, Marianne. Won't you read some more? I know you must be terribly hurt, but won't you read some more anyway?

MARIANNE   I think you ought to go home to bed now. *(With a smile)* I'm not a bit hurt. Really.

JOHAN   Yes, I'd better push off now.
(*They stand rather at a loss and unhappy. He fiddles with his pipe. She has picked up a coffee cup*)

MARIANNE   Perhaps you'll call up some time. If only for the children's sake.

JOHAN   Yes, sure. Yes, of course I will.

MARIANNE   It's always nice to see you, you know that.

JOHAN   If only Paula weren't so goddamn jealous. But still, she has reason. It's hard on her too.

MARIANNE   When will you know definitely about America?

JOHAN   In about a month.

MARIANNE   You can let me know what happens.

JOHAN   Yes, I'll phone you. Or write.

MARIANNE   And what are we going to do about the divorce? We must make up our minds.

JOHAN *(Wearily)* Are you going to marry again?

MARIANNE *(Wearily)* I don't know yet.

JOHAN   I'd rather wait before deciding. Don't you think so too?

MARIANNE   I don't know what I think. Sometimes I'm in despair. And then I think we ought to get divorced at once. And then sometimes I think rather hopefully that perhaps there's a chance we'll make it after all. *(At last they go out into the hall.* MARIANNE *is now very low.* JOHAN *embraces her; he too is in a state of utter confusion. Suddenly they start kissing each other.* MARIANNE *clings to him. They stagger against the wall. Smiles)* You'll stay the night. Won't you?

JOHAN   Yes, I'll stay the night.
(So they go to bed, and lie for a long time caressing each other with great tenderness and in silence. Then the phone rings in the study)

MARIANNE   Never mind the phone. It's nothing.

JOHAN *(In a rather forced tone)* Perhaps it's your lover. What can he want at this hour? Does he know I'm here?

MARIANNE   Of course he knows.

JOHAN   My God he's persistent.

MARIANNE   I'd better go and answer it after all. *(The telephone keeps on ringing.* MARIANNE *gets up quickly and puts on a dressing gown.* JOHAN *sees her go into the study—she leaves the door open—and hears what she is saying)* Hello. I can't talk now. Yes, Johan is still here. We've gone to bed, if you must know. So I imagine. What do you expect me to say? Yes, I'm sorry, it's true. I don't know. I'd be awfully glad if you didn't call up any more. I mean ever again. Try *for once* to behave like a grown-up man. Yes, it *is* a pity, I quite agree, but I really don't want to talk any more now. So long, David, take care of yourself.
(She flings down the phone and stands for a moment in thought, with her long red dressing gown and her hair loose, her right index finger against her cheek and illuminated by the table lamp. Then she gives a dry little laugh and puts the light out. She goes back to JOHAN *and sits on the edge of the bed. A smile)*

JOHAN   I couldn't help overhearing.

MARIANNE   You were meant to.

JOHAN   It was your lover, I gather.

MARIANNE   It was my *former* lover.

JOHAN   There was no need to say I was here.

MARIANNE   Perhaps you think I should have invited him. He was very anxious to come.

JOHAN   Are you in love with him?

MARIANNE   *(Gives him a long look)* Sometimes you ask such goddamn silly questions that I could kill you on the spot.

JOHAN   Sorry, I'm sure.

MARIANNE   If you want to know all about my love life I'll gladly tell you.

JOHAN   Are you angry with me now?

MARIANNE   I'm not angry but I'm about to cry. The trouble with me is that I can't get angry. I wish that one day I could really lose my temper, as I sometimes feel I have every right to do. I think it would change my life. *(Pause)* But that's by the way. *(Sighs)* When you left me I had only one thought in my head: I wanted to die. I walked about that morning, it was just at dawn, and I thought: I'll never live through this. In a sudden mood of spite I wanted the children to die too. But then Karin woke up feeling peculiar and was sick and had a temperature. It was a blessing in disguise, let me tell you. Then she broke out in spots, it was the measles, and the best thing that could have happened. She was really quite ill, with a touch of pneumonia, so what with nursing her in the evenings and at night, and with my work at the office in the daytime, I was kept pretty busy and had no time left over to brood. Then I got a stomach ulcer and that was a good thing too, though I felt lousy. *(Pause)* Well, so the weeks passed. Then I met the doctor at a dinner party. I can't say I was particularly attracted, but he wouldn't leave me alone and talked to me about myself. So I was hooked. Since then I've been pretty unsettled, to be quite honest. There have been times when I've gone around in a state of almost insane erotic excitement. I even got myself a massage gadget and read pornography to try to ease the pressure, but it only made it worse. Nothing helped. Do you know why? I was so bound to you that every time I had someone else in bed I thought only of you. I'm not saying this to give you a bad conscience, but merely to tell you just how it was. Since you wanted me to be frank. I got tired of those men too, not only in bed. Sometimes I got a kick out of it while it lasted, especially if we'd been drinking. But I got tired of their talk too. You and I have always got along so well together when we've been talking or working or just sitting quietly. I got fed up with their talk, their bodies, their gestures and movements. To my mind they made fools of themselves and I felt sorry for them. *(Pause, reflection)* It was all pretty humiliating, to tell the truth. *(Pause again)* Well, then I met David and he was rather different. Also, he was younger than I and a bit childish. He was quite unlike the others, anyway. Moreover, he was inclined to be wild. I found it hard to defend myself, so I rather fell for him. He was an extraordinary mixture—kind and gentle and considerate and ruthless and violent, so I must admit he swept me off my feet. He was so nice to the children, too. We all got along awfully well together, and the girls liked him. It wasn't such a bad set-up and I began to forget you. *(Sits in silence, thinking)*

JOHAN   And it was good in bed, I gather?

MARIANNE   Not at first. He was so fierce that he scared me and everything went wrong. He made so many demands on me and wasn't in the least considerate or thoughtful or anything. Then suddenly I *liked* the way he didn't give a damn about me—though oddly enough he did in a strange intuitive way. I'm pretty sure he was unfaithful at times. Not that I cared. I never asked.

JOHAN *(Gloomy)*   And now you've finished it off. What a pity!

MARIANNE *(Gravely)*   I don't know that it is, really.

JOHAN   You'll probably make it up next week.

MARIANNE   I'm not so sure I want to. It's not him I want. You were talking about loneliness—about admitting that one is lonely. I don't believe in your gospel of loneliness. I think it's a sign of weakness.
(All this time she has been sitting at the foot of the bed with her back against the bed-end. Now she lifts both her hands and holds them in front of her face in a helpless gesture)

JOHAN   What is it? *(Pause)* What's wrong, Marianne?

MARIANNE   It's so humiliating . . .

JOHAN   *(After a pause)*   What is?

MARIANNE   I don't know. *(Pulls herself together)* I'm thinking of the future, and then I think of you and me. I can't see how you're going to cope without me. Sometimes I feel quite desperate and think: *I must look after Johan.* He's my responsibility. It's up to me to see that Johan is all right. Only in that way will my life have a worthwhile meaning. One can't live alone and strong. One must have someone's hand to hold. Can't you *begin* to understand? I think we're making a mistake. I think we should work like hell to repair our marriage. As things are now we have a unique opportunity. We're wasting time. You're not to go away for three years without me. It would be too much for you. You're going to be so awfully afraid and uncertain if I don't look after you. I'm sorry to cry. I didn't mean to.
(JOHAN has sat up in bed and is caressing her knee clumsily. He sits bending forward with his head sunk, distressed and upset)

JOHAN   Sometimes I've puzzled over what can be wrong with me. I've wondered why I broke away from our marriage and why I fell in love with Paula and why I can't go back to you, now that it's over with Paula. But I can't arrive at an explanation. I'm completely in the dark. I'm fond of you, you know that, and sometimes I long for you most desperately. Yet it's as if there were a thick glass wall between us. I can see you, but I can't reach you. It's a sort of contempt—no, no, Marianne, I didn't mean that. You musn't take it literally. I express myself so badly. It's useless trying to explain. I only say the wrong things. I'll go now anyway.

MARIANNE   Can't you stay? We can lie side by side and hold hands. And we can talk about all sorts of unimportant little things. And by and by we'll fall asleep.

JOHAN *(Giving in)*   All right then. I'm terribly tired, as a matter of fact. I must just go to the bathroom. *(He gets up and shuffles out.* MARIANNE *smooths down the bed and opens the window a crack. Then she sets the alarm. She goes out into the kitchen and gets a bottle of mineral water and two glasses.* JOHAN *comes back)* I found some of my old pajamas in the cupboard. How nice to see them again.

MARIANNE   Good night, Johan. Sleep well.

JOHAN   Sleep well.

———————

A few hours pass. Then MARIANNE *wakes up to find that* JOHAN *has switched on the bedside lamp and gotten up.*

MARIANNE   What is it? Can't you sleep?

JOHAN   No, not a hope, I'd better go home. I feel miserable lying here. I'm sorry. *(He has begun to dress.* MARIANNE *also gets out of bed. She opens the drawer of the bedside table and takes out a letter which she hands to him. He checks himself and looks at the envelope in astonishment)* Why, that's Paula's handwriting.

MARIANNE   It's a letter to me from Paula.

JOHAN   What nasty things has she been writing?

MARIANNE   Read the letter yourself. It came before she went to London. I wasn't going to show it to you, as she didn't want me to. But I feel I must after all. Read it. No, read it out loud—now.

JOHAN *(Reading aloud)*   "Dear Marianne—I suspect that you'll be surprised to get a letter from me and I want to say at the outset that I'm not writing with any ulterior motive. I took this assignment in London so that I could get away for a week and thereby break a vicious circle of jealousy and suspicion. I know that Johan will look you up the minute I've gone. I have only myself to blame, as I've consistently stopped him from seeing you and the children. If only one could rectify mistakes. But what is done cannot be undone. If one could only wipe out suffering that one has caused other people . . ." (JOHAN *stops reading. He hands the letter back to* MARIANNE *and gives a laugh*) Just like Paula. As smart as ever.

MARIANNE   I think she means what she's written. She says that she wants us to be friends. She says that she can't endure hostility and silence. And here at the end: "If Johan does wants to go back to his family now, I won't prevent him."

JOHAN   How touching. And most touching of all is that you believe her.

MARIANNE   Don't tell her I've shown you the letter! Please!

JOHAN   (*Taking the letter and reading*)   "Johan is the gentlest, kindest, and most affectionate person I have ever met. If there is such a thing as love, then I think I love him. Johan's difficulty is that deep down he is so unsure of himself. He is utterly lacking in self-confidence, although he tries to seem so capable and courageous and never complains." (*Finishes reading*) I've noticed that actually you can say anything you like about anyone at all. Somehow it always fits. Here, you can take the letter.
(*He finishes dressing in silence, goes out into the hall, and puts on his coat.* MARIANNE *remains sitting on the bed holding the letter.* JOHAN *comes back into the bedroom, stands in front of her, and lays his hand on her shoulder. She looks up at him. They don't know what to say. He strokes her cheek. She kisses his hand. Then he goes*)

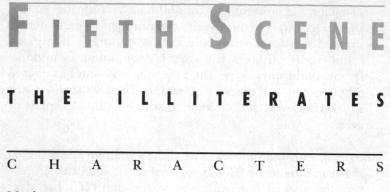

FIFTH SCENE

THE ILLITERATES

CHARACTERS

Marianne
Johan
Night Watchman

An extremely neutral room (regulation size). It is an evening in June.
JOHAN *sits reading a report. He has a cold. There's a knock at the door.*
Before JOHAN *has time to answer,* MARIANNE *storms in.*

MARIANNE Sorry I'm late. But Daddy called just as I was
leaving, and he went on and on and on. I said several
times I was in a hurry, but he wouldn't listen. How are
you?

JOHAN I have a cold.

MARIANNE Yes, you look pretty wretched.

JOHAN At first I just had a sore throat that might have been
anything and I thought, oh, it will go away. Then it turned
into a runny nose and then went down into my chest. So
now I cough all night long. I have a slight temperature and
feel lousy. I very nearly phoned and put you off, but since
you're going abroad I suppose it's essential to file the papers
with the court before you leave, isn't it?

MARIANNE Poor Johan. My heart bleeds for you. I hope Paula
is looking after you properly.

JOHAN She's also down with a cold. But with her it's a sort of
gastric flu. It's all terribly romantic.

133

MARIANNE   You'll pull through, don't worry.

JOHAN   You seem in very good spirits.

MARIANNE   Hmm, I am, at that.

JOHAN   Any special reason?

MARIANNE   Oh, I'm always excited before a trip. And then it's spring. And I have a new coat and skirt. How do you like it, by the way? Smart, isn't it? Of course in this light you can't see the color properly, But do you like it?

JOHAN   Yes, it's very nice.

MARIANNE   I'm glad we could meet here in your workroom. It saves time, I mean.

JOHAN   It's not exactly cozy.

MARIANNE   Just the place for going through divorce papers. Now, if you'll just look at this. Here's the actual agreement that Henning has drawn up. It's word for word as we dictated it together.

JOHAN   Then I needn't read through it.

MARIANNE   One should always read before signing. Don't look so grumpy, Johan.

JOHAN   I'm not grumpy.

MARIANNE   You're as sulky as can be. Here's the inventory of goods and chattels we acquired jointly and how we've divided them up between us. It's only a reminder list. You needn't sign it.

JOHAN   It says here that you're to have Granny's wall clock. That's a mistake, anyway.

MARIANNE   My dear Johan, your grandmother gave it to me. We've discussed it, for that matter.

JOHAN   I can't recollect having discussed Granny's wall clock.

MARIANNE   If you're so attached to it, then keep it by all means. But it is actually mine.

JOHAN   No, for Christ's sake. You're right as always. Take the damned clock, I'm not going to squabble over trifles. *(Coughs)*

MARIANNE   Is there anything else you think I have wrongfully appropriated?

JOHAN *(Sulkily)*   Your sarcasm is wasted. I have a cold and I'm depressed. So there. Would you like a glass of fine old brandy?

MARIANNE   That's just what the doctor ordered.

JOHAN   Egerman gave me a bottle. He had been in Paris lecturing and was presented with a whole case by grateful colleagues. There we are. Skoal! Well, what do you say? God, I needed that!

MARIANNE   Mmm. I don't really care for brandy, but this is something special.

JOHAN   I feel better now.

MARIANNE *(After a pause)*   It's hard all the same.

JOHAN   What's hard?

MARIANNE   Getting divorced.

JOHAN   It's only a few goddamn papers.

MARIANNE   I still think it's hard. We've been living apart for ages. We've seen practically nothing of each other. We're agreed. Yet one has a bad conscience. Isn't it strange. Johan! Don't you think it's—

JOHAN *(Sadly)*   Yes, it's strange.

MARIANNE   On my way here I was in a good mood. I was determined not to cry. I wasn't going to let the situation get me down.

JOHAN   You said you had a bad conscience.

MARIANNE   Can't we sit over there on the sofa and put the overhead light out? The glare is frightful. How can you work in such a bleak room?

JOHAN   The sofa's not very comfortable either.

MARIANNE   Yes it is, if you put your feet up on a chair.

JOHAN   Is that comfy? Like some more brandy?

MARIANNE   Yes, please. Are you all alone here this evening? Is the whole place empty?

JOHAN   There's a night watchman.

MARIANNE   How nice.

JOHAN   What do you mean, nice?

MARIANNE   I don't know, just nice.

JOHAN   When you have a cold, nothing's nice.

MARIANNE   Oh, stop feeling sorry for yourself! You're not going to die of it. Skoal! This gets better and better.

JOHAN   You *are* in good spirits. I envy you.

MARIANNE   Yes, I think I am, though I'm not sure. *(Smiles)* To tell the truth, I'm rather in love.

JOHAN   Still that David?

MARIANNE   David? Oh, him! No, that's over and done with.

JOHAN   Oh.

MARIANNE   For another thing, I'm beginning to feel free of you. And that's a relief. A *great* relief.

JOHAN   What do you mean by that?

MARIANNE   Never mind. Give me a kiss.

JOHAN   I have a cold.

MARIANNE   Don't you remember that I never catch your germs? Give me a kiss. I want you to.

JOHAN *(Kissing her)*   Well, was it what you expected?

MARIANNE   Better. *(Unbuttoning her blouse)* Now put your hand on my breast. Like that. Nice?

JOHAN   Are you going to seduce me?

MARIANNE   That's exactly my plan. In this very place, at this very moment. On the carpet, wall-to-wall and everything. What do you say to that? Wouldn't that be nice? Why do you look so anxious? Scared of the night watchman? After all, we're still married. Come and lie on top of me. One should make love on the floor much more often. Can you lock the door? Come and lie down, my darling. There, isn't that a lovely feeling? *(Smiles)* My poor little husband, who leads

such a miserable life. There, there, this is more like it, isn't
it? Kiss me. I've always liked it when you kiss me. Now you
lie on your back and I'll sit on top, then we'll come together.
Shut your eyes. If you look at me I get so self-conscious. And
hold your hands on my hips, like this. That's it. That feels
lovely. Imagine if the night watchman came in! *(Smiles)*
We'd ask him to join the party. We're so broadminded these
days. And we have all night. Let's just drink and make love.
And tomorrow we'll file the divorce papers.
(After they have made love they lie side by side facing each other.
JOHAN*'s hand rests against her cheek.* MARIANNE *has closed her eyes*
but is still smiling)

JOHAN   A penny for your thoughts.

MARIANNE   Mmm, I'm not telling.

JOHAN   Perhaps you're hungry?

MARIANNE   I always am.

JOHAN   What about a mixed grill and some beer? Doesn't that
sound good?

MARIANNE   But you're not allowed to take me out to a restaurant.

JOHAN   I'm in Uppsala this evening with my students.

MARIANNE   In that case you may stand me to supper by all
means. *(They are hilarious, tousled, and tipsy. They start putting*
*their clothes and faces in order)*Is there a bathroom anywhere
near?

JOHAN   Along the corridor to the left. You can't miss it.
*(*MARIANNE *unlocks the door and disappears into the corridor.* JO-
HAN *goes over to the desk and begins to fill his pipe. He lights it,*

glancing rather absentmindedly at the divorce papers which lie strewn over the desk. Suddenly the NIGHT WATCHMAN *is standing in the doorway)*

NIGHT WATCHMAN   Good evening, Professor.

JOHAN *(With a start)*   Heavens, it's you! Good evening.

NIGHT WATCHMAN   Working overtime, are we?

JOHAN   Er, yes.

NIGHT WATCHMAN   It's your secretary in the bathroom, I presume?

JOHAN   Eh? Oh yes, it's my secretary.

NIGHT WATCHMAN   Well, good night, Professor.

JOHAN   We're just going.

NIGHT WATCHMAN   You can stay all night, as far as I'm concerned.

JOHAN   We hadn't thought of doing so.

NIGHT WATCHMAN   Well, I wish you a nice Midsummer's Eve sir.

JOHAN   Same to you. Thank you. Good night.
(The NIGHT WATCHMAN *leaves.* JOHAN *sits down at the desk and begins to read the divorce agreement in earnest.* MARIANNE *comes in quietly and stands behind him, reading over his shoulder)*

MARIANNE   Let's sign the agreement and then go out and celebrate. Wouldn't that be a worthy end to a long and happy marriage?

JOHAN   I'd rather take the papers home and read through them quietly.

MARIANNE   What's this? Are we going to start chopping and changing after all our discussions?

JOHAN   You said yourself just now that one shouldn't sign anything without having read it through carefully. Didn't you?

MARIANNE *(Irritated)*   All right, we'll sit down opposite each other and read through the whole thing from A to Z. So that you can see I haven't cheated you in some mysterious fashion. *(Sits down crossly)*

JOHAN   Why are you so cross?

MARIANNE   I'm not in the least cross. Well, let's start.

JOHAN   You are. You're in a filthy temper.

MARIANNE   All right, I'm in a filthy temper, but I shall try to control it, since I'm used to controlling myself toward you and your whims. *(Blandly)* Can we leave this boring discussion now and get on with the reading. It's rather late, at that, and I have a busy day tomorrow.

JOHAN   So now we're not going to have supper?

MARIANNE   No, thank you. I'd rather not. I'm so grateful for the favors already bestowed upon me.

JOHAN   Whose whims now?

MARIANNE   Look here, Johan. *(Controlling herself)* No, don't speak. There's no point. I'll try to keep my temper. *(Sweetly)* Now, we'll put the papers in this envelope, like this, and you take them home with you and then you and Paula can go through the wording carefully together and see that I haven't diddled you.

JOHAN   Why, Marianne, what the hell's the matter?

MARIANNE   Nothing.

JOHAN   We were such good friends a moment ago.

MARIANNE   *(Holding a tight rein on herself)*   Exactly. By the way, don't forget it's Eva's birthday on Tuesday.

JOHAN   Am I in the habit of forgetting the children's birthdays?

MARIANNE   No, it has never happened, as I have always re-
minded you in good time. I'd be grateful if you'd kindly pay
for her trip to France this summer. I can't afford it.

JOHAN   How much will it cost?

MARIANNE   I think about two thousand kronor.

JOHAN   What! Are you out of your mind? Where am I going
to get two thousand kronor suddenly? It's out of the question.

MARIANNE   Then you can ask your mother.

JOHAN   I've already borrowed far too much from her.

MARIANNE   Well, I have no money anyway. It cost me over a
thousand kronor to have Karin's teeth fixed.

JOHAN   Can't they get their teeth seen to at school?

MARIANNE   You know as well as I do why Karin refuses to go
to the school dentist.

JOHAN   Eva will just have to cancel her trip. *I* don't have any
money. It won't hurt her to learn that you can't have everything you point to in this world. She's so goddamn spoiled
for that matter that it's not true. *And* ill-mannered. She went
to see Mother last week and Mother phoned me afterwards
and was quite shattered at the kid's behavior.

MARIANNE *(Capitulating)*   Oh, did she say that? Yes, it's hopeless. But she's at a difficult age.

JOHAN   I do think you might teach the girls a few manners.
But you let them boss you around just as they like.

MARIANNE   It's not so easy, let me tell you. They say I'm never at home to look after them. But I do try to be with them as much as I can. They're always angry with me. It's as if everything were my fault.

JOHAN   You should make them respect you. Anyway, they don't thank you for letting them do just as they like.

MARIANNE   Oh, don't talk nonsense. Isn't it better that I have their confidence? We do talk about everything. And for that I'm grateful. Why worry about trifles like manners and discipline and what you call being spoiled.

JOHAN   Anyhow, I'm not going to pay for Eva's trip to France. You can tell her that.

MARIANNE   Tell her yourself.

JOHAN   Why? You have the custody of the children. I have to fork out a hell of a big maintenance, which incidentally I have to pay taxes on and which is completely ruining me. So I don't see why I should have a lot of idiotic expenses on top of that. There's nothing to that effect in the divorce agreement, at any rate. Or is there?

MARIANNE   It's not the children's fault if we're worse off because you went off with another woman.

JOHAN   I never expected that remark from you.

MARIANNE   No, I'm sorry. It was crude of me.

JOHAN   Forget it. I will speak to our daughter. The difficulty is that we have no means of communication. Whenever she visits me she lolls on the sofa and reads *Donald Duck*. Or sprawls in an easy chair and watches TV. If I try to talk to her she mumbles something in a monosyllable as if she were a half-wit. Paula can't get any answer out of her at all. I think the girl is detestable, to be blunt. The only thing that makes her condescend to answer in a sentence with subject, predicate, and direct object is if I bribe her with money or treat her to the movies. Otherwise she chatters away on the phone to her friends for hours. At any rate I have no paternal feelings. Though I must admit she has grown pretty. No, it's much easier with Karin. Though she's so damned childish. Do you think perhaps she's a bit retarded? I'm beginning to be worried.

MARIANNE   How stupid you sound when you talk about the children like that. Stupid and childish.

JOHAN   Well, I am *not* amused. I brought them into the world by mistake and since then I've paid a small fortune for their upkeep. That must suffice. I refuse to play the fond father and I permit myself to dislike the children as much as they dislike me. Who has said that *I* must always be the one to take the first step toward contact and affection and love and all that? No, I prefer to act my part of wallet on two legs. At least that doesn't give me a bad conscience, seeing that I'm practically bankrupt with all I have to cough up. And that's as it should be. If you make a blunder, you have to pay. And if, as in this case, you make two blunders, then it costs you double. I don't mind telling you that I loathe my stupid, spoiled, brainless, lazy, and selfish daughters. Anyway, the feeling is reciprocated. *(Pause)* Why don't you say something? Are you angry now?

MARIANNE   I'm thinking back.

JOHAN   Thinking back?

MARIANNE   It used to be different. *(Quickly)* I mean as regards the children. Do you remember? How pleased you were when I plodded around with my big belly. And how eager you were for Eva to have a baby sister or brother. Do you remember all you used to do for the girls when they were little? Do you remember how you helped me look after them? You and I did everything between us and as a result the nanny that Mother had hired gave notice in sheer desperation. You spent all your time with the children, you played with them, read them fairy tales, you were so gentle and kind and patient. Much more patient than I was. Do you remember how worried you were over every little illness? You had a much better way with them than I did. And they loved you. Do you remember our Saturday evenings together? *(Sadly)* Why did things turn out like this? What went wrong? When did the children get bored with you? When did you get bored with them? What became of all the love and solicitude? And all the joy? Think of that summer when we gadded about the Mediterranean in your old rattletrap of a car and had the two small girls with us. And camped out. Remember those August nights on the coast of Spain, when we slept in the open, all four of us close together? Remember how nice and warm it was and what fun we had?

JOHAN   There's no use crying over spilt milk. Children grow up, relations are broken off. Love gives out, the same as affection, friendship, and solidarity. It's nothing unusual. It just is so.

MARIANNE   Sometimes I feel that you and I were both born with silver spoons in our mouths, but we've squandered our resources and suddenly find ourselves poor and bitter and angry. We must have gone wrong somewhere, and there was no one to tell us what we did.

JOHAN   I'll tell you something banal. We're emotional illiterates. And not only you and I—practically everybody, that's the depressing thing. We're taught everything about the body and about agriculture in Madagascar and about the square root of pi, or whatever the hell it's called, but not a word about the soul. We're abysmally ignorant, about both ourselves and others. There's a lot of loose talk nowadays to the effect that children should be brought up to know all about brotherhood and understanding and coexistence and equality and everything else that's all the rage just now. But it doesn't dawn on anyone that we must first learn something about ourselves and our own feelings. Our own fear and loneliness and anger. We're left without a chance, ignorant and remorseful among the ruins of our ambitions. To make a child aware of its soul is something almost indecent. You're regarded as a dirty old man. How can you ever understand other people if you don't know anything about yourself? Now you're yawning, so that's the end of the lecture. I had nothing more to say anyway. Some more brandy? Then we'll decide what to do about that supper.

MARIANNE   Yes, please. Incidentally I don't agree with you, but never mind. I don't believe in all that talk about awareness. What's the point of making people more nervous than they are already? You say that knowledge is security. Nonsense. Knowledge gives a wider choice and more anguish.

JOHAN *(Coughing)* Damn this cough. Oh, before I forget. I have something funny to tell you. That guest professorship has gone to hell. Not that it matters. But still.

MARIANNE   Why, Johan, what a terrible shame!

JOHAN *(Drinking)* Oh, I don't know. I was pretty disappointed, naturally. As usual there has been some goddamn hanky-panky. First the trip was postponed, and that was nothing to make a fuss about. Then suddenly there was no money. Then next thing I knew they'd sent Akerman! And fuck me. *(Laughs)* Just goes to show. Skoal!

MARIANNE   Poor old Johan. When did that happen?

JOHAN   In May. I had to request a new leave of absence, and it was difficult. Then Öhberg suggested that I apply directly to the chancellor of the university. Well, eventually they told me that Akerman was going instead. Granted, he has done a bit more research recently. But obviously there's some funny business somewhere. It smells a mile away.

MARIANNE Poor Johan, I *am* sorry.

JOHAN *(Beginning to harp)* I don't understand the mentality. A couple of weeks ago we were supposed to go to a convention in Oslo. Suddenly the department butts in and tells us we can't go. A, we're not getting any money, and B, we're to stay at home and get on with our job. *(Sips his brandy)* That's no way to talk to us, for Christ's sake! We're not a lot of lazy school kids playing hooky. I went up to the department to have the matter out. I've never known anything like it. I asked to see the minister of education but he didn't have time, so I had to content myself with some confounded underlings. You should have seen them! You should have seen the way they behaved. At least I was taught manners. And I'm a good bit older. There they sat in their shirt-sleeves, smoking and looking bored and supercilious. And their language! That undersecretary is a complete nitwit. They practically laughed me down. In the end I didn't know what I was saying, so I walked out. That's how they treat you nowadays. You're just a cipher. *(Drinks)* People like me have become inconvenient. And of course we're not of the right political shade. Not progressive. Not to the left of left. Overage. Out of the race. I could die laughing. *(Drinks)* I'll be forty-five this summer. I can reasonably expect to live for another thirty years. But viewed objectively I'm already a corpse. For the next twenty years I'll go around embittering my own life and other people's merely by existing. I am regarded as an expensive, unproductive unit which by rights should be got rid of by rationalization. And this is supposed to be the prime of life, when you could really make yourself useful, when you've gained a little experience. Shit, no. Throw the bugger out. Or let him creep around until he rots. I'm so goddamn tired, Marianne. If I had the guts I'd make a clean break and move to the country or ask for a job as teacher in a small town. Sometimes I wish I could . . .

(Drinks) Well, that's my sad story. *(Laughs)* Paula has a very ambivalent attitude toward the situation. And sometimes she says I'm a shit and starts packing her things. I don't know which of the alternatives would give me most relief. Anyway, I think she has a lover. Not that I care. I'm not jealous any more. I'm not really anything any more. I hardly know who I am now. Someone spat on me and I drowned in the spittle. *(Laughs)*

MARIANNE   It's an extraordinary thing . . .

JOHAN   What's extraordinary?

MARIANNE   Here I sit listening to you. And by rights I should feel something. But I don't feel anything. Faint sympathy, at most. On my way here this evening I suddenly got the idea of sleeping with you to see if I felt anything. And all I felt was good-natured friendship. Do you know what I think, Johan? I'm in the process of becoming free from you. It has taken a long time and been horribly painful. But I think I'm free now and can begin to live my own life. And how glad I am!

JOHAN   Allow me to congratulate you.

MARIANNE   I don't know why I'm saying this. And I suppose it's pretty callous of me to say it now, just when you've told me that you're going through a bad stretch. But oddly enough I don't care. I've considered you far too much during our married life. I think consideration killed off love. Has it struck you that we never quarreled? I think we even thought it was vulgar to quarrel. No, we sat down and talked so sensibly to each other. And you, having studied more and knowing more about the mind, told me what I *really* thought. What I felt *deep down*. I never understood what you were talking about. I merely felt a heavy weight like a sorrow. Had I allowed myself not to react with a bad conscience, I'd have known that everything we said and did to each other was wrong. Do you remember after Karin was born? When we suddenly couldn't make love any more? We sat down so prudently and explained so prudently to each other that it was quite natural. That it was only to be expected after two pregnancies one on top of the other. And all our subsequent discussions as to why we didn't get any pleasure out of making love. Neither of us realized that they were warnings. Red lights and stop signals were flashing all around us. But we only thought that was as it should be. We declared ourselves satisfied.

JOHAN   I think that these retrospective expositions are awfully boring and unnecessary.

MARIANNE *(Shouting)*   Your idiotic sarcasms nearly drive me mad. Must you always be the one to decide what is suitable or convenient? It serves you right if things have gone wrong. I'm *glad* Paula has a lover. You can commit suicide for all I care, though I expect you're too much of a coward. Well, well, so there you sit with tears in your eyes. And it leaves me cold! You can be made to feel what it's like for once. Feel what I've gone through.

JOHAN *(Calmly)*   Jesus, how I hate you really. I remember thinking it quite often: Jesus, how I hate her. Especially when we had made love and I had felt your indifference and knew you'd been thinking of something else. And we'd be out in the bathroom, with you sitting there naked on the bidet washing and washing away that nasty stuff you had got from me which you said smelled so awful. Then I would think: I hate her, her body, her movements. I could have struck you. I was itching to smash that white, hard resistance that radiated from you. But we chatted away so amicably to each other, joking about the nice times we had together in spite of everything.

MARIANNE   Then perhaps you can explain to me why I now have a man. And I love him. I love his body, I like his smells.

I do everything he asks me to. I long for him to take hold of me, for him to touch my breasts. Do you remember I only allowed you to touch my breasts in a special way, I shuddered when you fondled me unexpectedly, when you did anything that hadn't been agreed on. It's not so any more.

JOHAN   Just you wait and see. After a time you will marry him and before you know where you are you'll start in the same way with him. You wait and see. It's deep-rooted, that is. You'll start looking around for a new lover who can once again free you from that loathing.

MARIANNE   I know you're wrong. And I know that we could have come through those difficulties. They were not confined to our sex life. They were symptoms of other tensions. And those we'd have tried to clear up together. But we were so hopelessly considerate, we failed before we'd even started.

JOHAN *(Angry)*   There's such a thing as ordinary simple affection. There's such a thing as normal, natural sensuality, physical desire. But you don't know that. For you it's all blocked, shut off.

MARIANNE   I agree it has been so with you, but can *I* help that? Do you imagine I wasn't just as miserable about it as you were? I used to think: Must it be like this for us? Must it be so wretched? Then we'd console ourselves with the thought that after all sex was only of secondary importance, and that we got along well together in every other way. What self-deception, Johan. Nothing could be right when we could no longer make love.

JOHAN   You're forgetting certain things which it may be unpleasant to mention in this connection.

MARIANNE   Then perhaps you would kindly enlighten me.

JOHAN   Do you know what you did all along? *You exploited your sex organs.* They became a commodity. If you let me make love to you one day, the implication was that you'd be spared the next day. If I had been nice and helpful, I was rewarded with a lay. If I had been disagreeable or dared to criticize in any way, you got your own back by closing shop. What I put up with! It's grotesque when I think of the way you carried on. Christ! You were worse than any whore.

MARIANNE   But you wouldn't face the truth.

JOHAN   What goddamn truth, may I ask? Is it some sort of female truth? A truth with patent pending?

MARIANNE *(Furious)*   You're crazy. I really think you're out of your mind. Do you imagine that you can go on wiping your feet on me indefinitely? Am I always to be a substitute for your mother? All that goddamn harping on how I neglected our home and put my job first.

JOHAN   That's not true!

MARIANNE   During the first years of our marriage it was nothing but nag, nag, nag, both from you and your parents and from my own mother. All you succeeded in doing was to give me a bad conscience. I had a bad conscience at work and a bad conscience at home. Then I was expected to have a bad conscience because I didn't make love properly either. I was hedged in on all sides. Nothing but grumbling and nagging and demanding and—*Oh!* you son of a bitch! And if I got my own back with my sex organs, as you say, was it so strange? I was fighting against hopeless odds all the time: you and my mother and your parents and the whole of this goddamn society. I could never do what I wanted. There was always something in the way. When I think of what I endured and what I've at last broken free from, I could scream. And I tell you this: *Never again, never again, never again, never again.* You sit there whining about intrigues and having been double-crossed. It serves you right, it serves you damn well right. And I hope you have it rammed down your throat that you're a useless parasite.

JOHAN   You're being utterly grotesque.

MARIANNE   So what? That's how I've become. But the difference between my grotesqueness and yours is that I don't give in. I intend to keep on, you see. I intend to live in reality just as it is. For if there's one thing I like more than anything else on earth, it's to *live*. I enjoy overcoming difficulties and setbacks. And I don't ask for consideration. I don't give a damn for fine words and diplomacy.

JOHAN   *(Snatching up the divorce agreement)*   I'm glad we don't need to feel sympathy any longer. Glad we can throw all our bad conscience on the garbage pile. We're getting quite human. The whole trouble was that you and I ever met in the first place. That we fell in love and decided to live together. What a glorious fiasco right from the start. So the sooner we sign this paper the better, then we have only to divide up the silver and old wedding presents and say good-bye, and a pity it was all such a ghastly mistake from beginning to end.

MARIANNE   I'm not responsible for you. I live my own life and I'm capable of looking after myself and the children. Do you suppose I don't grasp what you've been sitting here saying all evening: *You don't want a divorce!*

JOHAN   *(Caught)*   I never heard anything so absurd!

MARIANNE   If it's so absurd then you can prove the opposite by signing the papers here and now.

JOHAN   All right.

MARIANNE   Johan! Be honest now! Look at me! Look at me,

Johan. You've changed your mind? You don't want us to divorce, do you? You thought we might pick up our marriage again. You were going to suggest something of the kind this evening. Go on, admit it.

JOHAN   Well, suppose I did have thoughts in that direction. Is it a crime? I confess I'm beaten. Is *that* what you want to hear? I'm tired of Paula. I'm homesick. Oh, I know, Marianne. You needn't put on that smile. I'm a failure and I'm going downhill and I'm scared and homeless. This isn't the right moment to ask you to go on with the marriage. I know what you're going to say. But you asked me. And I'm giving you a straight answer. I was bound to you in a different and deeper way than I realized. I was dependent on all those things that are called home and family and regular life and quiet everyday routine. I'm tired of living alone.

MARIANNE   Alone?

JOHAN   Loneliness with Paula is worse than real loneliness. I can't endure either of them. I can't talk about this. You know it all anyway. *(Silence)*

MARIANNE *(After a pause)*   I wonder how it would turn out.

JOHAN   I know that it would turn out much better than it has ever been. I know that we would be much more concerned about each other. Don't you think so? *(Pause)* Don't you think so?

MARIANNE   After a week or two we'd slip back into the old groove, our old nagging, our old aggressions. All our good resolutions would be forgotten. We wouldn't have learned anything. Everything would be the same as before. Or worse. It would be a mistake.

JOHAN   How can you be so sure?

MARIANNE   How many times must I repeat that I don't feel anything for you, other than rudimentary sympathy. *(Indignant)* I don't want you to entreat me. I'm not certain that . . . I'm not certain that I could cope. And that would be the worst thing that could happen.

JOHAN   Well, let's try.

MARIANNE *(Angry)*   Do you remember when I begged and implored you to come back? Do you remember how I groveled and wept and pleaded? I even turned religious for a time and prayed to God to let me have you back. Do you remember our meetings and your pretexts and half-truths, which merely showed your complete indifference all the more clearly.

JOHAN   I didn't know any better then. You can't reproach me for that now.

MARIANNE *(Angry)*   Reproach! What a fantastic word, Johan. Do you know what I think? I think you are feeble-minded and naïve. Do you suppose that I've gone through all I have and come out on the other side and started a life of my own which every day I'm thankful for, just to take charge of you and see that you don't go to the dogs because you're so weak and full of self-pity? If I didn't think you were so deplorable I'd laugh at you. When I think of what you've done to me during the last few years, I feel sick with fury. Go on, look at me. I'm proof against that gaze of yours. I've hardened myself. If you knew how many times I've dreamt I battered you to death, that I murdered you, that I stabbed you, that I kicked you. If you only knew what a goddamn relief it is to say all this to you at last.

JOHAN *(Smiling suddenly)*   You know, you're awfully pretty when you're angry like that.

MARIANNE   That's nice to know. *(More graciously)* Though *you* just look comical. What's more, you have lipstick on your cheek.

JOHAN   If I understand correctly, you'd prefer to see the divorce go through.

MARIANNE   *(On the verge of laughing)*   That's *exactly* how I'd like to sum up what I've already said.

JOHAN   Some more brandy?

MARIANNE   Heavens, we've nearly emptied the bottle! It's not surprising that I feel emancipated and a little peculiar. How do *you* feel?

JOHAN   Oh, not so bad. I think my cold has gone. At any rate, I haven't coughed for some time.

MARIANNE   *(Drinking)*   Well, to talk sensibly . . .

JOHAN   So what you said earlier wasn't sensible?

MARIANNE   It wasn't sensible, but it was true and necessary, as you must see.

JOHAN   I'm sitting here seeing as hard as I can.

MARIANNE   To talk sensibly, then. To say something reasonable, you should be glad I've made myself free and that I want to live my own life. I think you should do exactly the same. You should free yourself from the past, every bit of it. And start fresh under completely different conditions. *At this very moment* you have a marvelous chance.

JOHAN   Will you answer me something?

MARIANNE   Now you're sounding all pathetic again.

JOHAN   What's the use? I mean, to start fresh, as you say. I have no desire to.

MARIANNE *(Hesitating)*   What do you mean now?

JOHAN   Only what I've already said three or four times this evening, though you haven't bothered to listen. I have no desire to start fresh, I have no curiosity about what's ahead of me.

MARIANNE *(Beaten)*   You're only saying that because you're depressed and have had setbacks. You just want sympathy.

JOHAN *(With a smile)*   You've hit the nail on the head.

MARIANNE   When I think of the person I was only a few years ago, it's like someone altogether different. When you and I made love this evening I felt as if I were doing it with a stranger. Funny, isn't it? To be honest, it was rather exciting. Perhaps one day we'll be very good friends. And we'll gradually learn to know each other as the people we *really* are and not that horrible . . .

JOHAN   Horrible what?

MARIANNE   I mean that masked thing.

JOHAN   Masked thing?

MARIANNE   If only we could meet as the people we were meant to be. And not as people who try to play the parts that all sorts of powers have assigned us.

JOHAN   I'm afraid it's impossible. The masking starts in the cradle and goes on all through life. No one in the world can find himself, as you say.

MARIANNE   It's not true. I live a much more honest life now than I've ever done.

JOHAN   And happier?

MARIANNE   All that talk about happiness is nonsense. My greatest happiness is to eat a good dinner.

JOHAN *(Shaking his head)*   I'm not like you.

MARIANNE *(Suddenly, after a long pause)*   Don't you see that the whole of this situation frightens me? I feel horribly tempted to put out my hand and tear up that divorce agreement. Time and again I think: Why do *I* think I have the right to maintain a selfish life of my own? Do I really *imagine* I have a mission outside you and the children? Wouldn't it be tempting to start all over again together? I'm much stronger now and more independent. I could really be of help to you when you're having a rough time of it. *(Her hands in front of her face)* I feel such tenderness for you, Johan. *(Desperately)* I must be out of my mind. I know that we must get a divorce. Wisdom and common sense tell me that we must. *(Taking his hands)* It's intolerable.

JOHAN *(Humbly)*   I think I understand.

MARIANNE *(Shaking her head)*   Let's not talk about it.

JOHAN   No.

MARIANNE   Well, what shall we do about that supper?

JOHAN   I'm too drunk to go anywhere. Can't we sit here together for a while longer?

MARIANNE   Why not. As long as you don't make me sentimental.

JOHAN   Can't we go home?

MARIANNE   You mean home to my place?

JOHAN   Of course I mean home to your place.

MARIANNE *(Shaking her head)*   No.

JOHAN *(Drunk)*   Why not?

MARIANNE   Because I have a man who is sitting waiting for me, and he's going to be pretty upset that I reek of brandy and that I'm so late and that the papers aren't signed.

JOHAN   Is he jealous?

MARIANNE   Not particularly. *(Smiles)* But he knows my maso-
chistic nature. Do you know what he said before I left? He
kissed me and said: "You and your husband will make love.
And you'll come home with a guilty conscience and you
won't have signed the papers. And you'll give me up."

JOHAN   Are you going to tell him we've made love together?

MARIANNE   No. *(Smiles)* No, I don't think I will.

JOHAN   God, I'm tired.

MARIANNE *(Matter-of-factly)*   We've had too much to drink. If
we were sensible we'd go for a brisk walk in the fresh air
before going home to our respective soulmates.

JOHAN   You really are fantastic.

MARIANNE   No, I just have an incurable passion for what's
healthy. Come along, my dear. Let's go.

JOHAN   And the papers?

MARIANNE   When I came here I was determined to have our
divorce put through at all costs. In some way I've changed
my mind.

JOHAN   That's generous of you.

MARIANNE   Not in the way you think.

JOHAN   In what way then?

MARIANNE   I think I had an idea of remarrying. I'm not sure,
but I think so. My friend who's at home waiting for me now
suits me in every way. We get along well together and the
girls like him. He himself has been divorced for many years
and not long ago he suggested that he and I should get

married. I must say I was tempted. *(Pause)* It's so silly with these papers. They mean nothing at all really. Take them, Johan. Tear them up if you like. It's all the same to me whether I bear your name or my own or someone else's.

JOHAN   God, what a sermon!

MARIANNE   You're right. Shall we go?

JOHAN   I don't mind signing the papers.

MARIANNE   Do as you like. I don't care.

JOHAN   Don't go!

MARIANNE   It's late. Can I call a cab?

JOHAN   You must dial zero first, then you'll get an outside line.

MARIANNE   *(Phoning)* Good evening. Will you send a cab to Malmrosgatan forty-five, please? It's coming at once? Thank you. *(Puts down the receiver)* Can I give you a ride? You'd better not take your own car. You've had too much to drink.

JOHAN   I'll stay for a while.

MARIANNE   No, don't, Johan. Come with me now. It's not good for you to sit here alone brooding.

JOHAN   Never mind what I do.

MARIANNE   Come along, Johan.

JOHAN   Why don't you stay a while longer?

MARIANNE   I don't want to stay any longer.

JOHAN   Please don't go.

MARIANNE Please don't start that, Johan. You're just tired and drunk.

JOHAN Don't go, please.

MARIANNE Let me past!

JOHAN I'm not letting you go.

MARIANNE Don't be a fool!

JOHAN Don't be a fool yourself.

MARIANNE Even in our marriage we never behaved in this stupid way, Johan. Don't let's start now. Please give me the key.

JOHAN I don't give a damn what you say. Now I can see Marianne's well-ordered brain clicking away! What do I do now? Has he gone mad? Is he going to hit me?

MARIANNE If you really want to know, all I think is that you're screamingly funny.

JOHAN Oh, funny am I? Then why don't you laugh? I think you look scared if anything.

MARIANNE At least let me call and cancel the cab.

JOHAN Why? It will wait for ten minutes and then drive off. Sit down and take it easy. This is going to take a long time, I promise you.

MARIANNE All right, I don't mind. Well, what do you want to say now?

JOHAN Nothing. I just want to look at you.

MARIANNE   Go ahead. *(With a mocking smile)* As a matter of fact, it's just what I might have expected from someone like you. I wonder how many times in my profession I've warned wives seeking a divorce against being alone with their wronged husbands. I must confess I never thought I'd land in that situation myself.

JOHAN   Shut up!

MARIANNE   Do you think I'm afraid? *(Shakes her head)* If you want to know, I couldn't care less about what you're going to do.

JOHAN   Shut up, I said! *(He strikes her)*

MARIANNE   You crazy fool! *(She strikes back. A fight breaks out. A brutal, reckless, vicious brawl, which goes on and on until they are both exhausted. They are in a violent fury, but played out and covered in blood. They have sunk down panting in different corners of the room)* You must give me the key so that I can go to the bathroom and try and stanch the blood.

JOHAN   I'm not letting you out.

MARIANNE   Give me the key, you big fucking slob. You goddamn shit.
(He knocks her down on to the floor and kicks her savagely. She tries to shield her face with her hands)

JOHAN   I could kill you. *(Shouts)* I could kill you! I could kill you! *(Then he tires. She is lying motionless, huddled up. Suddenly it is very quiet in the white, bare room. The light glares from the ceiling. Overturned furniture. Blood-stains on the carpet. The objects from the desk strewn everywhere. Silence)* Are you all right?

MARIANNE   It was my own fault. Will you please let me out now?
(JOHAN unlocks the door and she goes out into the dark corridor. He

sits down, his hands trembling violently. Again and again he takes
very deep breaths, as though he were suffocating in rarefied air)

JOHAN *(Calling)* Shall I help you?

MARIANNE *(From outside)* No, please don't come here.
(He gets up slowly and goes over to the desk. Hunts about for a
while. Finds the divorce papers and signs his name on the original
and copies. MARIANNE *comes in, having patched herself up as well*
as she could. She signs her name beside his. Then she folds the papers
and puts them into her briefcase, which she clips shut. She puts on
her gloves) I'll see that the papers are filed in court as soon
as possible.

JOHAN Thank you, I'd appreciate that.

MARIANNE Well, so long.

JOHAN So long.

MARIANNE *(Turning in the doorway)* We should have started
fighting long ago. It would have been much better.

SIXTH SCENE

IN THE MIDDLE OF THE NIGHT IN A DARK HOUSE SOMEWHERE IN THE WORLD

CHARACTERS

Marianne
Johan
Eva
Arne
Marianne's Mother

A few years later. MARIANNE *is paying a visit to her mother.*

MARIANNE Hello, Mummy dear.

MOTHER Hello.

MARIANNE How's your foot?

MOTHER Oh, the pain has gone. But naturally I feel handi-
capped.

MARIANNE When did the doctor think you could start work
again?

MOTHER Not until next week.

MARIANNE Then you must arm yourself with patience.

MOTHER I just sit here and get nowhere.

MARIANNE Can you get any sleep at night?

MOTHER Well, the foot makes it difficult for me to turn in bed.
But I mustn't complain. Would you like some tea? Miss Alm
got the tray ready half an hour ago. So I've already had mine.

MARIANNE My dear, I'm awfully sorry to be so late, but I had a client I couldn't get rid of. And occasionally one must make time to listen.

MOTHER   Why, of course. I quite understand.

MARIANNE   The tea is still hot.

MOTHER   Shall I make you some toast?

MARIANNE   No thanks.

MOTHER   A piece of cake then?

MARIANNE   No thanks. I'm dieting.

MOTHER   How ridiculous.

MARIANNE   And I do exercises for half an hour every morning. And Henrik and I play tennis twice a week. It's very good for me.

MOTHER   Oh, there's something I must ask you since you're here. Are you coming to the interment of the ashes?

MARIANNE   When will it be?

MOTHER   We thought the eighteenth.

MARIANNE   Let me see now... *(Refers to her pocket diary)* Hmm, that's difficult. I have a court case that morning and it's bound to drag on. Is Daddy to be buried at Uppsala?

MOTHER   That was his wish. Your brothers and sisters are coming.

MARIANNE   But Mummy dear, the interment is merely a formality. You can't expect me to play hooky from work just because of that.

MOTHER   It depends how you look at it.

MARIANNE   Can't we change the day then?

MOTHER   All the others could come. And as you know, April eighteenth was your father's and my anniversary. We were married on April eighteenth thirty-nine years ago. Perhaps you had forgotten?

MARIANNE   Won't it all be needlessly upsetting?

MOTHER   Not for me.

MARIANNE   In any case, I can't come.

MOTHER   Well then, that's that.

MARIANNE   Karin and Eva send their love. They promised to look in after school tomorrow.

MOTHER   *(Brightens)*   Oh, how nice. Just imagine—Eva called to see me the day before yesterday with her boyfriend. She was actually wearing a dress and was quite the young lady. Her friend seems nice too. They stayed talking for a whole hour. I find it harder with Karin. But then she's the image of her grandfather.

MARIANNE   Poor Daddy.

MOTHER   I didn't mean to say anything disparaging about your father. Especially now that he is dead.

MARIANNE   I didn't think you did.

MOTHER   I've thought quite a lot about our marriage. Particularly sitting here with my foot, when I've had time to reflect.

MARIANNE   And what conclusion have you reached?

MOTHER   None at all, really. And that's what surprises me.

MARIANNE   What do you mean?

MOTHER   We had a good life. Sometimes we fell out, it's true, but we never quarreled. We never stooped to humiliating and insulting each other. We kept silent instead. And it was best like that. By degrees the hostility faded away and we forgot our differences. Neither Fredrik nor I was one to nurse a grievance.
(Pause)

MARIANNE   No.

MOTHER   Of course I miss him. But actually I don't feel any more alone now than when he was alive.

MARIANNE   I'm sorry to hear that.

MOTHER   Why? Both of us were kept busy. He with his affairs, I with mine.

MARIANNE   May I ask you something, Mummy?

MOTHER   Ask me anything you like.

MARIANNE   But please don't think I'm being tactless.

MOTHER   I won't think that.

MARIANNE   How was it in bed, for you and Daddy?

MOTHER   *(Pause)*   He was more interested than I was.

MARIANNE   Well?

MOTHER   *(Irritated)*   What more do you want to know? He took what he wanted. And I let him have his way. I never refused him. I considered it my duty to be at his disposal. Anyway, he had other women. At times it was rather horrible.

MARIANNE And you?

MOTHER I?

MARIANNE Did you have other men?

MOTHER After Fredrik and I were engaged I fell in love with another man and wanted to break it off. But Mother and Father didn't want me to do anything rash. So that was that.

MARIANNE Haven't you ever hated Daddy?

MOTHER Hated him? What do you mean?

MARIANNE When you got married, you both signed a contract entirely in his favor. Haven't you ever hated him for that transaction?

MOTHER I liked him. Besides, we were as blind as kittens. Neither of us realized what we were embarking on.

MARIANNE But Mummy, it's not possible!

MOTHER He had his faults. So did I. *(Pause)* No, it's not that.

MARIANNE What is it then?

MOTHER I wonder how it would have been had we confided in each other. If we had talked over everything that occurred to us.

MARIANNE And you never did?

MOTHER No. We had a rule that our parents taught us: *Each one copes with his own troubles.*

MARIANNE   Do you regret it?

MOTHER   Not regret exactly. I can't say that. But I can't help thinking about our heroic silence. I'm sure it must have tormented him quite a lot. He was such a lively person. Much gayer and more open than I.

MARIANNE *(Moved)*   Do you reproach yourself, Mummy?

MOTHER   I don't know. But it *is* ghastly. No, not ghastly, that's far too dramatic a word. It's extraordinary that two people live a whole life together without . . .

MARIANNE   Without touching each other.

MOTHER   Perhaps that's what I mean.

MARIANNE   And now you think it was your fault?

MOTHER   You mean I'm sitting here with a guilty conscience? No, I'm not. We did our best. All the same . . .

MARIANNE   You can't help thinking of . . .

MOTHER   It sounds so stilted if you put it into words. He has vanished in the darkness and taken his life with him. But the funny thing is that he has taken my life too. *(Smiles)* This is what's called facing the truth, isn't it?

MARIANNE *(Deeply affected)*   You and I have never talked like this before.

MOTHER   We've never had time.

MARIANNE   Or inclination.

MOTHER   I've always been a little scared of you.

MARIANNE *(Smiling)* Scared? Of me?

MOTHER You've always been so capable.

MARIANNE What about yourself?

MOTHER *(Shaking her head)* If you only knew how anxious I've been about not doing everything perfectly.

MARIANNE *(Touched)* But you *are* perfect.

MOTHER Sometimes I'm a little girl of seven, walking in the woods with a father and holding his hand. I'm growing old and sentimental, that's the truth.

MARIANNE May I ask you something else?

MOTHER *(Smiling)* It can't be avoided, can it?

MARIANNE Why were you so furious with me when Johan and I were divorced five years ago? When it was he who got himself another woman and walked out on me?

MOTHER I wasn't furious at all. I was merely sorry.

MARIANNE But you criticized me all the time.

MOTHER I don't remember that.

MARIANNE It was all my fault.

MOTHER Did I say that?

MARIANNE Yes, you did.

MOTHER I've forgotten.

MARIANNE I think you might have sided with me that time.

And helped me a little. But you didn't. I wonder why.

MOTHER   I remember just the opposite. I know I said to your father that whatever we did we mustn't interfere and that at all costs we must behave as usual. It was he who was furious, not I.

MARIANNE *(Smiling)* It just goes to show. *(Looking at the time)* Heavens, I must fly. I'm late as it is.

MOTHER   Do you have to go already?

MARIANNE   I'll come again tomorrow. And we can have another talk. I'll be here about five.

MOTHER   Then we can have dinner together.

MARIANNE   I'm afraid I'm asked out to dinner. But I can stay until six thirty.

MOTHER   Can't you bring your dress with you, then you needn't go home and change?

MARIANNE   Yes, I could do that.

MOTHER *(Impulsively)* It was so nice to talk to each other.

MARIANNE *(On her way out)* Let's do it more often.

MOTHER   Do go out to the kitchen and say hello to Miss Alm. She'll be mortally offended if you go without seeing her.

MARIANNE   Heavens, yes! I'll go and say hello to her. So long, Mummy, take care of yourself.

MOTHER   Give my love to Henrik and the children.

MARIANNE   Henrik's away, he won't be home until Saturday.
Bye!

———————

JOHAN *is sitting in his workroom at the institute, busy with some typing. Nowadays he is clean-shaven and wears glasses.* EVA *looks in.*

EVA   Am I disturbing you?

JOHAN   Well . . .

EVA   What are you and your wife doing this evening?

JOHAN   We're busy, as a matter of fact.

EVA *(Smiling)*   What a pity.

JOHAN   Oh?

EVA   I'm throwing a little party and I thought you and your wife might care to look in if you had nothing better to do. There'll only be seven or eight of us.

JOHAN   I'm sorry, it's impossible.

EVA *(Smiling)*   Well, have a nice weekend anyway.

JOHAN   Thanks. Same to you.

EVA   Can't we meet some time?

JOHAN   I'm too busy.

EVA   Are you tired of me?

JOHAN   Why, Eva!

EVA   If you want to break it off, then say so properly and don't make excuses.

JOHAN   All right then. Let's break it off.

EVA   Thank heavens for a straight answer. I had a job getting it out of you.

JOHAN   I didn't want to hurt you.

EVA   *(Gives a laugh)*   No, exactly.

JOHAN   If you'll forgive me, I must finish writing this damned report.

EVA   *(Cheerfully)*   Why, of course, my dear, I won't disturb you. Well, thanks for everything. You were an awfully sweet lover, though a bit absent-minded.

JOHAN   *(Smiling)*   Thank *you*. You also get good marks.

EVA   Is there someone else?

JOHAN   To be honest, yes.

EVA   Who?

JOHAN   I'm not telling you.

EVA   Is it anyone I know?

JOHAN   Possibly.

EVA   Is it Lena?

JOHAN   I'm not saying any more.

EVA   Then it is Lena.

JOHAN   No, it's not Lena.

EVA   Oh, the girl's pretty if it comes to that. But isn't she a shade too young and flighty for you, my sweet?

JOHAN   It's *not* Lena, I said.

EVA   I don't care anyway. Bye-bye, darling.

JOHAN   So long. All the best.
(EVA *goes out and shuts the door.* ARNE *looks in. He's beginning to put on weight, but youthful*)

ARNE   Hi.

JOHAN   Hi.

ARNE   Have a nice weekend.

JOHAN   Thanks. Same to you.

ARNE   These long weekends with the family are the goddamn end. By the way, I heard you were put on to a survey. Should I congratulate you?

JOHAN   There's not the slightest reason.

ARNE   I suspected as much.

JOHAN   I'll be practically cut off from the institute for two years.

ARNE   What a bore! For you.

JOHAN   Anyway, the whole survey's idiotic. In two years, when it's ready, it will be worthless. It's nothing but a political red herring.

ARNE   Can't you go to Hammarberg and say you don't want to do it?

JOHAN   I've already seen him.

ARNE   Well?

JOHAN   He's a clown. Clown number one of the Swedish civil service. Next thing we know he'll be a member of the government.

ARNE   Yes, but what did he say?

JOHAN   He spoke in ciphers. I didn't know what to make of it. Hardly encouraging.

ARNE   Oh, I see. Well, so long. Have you been to bed with Lena?

JOHAN   To tell you the truth, I haven't.

ARNE   But she turns you on, doesn't she?

JOHAN   What about yourself?

ARNE   Well, yes.

JOHAN   I don't think I'd dare.

ARNE   Have you given up?

JOHAN   Call it what you like.

ARNE   I keep fit, anyway. Exercise, tennis. Swimming. Sun lamp. Watch my weight. So that I needn't feel embarrassed. If it should come to a more intimate presentation, I mean. Bare facts and all that. So long.

JOHAN So long.

(ARNE *goes out and shuts the door. Quick footsteps are heard in the corridor.* EVA *flings the door open*)

EVA I suddenly lost my temper.

JOHAN So I see.

EVA I think you're a big shit. Not because you've broken it off with me. I'm not complaining. It was fun while it lasted and we both knew it wasn't for life. But to my mind you're a slob for not saying straight out that you'd had enough. Do you know what's wrong with you? You're so fucking spoiled and priggish that everything bores you. You'll end up by being so bored that you'll be anonymous. In a few years you'll become part of those bookshelves. You're smug and cocky and spoiled. You're bone lazy. You must have others who live for you. Do you remember when you went to the doctor for a check-up and he told you that you had shrunk an inch or two? So there.
(*Sits down*)

JOHAN (*Echo*) So there.

EVA (*No longer so fierce*) Why don't you hit back? Why don't you raise Cain? Why do you make yourself out so meek, when you're so pompous and stuck-up?

JOHAN This is really very interesting.

EVA The explanation is that you're so pompous that . . . You're so spoiled and priggish that . . .

JOHAN Well, what?

EVA I'm fond of you, you silly old thing. That's why I'm bawling you out. And I feel sorry for you somehow.

JOHAN That's kind of you.

EVA   So long. Let me know when you're tired of Lena's melon breasts and long for my flatter but much more motherly charms.

JOHAN *(Sighing)*   It's not Lena.

EVA   She's an efficient secretary, I grant you. And I'm sure awfully kind. But she's too young for you, Johan. You'll only ccme to grief with her.

JOHAN   I've told you, it's *not* Lena.

EVA   I have my intuition.

JOHAN   Yes, you have, haven't you?

EVA   And I can see that you're terribly involved.

JOHAN   Maybe I am.

EVA   And it can't be anyone else but Lena. So long.

JOHAN   So long.(EVA *goes out and closes the door.* JOHAN *goes on working. The phone rings and he seizes it*) Hello. Hi! Are you ready now? I'll call for you. Oh, you'd rather not. Well, what about the corner of Karlavägen and Grev Turegatan? Will that do? I'll be there in two minutes. Fine. Bye!

————

JOHAN *has parked at the street corner. He sits huddled up waiting. After a minute or two* MARIANNE *walks along on the other side of the street. When she catches sight of him she beams and starts to run. She gets in beside him, breathless and smiling. She kisses him quickly on the lips. He starts the car.*

MARIANNE   Been waiting long?

JOHAN   No, I just got here.

MARIANNE   I went to see Mummy.

JOHAN   Oh. How is the old girl?

MARIANNE   I think that . . . Oh, I'll tell you later.

JOHAN   Let's go then.

MARIANNE   Oh, what fun this is! I'm so excited! I went out to the country house yesterday and got it ready. Turned on the heating and the refrigerator and straightened up and got in some food. It was just like old times.

JOHAN   Let's see now, how many years is it since I was there?

MARIANNE   Seven, I think.

JOHAN   And you?

MARIANNE   Well, you see, Henrik doesn't care much for the house. He prefers the real country. So as a matter of fact we usually rent it. Occasionally the girls and I go out there for the weekend, but less and less often. Eva and Karin live their own lives nowadays. It's best that way.

JOHAN   And how's your husband?

MARIANNE   He's overworked, of course. And has high blood pressure, but so does everyone. How is your wife doing?

JOHAN   Oh, all right, I think. She's in Italy on a rest cure.

MARIANNE   Isn't it fantastic that our respective spouses are away at the same time!

JOHAN   It strikes me rather as being slightly indecent.

MARIANNE   But that's just what is so delightful.
(*They arrive at the country house. It hasn't changed much.* MA-RIANNE *unlocks the door. They go in*)

JOHAN   It looks much the same.

MARIANNE   A bit dilapidated, that's all. It needs fixing up. But right now we can't afford it, so it will have to wait.

JOHAN   How does it feel?

MARIANNE *(Evasively)* I don't want to know. It's better that way. You'd better drive the car into the garage so that Gustav doesn't see that we're here. He'd be over like a shot to say hello. And the fat would be in the fire if he saw you.

JOHAN I'll put the car away later. We're going straight up to the bedroom.

MARIANNE *(With a smile)* It's ridiculous, but I'm as nervous as if it were the first time.

JOHAN But as a matter of fact it's not.
(They lie on the big double bed and hold hands, at first without speaking)

MARIANNE A penny for your thoughts.

JOHAN I was trying to think whether it was you who seduced me or I who seduced you.

MARIANNE It was almost a year ago. Yes, it was. The eighth of May, the day before my birthday. Just fancy that. And today's the twenty-eighth of April.

JOHAN It was you who seduced me.

MARIANNE Yes, it was.

JOHAN Did you ever go and see the second act of that play?

MARIANNE No. It must have looked odd when we sneaked off like two criminals at the intermission.

JOHAN What decided you?

MARIANNE I don't know. The second I entered the theater I saw you sitting there all alone. You looked so lonely. So it seemed quite natural to pounce on you at the intermission.

JOHAN   I was awfully pleased, actually.

MARIANNE   And I was pleased that you were pleased.

JOHAN   And you said right off, let's get out of here and go back to my place. My husband's away and won't be home until Friday.

MARIANNE   You blushed.

JOHAN   You bet your sweet life I did. I got such a hard-on that I could hardly stand up straight.

MARIANNE   *(Smiling)*   It was nothing to the way I felt.

JOHAN   We hadn't seen each other for about two years.

MARIANNE   Two years. That's right.

JOHAN   And now we're celebrating our first anniversary.

MARIANNE   No.

JOHAN   What do you mean?

MARIANNE   We're celebrating our twentieth anniversary. We got married in August twenty years ago.

JOHAN   So we did. Twenty years.

MARIANNE   A whole life. We've lived a whole grown-up life with each other. How strange to think of it.
(Weeps suddenly)

JOHAN   *(Gently)*   Dearest. Dearest heart.

MARIANNE   Oh, Johan, isn't it funny? I mean, lying here in this wretched old bed again. It has been different this last year

when we've had our hotel rooms. They were suitably imper-
sonal. But this . . .

JOHAN *(Kindly)* Perhaps it was silly of us to come here. Perhaps we should have gone to Denmark instead, as I first
suggested.

MARIANNE We didn't have time. And this is quite all right.

JOHAN No, it isn't all right at all. Do you know what I'll do?

MARIANNE I'll soon get used to it.

JOHAN I'll call up Fredrik. He has a cottage not far from here
down by the water. You know.

MARIANNE But how can we get in?

JOHAN   There's sure to be a neighbor who has a key. I'm going to phone anyway.

MARIANNE   No, what's the point?

JOHAN   There's no harm in trying. *(Leafs through an address book, dials a number)* Fredrik? Hello, it's Johan. How are you? *(Pause)* Oh, I'm fine. *(Clears his throat)* Look, this is rather a delicate matter. Are you alone? I mean, can we talk freely? Do you think you could lend me your fishing cottage over the weekend? *(Pause)* Hahaha. Yes, right the first time. Though it's not what you think. Hahaha. Very pretty, let me tell you. Young? Well, damn it, she *is* a bit young perhaps. Hahaha. It's all rather tricky, you see. Thanks a lot. I hope I can do you a favor some time. Look, don't say anything to Birgit, will you. She wouldn't understand this sort of thing. Hahaha. You know how women are. Oh, the key's under the step, is it. *(Pause)* Fine. What? Blonde. Nice figure. I'm not saying. Not over the phone. Let's have dinner together one day, eh? I'll call you. Give my love to Birgit. No, better not, at that.(MARIANNE *and* JOHAN *giggle and laugh.* MARIANNE *has taken out a bag with nightgown and toilet things, and a shopping bag with food.)* Come on, let's go. What on earth's in that bag?

MARIANNE   It's only the food we have to take with us, silly. *(They drive off. Arrive at the cottage. It's in a wretched state.* JOHAN *tries to get the fire going.* MARIANNE *goes up to him. Her feelings get the better of her, tears come to her eyes.* JOHAN *turns around)*

JOHAN   What is it? Crying?

MARIANNE   It's so touching. I *am* a fool.

JOHAN   Touching, am I? I'll be damned!

MARIANNE   Yes, you are. Johan, my dearest. You've grown so small in some way.

JOHAN *(Embarrassed)* Do you too think I've shrunk?

MARIANNE You're much more handsome than before. And you look so gentle and kind. You always had such a tense look before, sort of anxious and on your guard.

JOHAN Oh, really?

MARIANNE Are people beastly to you?

JOHAN *(Smiling)* I don't really know. I think perhaps I've stopped defending myself. Someone said I'd grown slack and gave in too easily. That I diminished myself. It's not true. If anything, I think I've found my right proportions. And that I've accepted my limitations with a certain humility. That makes me kind and a bit mournful.

MARIANNE *(Tenderly)* And you with your great expectations.

JOHAN No, you're wrong. It was my father who had the great expectations, not I. But I wanted so desperately to please Daddy, so I tried all the time to live up to *his* expectations. Not mine. When I was little I had very modest and pleasant ideas as to what I would do when I grew up.

MARIANNE *(Smiling)* What were they?

JOHAN Have I never told you?

MARIANNE If so I've forgotten.

JOHAN Yes, of course. *(Pause)* Well, you see, I had an old uncle. He had a little store at Sigtuna that sold books and toys and stationery. I was often allowed to go and see him, as I was a sickly child and in need of quiet and fresh air. Sometimes he and Aunt Emma let me help them in the store. I liked that more than anything. My dream was to own a store like that. There you have my ambitions.

MARIANNE   Yes, we should have had a little store. *(Smiles)* How content we'd have been. We'd have grown fat and comfortable and had a lot of children, and slept well and been respected and have joined some local society and never quarreled.

JOHAN   How strange, talking about all that never was. Anyway, you'd never have settled down in some sleepy little place in the country.

MARIANNE   No, that's true. *(Serious)* I used to dream of pleading the cause of the oppressed. There were no limits to my ambitions. And then I became a divorce lawyer. Come on, let's straighten up.

———

MARIANNE *and* JOHAN *are sitting at the table. They have eaten, and are sipping wine. A paper lantern is lit.*

MARIANNE   A penny for your thoughts.

JOHAN   It just struck me that you and I have begun telling each other the truth.

MARIANNE   Didn't we before? No, we didn't. Why didn't we? That's odd. Why are we telling the truth now? I know. It's because we make no demands.

JOHAN   We have no secrets from each other.

MARIANNE   Nothing to guard.

JOHAN   In other words, we can tell the truth. After twenty years.

MARIANNE   After twenty years.

JOHAN   Do you think two people who live together day in and day out ever tell the truth to each other? Is it possible, at that?

MARIANNE   It wasn't for us, anyway.

JOHAN   Is it even necessary?

MARIANNE   You mean, suppose that you and I had always told the truth and not kept anything secret from each other?

JOHAN   Did we even know that we kept things secret?

MARIANNE   Of course we lied. I did, anyway.

JOHAN   You! You don't mean it.

MARIANNE   Listen to your tone of voice, Johan.

JOHAN   What goddamn tone of voice?

MARIANNE   The tone of injured innocence. *(Smiles)* At the beginning of our marriage I was unfaithful to you several times. As a matter of fact.

JOHAN   Indeed!

MARIANNE   Are you shocked?

JOHAN   I don't quite know. Yes, I think I am.

MARIANNE   It was all rather harmless. I felt that I was stifling under marriage and childbirth and other duties. So I went in for a spot of adultery.

JOHAN   I'll be damned.

MARIANNE   In pretty quick succession I had three rather cozy little affairs with men you don't know. If you ask me about my conscience, it never said a word.

JOHAN   I see. Well, well. Just goes to show.

MARIANNE   I felt that my affairs were a slight recompense for the suffering I was caused.

JOHAN   If only we'd told the truth.

MARIANNE   If I had told the truth in the spring of nineteen fifty-five, the truth would have pulverized our marriage. I would have broken with our families, sold our two daughters, and killed you. Although in fact I loved you. For I did.

JOHAN   But later?

MARIANNE   Later I got tired.

JOHAN   Of me?

MARIANNE   No, I got tired of my lovers. It wasn't that kind of liberty I longed for after all. So I tried to adjust myself.

JOHAN   And you said nothing.

MARIANNE   What was the use? Anyway, you were working on your doctoral thesis. And you had a stomach ulcer. So we had to tiptoe around to avoid disturbing you.

JOHAN   But all the same!

MARIANNE   All that mattered just then was for you to get your Ph.D. So truth had to take second place. Superficially, the relationship between men and women has changed. But in reality it's the same as a hundred years ago. Ridiculous, isn't it?

JOHAN But afterwards?

MARIANNE Oh, we talked. Quite often.

JOHAN Without any real openness.

MARIANNE We made do with convenient half-truths. And both of us had studied psychology, so we could explain almost anything. And we couldn't be bothered to have fights. Now and then, when we really lost our tempers, we had a few words, of course.

JOHAN But we took them back. Afterwards. It would have been carrying things too far to untangle everything.

MARIANNE So we resorted to lying. Sometimes more, sometimes less, as it suited us.

JOHAN Do you apply these experiences to your new marriage?

MARIANNE Why, of course. I lie all the time.

JOHAN So do I.

MARIANNE There, you see.

JOHAN That is to say, my wife isn't interested in the truth. She has arranged the marriage to our mutual convenience.

MARIANNE Do you love Anna?

JOHAN This eternal woman's question. I think she's kind, intelligent, pleasant, clean, well-mannered, presentable, and sexually attractive. I like having breakfast with her.

MARIANNE And she's willing to look after you?

JOHAN   She says she's fond of me. She doesn't care if I'm clever or not. I can be as tired and insufferable as I like. She says it doesn't matter. She says she feels safe with me. She doesn't want anyone else. It's quite beyond me.

MARIANNE *(Another tone of voice)*   You've had luck with your lottery ticket, Johan!

JOHAN   Then I suppose I shouldn't be unfaithful to her with you.

MARIANNE   Perhaps you love us both.

JOHAN   There you go, all sententious again. I suppose you have to have a gift for feeling love. I don't have that gift.

MARIANNE   First it was your mother who adored you and thought you were a genius. And then the whole succession of women who have behaved in exactly the same way as your mother. Including me. I wonder what it is in you that sabotages all natural maturity. I'm not saying this to be spiteful, but merely because the question never stops puzzling me.

JOHAN *(Candidly)*   Nowadays I know the cause and it's not particularly encouraging.

MARIANNE   It would be interesting to hear.

JOHAN *(Gaily)*   Now you shall hear my hideous secret. I'm a middle-aged boy who never wants to grow up.

MARIANNE   I've known that all along.

JOHAN   I have found it very hard to grasp that I'm a child with genitals. A fabulous combination when it comes to women with maternal feelings.

MARIANNE   Heavens, how banal! I thought at least you were going to confess to some criminal tendencies.

JOHAN *(Continuing)*   And for that reason I never grew up. Why should I? It would mean that I was forced to manage on my own. I might even have to accept responsibility.

MARIANNE   What an awful anticlimax, Johan dear.

JOHAN   I don't *want* to mature, you see. That's why Anna is a good wife.

MARIANNE   Poor Anna.

JOHAN *(Smiling)*   Your sympathy doesn't ring true. Now let's talk about you instead.

MARIANNE *(Laughing)*   Weren't we going to have dinner?

———————

They have now had dinner and have settled down comfortably in front of the fire. It is dusk. They are sitting in easy chairs and smoking in silence

MARIANNE   You want to know how I get along with Henrik, my husband?

JOHAN   Not any more.

MARIANNE   It was silly of us to get married at all. Or shall I say it was rash? We looked on it more or less as a joke. Two people can live together year in and year out without being married and it's quite a different matter from living together when they *are* married.

JOHAN   When did you meet?

MARIANNE   Oh, some years ago. If you'll forgive my saying so, it was a purely sexual affair.

JOHAN   Oh. Oh, I see.

MARIANNE   Henrik is very, how shall I put it, convincing on that point. *(Smiles)* Sex really turns him on and he persuaded me that I was just as avid as he was. As you know, I wasn't all that hot for it in the old days.

JOHAN   So I remember.

MARIANNE   You don't like my talking about this?

JOHAN   No, I don't. But it can't be helped.

MARIANNE   Frankly, I was obsessed by this new thing that I had never known. I found I was insatiable. *(Smiles)* It sounds crazy.

JOHAN   I think it sounds nice. For you, I mean.

MARIANNE   As you can imagine, I fell hard for Henrik and couldn't do without him. He was also pretty crazy about me. But I soon found out that he was having other women on the side.

JOHAN   Well I never!

MARIANNE   At first I was terribly hurt and humiliated. I even became jealous.

JOHAN   *You* did?

MARIANNE   We had a violent quarrel. That is to say, *I* was the violent one. I told him to go to hell.

JOHAN   And did he?

MARIANNE He said I was overwrought. And walked out. After a week or two I begged him on my knees to come back. On *any* conditions. He too thought it was time to resume. We went off on a vacation together. We were very happy. On our return we got married. Since then it has been up and down. Mostly down.

JOHAN I'm sorry.

MARIANNE Henrik is an overwhelmingly active person. He's senior physician at the General Hospital. He's also on dozens of committees and on top of that spends every spare minute doing research. I just don't know how he does it.

JOHAN Especially if he has a private practice with a lot of ladies at the same time.

MARIANNE His health isn't too good. He has high blood pressure and has to keep taking medicine. Sometimes I feel I can't stand him another minute. That he'll be the death of me with all his demands.

JOHAN That's not very nice for someone with your insistence on liberty, is it?

MARIANNE Oddly enough it's just the reverse.

JOHAN I don't get you.

MARIANNE Today I'm no longer dependent on him. I live with him. That's fine. I live with you. That's fine. If I meet some other man who attracts me I can live with him too.

JOHAN Do you call *that* liberty?

MARIANNE For the time being it's liberty.

JOHAN And you're happy?

MARIANNE   Sometimes I'm extremely unhappy when by rights I should be happy, and just the opposite. The feeling of happiness follows no rules. At least not with me.

JOHAN   There's something I'd like to ask you.

MARIANNE *(With a nod)*   You want to know if I'm still in the habit of getting my own back on the sexual plane. *(Laughs)* I tried all right. But he never paid any attention. He merely said I bored him with that sort of nonsense. And devoted himself to some other woman with the same all-absorbing interest. And there I was, high and dry with my revenge. So I've stopped all that. You and I also have it good nowadays. Don't we, Johan my darling?

JOHAN   Yes, of course.

MARIANNE   Are you jealous?

JOHAN   I feel both attracted and repelled.

MARIANNE   Do you remember what we had drummed into us as children? All that rubbish about physical love being the most sacred and beautiful thing there was? That the body was a temple and that you mustn't cheapen yourself. Or something equally idiotic. To make love to someone was almost a sacrament. Everything was so precious and delicate and wonderful that we got the jitters when we tried to put it into practice. At the other extreme was pornography, with lurid descriptions of the sex act and colossal feats of incessant orgasm. That was also pretty depressing. *(Pause)* What's up, Johan? You look so thoughtful.

JOHAN *(Smiling suddenly)*   I was thinking that everything's fine. Just fine. Tremendously good. Couldn't be better. It's just that I can't stand it.

MARIANNE   I knew you didn't want to hear the truth.

JOHAN *(Fiercely)*   Do you think I care about your orgasms with that goddamn slob and his blood pressure? You're welcome to them. I'm full of admiration for your complete emancipation. It's most impressive. You should damn well write a novel. I bet you'd be applauded by Women's Lib.

MARIANNE   You can't mean to be as stupid as you sound.

JOHAN   I tell you I couldn't care less about it all.

MARIANNE   But it suddenly mattered so terribly.

JOHAN   No, not really. It's just a little bit of all the marvelous things life has to offer. Think of all our knowledge! Think of all the wisdom and awareness that we've arrived at through tears and misery. It's magnificent. Fantastic. We've discovered ourselves. It's out of this world. One perceives his smallness. The other her greatness. Could it be better? Here we sit so sensibly, talking rubbish about our better halves. They're almost with us in the room. We wave to them. It's mental group sex on the top level. It might all be taken from a textbook on lifemanship. It's unheard-of, Marianne. Analysis is total, knowledge is boundless. But I can't stand it.

MARIANNE *(Sad suddenly)*   I know what you mean.

JOHAN   Do you really?

MARIANNE *(Sadly)*   I know what you mean, but I don't think it's so terrible.

JOHAN   Hmm, that's the big difference between you and me. Because I refuse to accept the complete meaninglessness behind the complete awareness. I can't live with that cold light over all my endeavors. If you only knew how I struggle with my meaninglessness. Over and over again I try to cheer myself up by saying that life has the value that you yourself ascribe to it. But that sort of talk is no help to me. I want something to long for. I want something to believe in.

MARIANNE   I don't feel as you do.

JOHAN   No, I realize that.

MARIANNE   Unlike you, I stick it out. And enjoy it. I rely on my common sense. And my feeling. They cooperate. I'm satisfied with both of them. Now that I'm older I have a third coworker: my experience.

JOHAN *(Gruff)*   You should be a politician.

MARIANNE *(Serious)*   Maybe you're right.

JOHAN   Good Lord!

MARIANNE   I like people. I like negotiations, prudence, compromises.

JOHAN   You're practicing your election speech, I can hear it.

MARIANNE   You think I'm difficult.

JOHAN   Only when you preach.

MARIANNE   I won't say another word.

JOHAN   Promise not to tell me any more homely truths this evening?

MARIANNE   I promise.

JOHAN   Promise not to harp on that orgasm athlete?

MARIANNE   Not another word about him.

JOHAN   Do you think that *for just a little while* you can restrain your horrible sententiousness?

MARIANNE   It will be difficult, but I'll try.

JOHAN   Can you possibly, I say *possibly*, ration your boundless female strength?

MARIANNE   I see that I'll have to.

JOHAN   Come on then. Let's go to bed.

————

During the night MARIANNE *wakes up and screams with horror.* JOHAN *puts on the light and tries to put his arms around her to calm her, but she breaks loose, leaps up, and starts pacing to and fro.* JOHAN *waits in silence for her to say something.*

MARIANNE   I can't think why it is I dream like that. What do you think causes it?

JOHAN   Perhaps you ate something that didn't agree with you.

MARIANNE   Do you think so?

JOHAN   Or else, dearest Marianne, in your extremely well-ordered world there is something you can't get at.

MARIANNE   What would that be?

JOHAN   How should I know?

MARIANNE   Put your arms around me. I'm shivering so terribly. Although I'm so hot. Do you think I'm catching something? The children have just had colds.

JOHAN *(Gently)*   There, there. You'll soon feel better.

MARIANNE   Pull the blanket up over my shoulders, will you? Like that, that's lovely. Now I feel much better.

JOHAN   Don't you remember what frightened you?

MARIANNE   We have to go along a dangerous road or something. I want you others to take my hands so that we can hold on to each other. *(Frightened)* But it's no good. I no longer have any hands. I only have a couple of stumps that end at the elbows. At that moment I am slithering in soft sand. I can't get hold of you. You're all standing up there on the road and I can't reach you.

JOHAN *(Tenderly)*   What a horrible dream.

MARIANNE *(After a pause)*   Johan!

JOHAN   Yes, my dear.

MARIANNE   Do you think we're living in utter confusion?

JOHAN   You and I?

MARIANNE   No, the whole lot of us.

JOHAN   What do you mean by confusion?

MARIANNE   Fear, uncertainty, folly. I mean confusion. That
we realize secretly that we're slipping downhill. And that
we don't know what to do.

JOHAN   Yes, I think so.

MARIANNE   Perhaps it's like a poison.

JOHAN   Inside us, you mean?

MARIANNE   Just think if everything really is too late.

JOHAN   We mustn't say things like that. Only think them.

MARIANNE   Think how we exert ourselves all the time.

JOHAN   Especially you.

MARIANNE   Johan . . .

JOHAN   Yes?

MARIANNE   Have we missed something important?

JOHAN   All of us?

MARIANNE   You and I.

JOHAN   What would that be?

MARIANNE   Sometimes I know exactly how you're feeling and thinking. And then I feel a great tenderness for you and forget about myself, even though I don't efface myself. Do you understand what I mean?

JOHAN   I understand what you mean.

MARIANNE   Sometimes I can identify myself with a complete stranger too, and understand him. Those are brief moments of insight.

JOHAN   If we were to trust in that sort of sentimental fellow-feeling, nothing would ever get done, I can assure you.

MARIANNE   Johan.

JOHAN   Yes?

MARIANNE   Sometimes it grieves me that I have never loved anyone. I don't think I've ever been loved either. It really distresses me.

JOHAN   I think you're too tense about this.

MARIANNE   *(Smiling)*   Do you?

JOHAN   I can only answer for myself. And I think I love you in my imperfect and rather selfish way. And at times I think you love me in your stormy, emotional way. In fact, I think that you and I love one another. In an earthly and imperfect way.

MARIANNE   Do you really think so?

JOHAN   You're so damned hard to please.

MARIANNE   Yes, I am.

JOHAN   But here I sit with my arms around you, without any fuss, in the middle of the night in a dark house, somewhere in the world. And your arms are around me. I can't honestly say I have any great insight or fellow-feeling.

MARIANNE   No, you haven't.

JOHAN   Presumably I don't have the imagination for that.

MARIANNE   No, you're rather unimaginative.

JOHAN   I don't know what the hell my love looks like. I can't describe it and I hardly ever feel it in everyday life.

MARIANNE   And you think I love you too?

JOHAN   Yes, perhaps you do. But if we harp on it too much, love will give out.

MARIANNE   We're going to sit like this all night.

JOHAN   Oh no, we're not!

MARIANNE   Why not?

JOHAN   One leg has gone to sleep and my left arm is practically dislocated. I'm very sleepy and my back's cold.

MARIANNE   Well then, let's snuggle down.

JOHAN   Yes, let's.

MARIANNE   Good night, my darling. And thanks for the talk.

JOHAN   Good night.

MARIANNE   Sleep well.

JOHAN   Thanks, the same to you.

MARIANNE   Good night.

FACE TO FACE

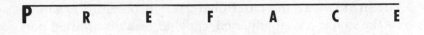

Ingmar Bergman wrote the following letter to his cast and crew before they began filming Face to Face.

Fårö, Sweden
September, 1975

Dear Fellow Workers:

We're now going to make a film which, in a way, is about an attempted suicide. Actually it deals ("as usual" I was about to say!) with Life, Love, and Death. Because nothing in fact is more important. To occupy oneself with. To think of. To worry over. To be happy about. And so on.

If some honest person were to ask me honestly just why I have written this film, I, to be honest, could not give a clearcut answer. I think that for some time now I have been living with an anxiety which has had no tangible cause. It has been like having a toothache, without the conscientious dentist having been able to find anything wrong with the tooth or with the person as a whole. After having given my anxiety various labels, each less convincing than the other, I decided to begin investigating more methodically.

Another person's vicissitudes came to my aid; I found similarities between her experiences and my own, with the difference that her situation was more obvious and more explicit, and much more painful.

In this way the chief character in our film began to take shape: a well-adjusted, capable, and disciplined person, a highly qualified professional woman with a career, comfortably married to a gifted colleague and surrounded by what are called "the good things of life." It is this admirable character's shockingly quick breakdown and agonizing rebirth that I have tried to describe. I have also, on the basis of the material at my disposal, shown the causes of the disaster as well as the possibilities available to this woman in the future.

For my own part I have benefited greatly by this process. The torment, formerly diffuse, has acquired name and address, and so has been deprived of its nimbus and alarm. If this opus can be of similar use to someone else, the effort is not in vain.

To recognize a distant or close acquaintance with a malicious or pitying smile is of course not so bad either and can give rise to strengthening comparisons, in which one's own excellence can be measured by someone else's wretchedness.

Nor in fact is there any harm in simply letting oneself be entertained for a couple of hours. Good-looking and talented actors, who in a credible manner portray sad, dramatic, or amusing situations, are almost always entertaining, however painful the complications happen to be.

On the other hand, ennui or indifference affect the film's originator in a terrible way, and it is only fair in that case that he should be put to shame, publicly mocked, and the victim of thumping financial reprisals.

What more shall I say? Oh yes, as you can see from the mere bulk of this book, it will be a pretty long film, several kilometers by the time it's finished. I've tried in vain to condense it, but each thing has its size and I have learned to be cautious about interfering in my charac-ters' actions and conversations and steering them. During rehearsal we always find points that turn out to be overclear or unnecessary.

The first part of the film is almost pedantically realis-tic, tangible. The second part is elusive, intangible: the "dreams" are more real than the reality. In this connec-tion let me add a somewhat bizarre comment. I am ex-tremely suspicious of dreams, apparitions, and visions, both in literature and in films and plays. Perhaps it's because mental excesses of this sort smack too much of being "arranged."

So when, despite my reluctance and suspicion, I go to depict a series of dreams, which moreover are not my own, I like to think of these dreams as an extension of reality. This is therefore a series of *real* events which strike the leading character during an important mo-ment of her life. Here something remarkable occurs.

Although Jenny is a psychiatrist she has never taken this extended reality seriously. Despite her wide knowl-edge she is, to a pretty great extent, mentally illiterate (a common ailment with psychiatrists; one could almost call it an occupational disease). Jenny has always been firmly convinced that a cheese is a cheese, a table is a table, and, *not least*, that a human being is a human being.

This last conviction is one of the things she is forced to modify in rather a painful way when she realizes in a flash that she is a conglomeration of other people and of the whole world. Frankly, I don't know whether she will be able to bear her realization.

In that case there remains only one fairly poor alterna-tive: she reverts to what, for the sake of simplicity and security, is called Jenny Isaksson, a stifling, static combi-nation of mapped-out qualities and patterns of behavior.

If, on the other hand, she accepts her new knowledge, she lets herself be drawn farther and farther in toward the center of her universe, guided by the light of intuition, a voyage of discovery which at the same time opens her up to the other people in an endless design.

There is a consequential alternative: the endlessness becomes unbearable, the mechanism breaks down under the hardships of the voyage, she tires of her increasingly broadened insight and of the ennui that results from such an insight. She tires and puts out the light, in the respectable certainty that if you put out the light it will be dark at any rate—and quiet.

I think it's important to have said all this, since it is significant for our attitude to the film we are going to make, both humanly and artistically.

I mean that the kind of film we are embarking on offers dangerous possibilities of artistic idea-diarrhea. To decide at every moment what is right and true and proper can be rather tricky. And the effort must not be noticeable either. Everything must give an impression of being natural—and yet be possible for us to create with our limited material resources.

So let's set off on a new adventure.

The scene is the Psychiatric Clinic of the General Hospital. It is an afternoon in the middle of June.

MARIA *is* JENNY *'s last patient for the day. She has obviously been crying; she is sitting hunched up, her arms hanging loosely at her sides. Her dark hair falls over her shoulders, thick and tangled. Her beautiful face is blotchy and swollen.*

JENNY *gazes at the one adornment to the bare white room: an abominable oil painting, presumably donated by some artistically inclined patient, which only adds to the dreariness.*

JENNY (*After a long wait*) We've been sitting like this for half an hour. I have to go soon and we won't have a chance to talk until Monday.

MARIA Oh, come on!

JENNY I have no idea what you mean.

MARIA You know perfectly well I've lost a filling.

JENNY No, I didn't.

MARIA Yesterday the nurse came and said I had to go to the dentist.

JENNY   Well?

MARIA   You arranged it all, didn't you?

JENNY   Honestly, I don't know what you're talking about.

(MARIA *gets up slowly. Her face is very pale and her eyes smolder with hatred. She spits in* JENNY*'s face.* JENNY *remains seated, more astonished than upset*)

JENNY   Sit down, and let's thrash this out.

(*Quick as lightning* MARIA *seizes a thick looseleaf file that is lying on the table and slams it down as hard as she can at* JENNY*'s head.* JENNY *gets her arm up just in time to ward off the blow*)

JENNY   (*Angry*)   Don't be so stupid!

(*The contents of the file scatter all over the floor. She grips* MARIA*'s shoulder and pushes her down into a chair*)

JENNY   (*Angry*)   Quiet down, Maria!

(MARIA *does quiet down and leans back in the chair, looking at* JENNY *with a hurt expression.* JENNY *sits beside her on a yellow wooden chair*)

MARIA   You're always making excuses.

(*But her tone is no longer hostile. She raises her arm and first lays it against her forehead, then crosses both arms over her head like an unhappy child*)

JENNY   You thought I sent you to the dentist so that he'd give you an injection, didn't you? A sedative. Wasn't that it, Maria?

MARIA   I asked the nurse and she said that I might have to have an injection, and when I said I didn't think it was necessary because the root was already filled, she said I'd better be prepared for an injection anyway.

JENNY   You've made that all up. I've promised that you won't be given injections and pills, and I'll keep my word.

MARIA   Do you know what's so incredibly wrong with you? Well, I'll tell you, because I've figured it out: *You're unable to love!* And by love I mean love and not fuck, though I doubt if you're much good at that either. Do you know what you are? *You're almost unreal.* I've tried to like you as you are, because I thought that if I love Jenny uncompromisingly then perhaps she'll become a little more real, I mean less anxious and more sure of herself. Well, people do, don't they, if they know they are loved, even if it's only a dog that loves them. But not a hope! Jenny looks at me with her lovely big blue eyes, the most beautiful eyes in the world, and all I see is her anguish. Have you never loved *anybody*, Jenny? *(She laughs, stretching out her hand and laying it on* JENNY*'s thigh)* What would you say if I raised my hand and stroked your cheek? What would you say if I lowered my hand and began to fondle your breast? What would you say if I . . . if I lowered my hand still more and began to fondle you between your legs?

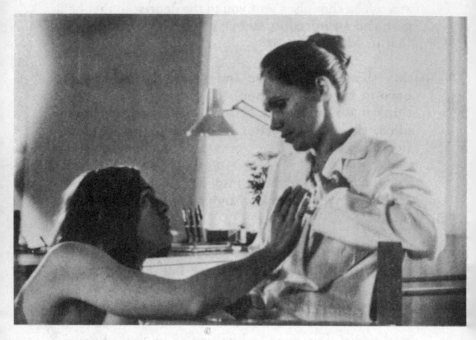

JENNY   You're sweet, really, and very persuasive. But you must remember that a psychiatrist often has to deal with this particular situation. The big problem—and it hasn't been solved yet—is how to avoid involvements between doctor and patient.

MARIA   *(After a short pause)*   Do you like being cruel in the course of duty?

JENNY   Now you're putting it on. You know as well as I do that neither of us would benefit from an affair.

MARIA   Anyhow, in the end you will betray me.

JENNY   What do you mean, betray you? I'm your doctor and I'm trying to make you well. It's *my* responsibility how that's to be done.

MARIA   *(Quickly)*   Are you sure? I mean, shouldn't we share the responsibility?

JENNY   That's just idle talk.

MARIA   I mean, shouldn't we share the responsibility—and the risks? Why should I take all the risks and you something vague and harmless called responsibility?

JENNY   It's not practically possible.

MARIA   Why not?

JENNY   Such experiments have been tried. With limited success.

MARIA   With limited success. You're fantastic!

JENNY   What are you doing now?

MARIA   *(Quietly)*   So you won't make love to me?

JENNY   *(With a smile)*   No, I certainly won't. But if you'd like to continue our inadequate attempts to make you well, I'll gladly do what I can.

MARIA   On your terms?

JENNY   Exactly. On my terms.

MARIA   Look at me for a minute. No, really look. Look me in the eyes, Jenny. What do you see?

JENNY   I see that you're putting on an act.

MARIA   What am I acting?

JENNY   Anguish. Fear. Anguish, I think.

MARIA   And what am I acting now? Look carefully.

JENNY   I don't know.

MARIA   I was imitating you.

   (Laughs)

JENNY   I couldn't tell that.

MARIA   No, you couldn't. (Pause) Poor Jenny!

JENNY   There's nothing poor about me.

MARIA   No, of course not. I'm the one to be sorry for. Isn't it awfully muggy?

JENNY   It looked like there might be a thunder storm this afternoon.

MARIA   Do you never feel helplessly, hopelessly, power-lessly helpless?

JENNY   How do you mean?

MARIA   I mean as a psychiatrist.

JENNY I don't think so.

MARIA I'm sure it says on the first page of your first textbook that a psychiatrist must never feel helplessly, hopelessly, powerlessly helpless. And if against all the rules he should feel powerlessly helpless, then he must not admit it. Doesn't it say that on the first page of your basic textbook?

JENNY Yes, it does actually.

(MARIA *tries to kiss* JENNY *but she pushes her away. Then* MARIA *starts to laugh. Shaking her head and laughing, she bends down to pick up the papers that are scattered over the floor.* JENNY *shoves her aside and picks them up herself. Suddenly* MARIA *leaves the room, shutting the door without a sound.* JENNY *sits down on the yellow chair. She is shaking)*

That same stormy June evening JENNY *moves in with her grandparents. They live in a spacious old-fashioned apartment on a quiet street near a park, which borders on the open water and has leafy waterside paths. At the other end is a Victorian church whose tall, slender spire, on early summer mornings, casts its shadow along the entire length of the street.*

On this particular evening the town is deserted and JENNY *has no trouble parking her car right outside the ornate entrance of the apartment house. She lifts her suitcase from the back seat and locks the doors.*

She walks into the lobby with its heavy and now rather shabby elegance: marble staircase, brass banister, thick red carpet, stained-glass windows, paintings on the walls, mosaic on the floor, oddly shaped wall sconces shedding a dreary light over all this splendor.

The elevator cage creaks down and stops with a sigh. The grille door is drawn aside and a large woman dressed entirely in black gropes her way out. She is holding a white cane. JENNY *checks her impulse to help the old lady, as she seems to be quite at home. With her feet now on firm ground she walks with astonishing speed toward the stairs, grasps the banister without hesitation, and begins her descent to the street door.*

She turns around as though aware that someone is watching her. Her face is strong and very pale. Her right eye socket is staring and empty. Spotting JENNY, *she gives a faint smile and turns at once to the door, which she opens without difficulty.*

GRANDMA *is a lively, handsome woman with clear eyes and cheeks that are still smooth and rosy. She embraces her granddaughter delightedly.*

GRANDMA   If you knew how pleased I am to see you! Both Grandpa and I have been quite excited all day. Come along and I'll show you. I've put you in Karin's room. You won't be disturbed there and now in the summer there's no noise from the street. Would you like a firmer pillow? I seem to remember that you—

JENNY   No, thank you, Grandma, that's fine.

GRANDMA   Let me see now . . . I've cleared out the bureau and one of the closets. I can empty the other one too if you don't have enough room. They're only old summer clothes, I don't know why they're still here, it would be much better to—

JENNY   Grandma dear, one closet and the bureau will be plenty.

GRANDMA   If you need a larger desk we can move in the one from Karl's room. He's not likely to come this summer and perhaps you—

JENNY   I can manage quite well with this desk.

GRANDMA   Promise to tell me if there's anything you need. Grandpa and I have been looking forward *so* much to your coming.

JENNY   So have I.

GRANDMA   Now let's go out and say hello to Grandpa.

JENNY   How is he?

GRANDMA   I think he's better. *(With a little laugh)* You know, he's become so terribly nice.

(Entering GRANDPA *and* GRANDMA*'s drawing room is like entering the world that died out with the First World War. Curtains, hangings, carpets, furniture, pictures, wall sconces, and a chandelier. The tall French doors, the ormolu clock, the open fireplace, the mirrors, the small statuettes, the countless photographs of children and grandchildren, friends and relations. The vases of flowers and the potted plants. Everything here lives its quiet, meek life in the soft daylight and the dusk of long evenings.*

GRANDPA is sitting in a large easy chair. The only sign of his recent illness is that he is very pale; he is immaculately dressed and shaved. Beside the chair is a low table cluttered with books, newspapers, and some old albums, as well as a glass of straight whisky.

GRANDPA reaches out with his hand and draws JENNY to him. As they embrace, his spectacles slide down crookedly. They are both somewhat moved)

JENNY   Hello, Grandpa! I've come to stay for two months. Erik sends his love. He's in Chicago at a conference. I just spoke to him on the phone and he said he has a lot to tell you when he comes home. Grandma says you're feeling much better, and you look it. You'll have a cup of tea too, won't you?

(GRANDMA *gives him the tea on a little tray, which she places over the arms of the chair. On a plate are two slices of toast with jam*)

GRANDMA   And how is little Anna?

JENNY   She went off to riding camp yesterday and has just fallen in love with a boy three years older than she is. He tells her all about the world revolution. Things couldn't be better.

GRANDMA   Is the boy at the camp too?

JENNY   Grandma dear, don't worry. Anna is fourteen and can take care of herself.

GRANDMA   Do you take sugar?

JENNY   Yes, please. Three lumps. Grandma! Have you made muffins! Just when I've decided to diet.

GRANDMA   I never heard anything so silly.

JENNY   Anyway, after riding camp Anna is going to stay with her best friend in Skåne and won't be home until school starts.

GRANDMA   And when will the new house be ready to move into?

JENNY   I *hope* at the beginning of August. The builders have sworn on the Bible at any rate. Though you never know.

GRANDMA   And you're going to work the whole summer?

JENNY   Yes.

GRANDMA   Won't you have any vacation at all?

JENNY   Oh, Erik and I might go to Taormina in October. We'll see.

GRANDMA   Just what sort of job is it?

JENNY   I'm filling in for the medical supervisor of the Psychiatric Clinic at the General Hospital.

GRANDMA   I hope you're well paid?

JENNY   Yes, thank you, Grandma, I'm very well paid.

GRANDMA   How do you like it?

JENNY   I'm the sort of person who likes it wherever I am. I take after you.

(GRANDMA, *who has finished her tea, has begun darning socks. She glances at her granddaughter over her spectacles*)

GRANDMA   What's the matter?

JENNY   With me? I'm just fine.

GRANDMA   Is something wrong between you and Erik?

JENNY *(Laughing)*   No, certainly not!

GRANDMA   There's something, anyway.

JENNY   I'm just a little out of sorts. I never really recovered from that bout of flu in the spring. So possibly I need vitamins or something.

(A grunt is heard from GRANDPA*'s chair.* GRANDMA *gets up at once and goes over to him. Then she calls to* JENNY.
GRANDPA *has opened an old photo album. There are pictures from a summer long ago, when* JENNY *was a little girl and the big house in the archipelago was full of children and grownups)*

GRANDMA   I think that was the summer of forty-eight. Yes, it must be that summer, because Greta is pregnant and Ragnar was born at the beginning of September. What a lot of us there were then! And that wretched boat we had that was always breaking down. How I detested it.

*(*GRANDMA *says this teasingly and* GRANDPA *gives a sardonic smile. Then he points a long lean finger at a snapshot of* JENNY, *eight years old. The little person stands there so incredibly thin and slight, looking delightedly into the camera. She is holding a man by the hand)*

GRANDMA   You were always your father's girl.

JENNY   Oh, there were reasons for that.

GRANDMA   Grandpa loves to pore over those old photographs. He can sit looking at them for hours.

(She strokes his cheek briefly and resumes her darning. JENNY remains standing by the chair, letting GRANDPA dip into the past)

It is later that evening and JENNY can't fall asleep. Finally she gets up and pads out to the kitchen. She heats some milk in a pan, takes liver pâté and gherkins out of the refrigerator, and butters a piece of crispbread. Then she sits down at the big kitchen table, switches on the little portable radio standing on a shelf by the window, and lets herself be soothed by a Mozart sonata. To divert herself further she fishes out an old magazine and spreads it on the table.

The window is slightly open to the warm night. It has begun to rain. Now and then thunder rumbles in the distance.

The door opens and GRANDMA *peeps in. She is wearing a dark green full-length dressing gown. Her hair, still tinged with red, has been plaited into a thick braid.*

JENNY   Hello! Would you like a sandwich and some milk?

GRANDMA   No, I think I'll make myself some coffee. Nothing puts me to sleep better than a nice strong cup of coffee at this time of night.

JENNY   Is Grandpa asleep?

GRANDMA   For fifty years I've never been able to figure out when Grandpa is asleep. He goes to bed, lays his hands on his chest, and looks like a king lying in state. It's useless talking to him then. He withdraws into himself and shuts himself in.

JENNY   I thought he looked awfully tired.

GRANDMA   The paralysis is much better and sometimes we can actually have a conversation. But you know how impatient he is. He gets so angry if you don't understand what he means.

JENNY   How do you cope with being a full-time nurse?

GRANDMA   Oh, he can't boss me around just because he's sick.

JENNY   Don't you ever wish you were a little freer?

GRANDMA   That Grandpa was dead, you mean? Having someone to look after like this, to get cross with or pat on the cheek or just to talk to—it's important.

JENNY   I think so too.

GRANDMA   I'll tell you something. Grandpa never became the famous scientist that everyone expected. He was much too impatient and arrogant. I grew pretty tired of him during those years. In fact I very nearly left home with all the children. He was really impossible.

JENNY   But you never did leave?

GRANDMA   No, I didn't.

JENNY   Did something special happen?

(GRANDMA *helps herself to the last of the coffee and glances at* JENNY. *She gives a short laugh, almost embarrassed.* JENNY, *who for the first time in ages feels warm and relaxed, also begins to laugh. She takes* GRANDMA*'s hand*)

JENNY   Tell me now.

GRANDMA   I went around feeling cross with Grandpa day after day because he kept grumbling about everything, about money and housekeeping and the children's clothes and my appearance and I don't know what. And I was pretty tired—I had my own teaching job to do, and we had just moved to Uppsala and everything was in a muddle. Well, one day I was hurrying along Garden Street, I think I had to go home during lunch for some reason . . . Oh yes, Linda had the measles and she was such a mama's girl.

JENNY   And then?

GRANDMA   Well, I happened to look up and there he was walking along on the other side of the street. I was coming from the school and he was on his way to Queen Street, so he had his back to me. Then he turned the corner.

JENNY   Was there anything special about the way he looked?

GRANDMA   Grandpa? No, not at all. He walked briskly along, his back straight and his nose in the air as usual. Very dapper and with his hat at the proper snobbish angle. Oh no, he looked just as stuck-up as usual. I expect you understand this much better than I do, having taken your doctor's degree in all the little quirks of the mind. Maybe it has a Latin name.

JENNY   There's nothing about love in our textbooks.

GRANDMA   I see. Hmm . . . Well, I wouldn't call it love exactly. Rather a kind of understanding. I suddenly grasped the meaning of all sorts of things: my own life and Grandpa and his life and the children's future and the next life and I don't know what.

JENNY   Have you known all that ever since?

GRANDMA I have to make a terrific effort to remember how I felt then.

JENNY It was a saint who said, "Love is a state of grace. Those who are in it usually do not themselves know they are among the chosen. Love influences through their actions just as naturally as the rose through its scent or the nightingale through its song." I think it was St. Francis.

GRANDMA A state of grace? Whose grace?

JENNY For St. Francis there was no doubt.

GRANDMA *(Respectfully)* Well, that just goes to show. For me life has been mostly practical considerations.

JENNY Oh, yes.

GRANDMA Well, it's bedtime. I'd better close the window, in case of thunder and more rain.

(GRANDMA *gets up quickly and shuts the window. They put out the kitchen light, kiss each other good night, and go their separate ways. The rain is heavier now and a faint rumble echoes over the rooftops)*

JENNY *stretches out on the large, comfortable bed. She picks up a book but finds at once that she is too sleepy. She gives up the attempt and puts out the light. Yawning, she turns over on her stomach and falls asleep immediately.*

She wakes up feeling completely paralyzed. Opposite her bed, in the changing, shadowless nocturnal light, she can make out a shapeless, gray, billowing mass. Now it takes form, rising, collecting itself. It is a large woman dressed in gray. One eye has been gouged out and the socket gapes black. With excruciating slowness she turns her terrible face toward JENNY *and gazes at her. Then she speaks. The thin black lips form words which* JENNY *cannot grasp but which seem very urgent, menacing. When* JENNY *doesn't understand, the expression on the woman's face changes to cruel impatience. With great effort she begins to rise from the sofa, looking fixedly at* JENNY, *who (still paralyzed) returns her stare. Now the woman is standing on the floor, her face distorted with fury. She approaches the bed with flowing, unreal movements.*

JENNY *tries to scream but can't make a sound. Just then the apparition vanishes and she wakes up, puts on the light, and sits for a long time bolt upright in bed. It is raining heavily and a gray light is framed against the blind. The time is three thirty in the morning. She gets out of bed and begins to pace up and down the room. Feeling cold, she puts on her bathrobe. She goes out into the drawing room, sits down in* GRANDPA's *chair, and tries to calm herself.* "What's wrong with me, I've never been like this, what's the matter with me?"

Day is breaking, harsh and gray, outside the big windows. The rain drives against the panes. The ormolu clock gives four quick strokes and is answered by the deep notes of the grandfather clock.

DR. JENNY ISAKSSON *and* DR. HELMUTH WANKEL *are sitting in* JENNY's *office at the Psychiatric Clinic of the General Hospital, going through the day's schedule. Wankel chain smokes frenziedly, wears thick glasses, and speaks forcefully but with a slight stammer.*

JENNY   Couldn't you try to stop smoking for a while? I'm almost dead from nicotine poisoning.

WANKEL   Jenny, my dear, please forgive me! Let's open the window. Oh, it's open already. I'll empty the ashtray and . . . By the way, how is Maria? I heard that you'd had trouble with her.

(Ceremoniously, his movements slightly exaggerated, he picks up the ashtray and empties it into the wastebasket)

JENNY   She has been in my care for two months. When she came in she couldn't make contact in any way and was almost catatonic, with violent attacks of anguish and aggressiveness. Now we can at least talk to each other. *(Pause)* Oh yes! We've stopped treatment of any kind—she is quite unresponsive to . . .

WANKEL   I know. You told me.

JENNY   It's almost incredible. I, at any rate, have never come across that sort of resistance.

WANKEL   You know as well as I do that we can't have people here untreated month after month. We have to do something to get her out.

JENNY   Maria is a gifted person. Sensitive, clever, emotionally well-equipped.

WANKEL   What's the use of all those excellent qualities if her mind is darkened by anguish?

JENNY   All the same, I think I've made a little progress.

WANKEL   You can hand her over to me when you've had enough.
    And realized how hopeless it is to cure psychoses of her kind. So far there are only mechanical solutions.

JENNY   Do you think they deserve to be called solutions?

WANKEL   My dear Jenny. A lunatic quack psychiatrist once wrote that mental illnesses are the worst scourge on earth, and that the next worst is the curing of those illnesses. I'm inclined to agree with him.

JENNY   *(Laughing)*   You *are* encouraging.

WANKEL   Twenty years ago I realized the inconceivable brutality of our methods and the complete bankruptcy of psychoanalysis. I don't think we can really cure a single human being. One or two get well despite our efforts.

JENNY   Man as a machine?

WANKEL   Exactly! We change spare parts and eradicate symptoms.

JENNY   Anyway, I'll keep Maria for a little longer. If you don't mind?

WANKEL   You're the boss. For the time being, at least. *(Smiles)* Will you excuse me if I go now? I'm having lunch with the housing minister (an incurably normal neurotic). Besides, I'm dying for a cigarette.

JENNY   Bye-bye.

WANKEL   Bye-bye. And as I said, hand Maria over to me when you're tired of her. Preferably before Erneman returns from his trip to Australia. It has dawned on him that this is a factory which must pay its way and he likes to see the lunatics turn over. That's why he's so well loved by all the politicians and can gallivant all over the world spreading his gospel.

(He sighs gently, gathers up his papers, and stuffs them into a brief case which seems already about to burst. Then he lights a cigarette and sucks at it frenziedly)

JENNY   Well, good-bye.

(Fans herself)

WANKEL   Oh, by the way. You're coming to my wife's little party, aren't you?

JENNY   As you see, I have on my Sunday best just in case. Are *you* going?

WANKEL   It would hardly be proper, as she's going to unveil a new lover. Young Strömberg.

JENNY   The actor!

WANKEL   The very same.

JENNY   Why, he must be—

WANKEL   He is exactly thirty-six years younger than my wife. It's all rather touching. *(Gravely)* I mean touching. Without any sarcasm.

JENNY   But isn't young Strömberg—

WANKEL   Yes, he is. Elisabeth loves Strömberg's little playmates too. She's like a mother to them all.

JENNY   Then I'll have to go.

WANKEL   You can tell her from me that I have a poor prognosis for young Strömberg and that I love her in spite of everything.

(He goes off, lighting a new cigarette)

MRS. WANKEL *opens the door herself. When she sees* JENNY *she bursts out laughing. (Should anyone wish to know what she looks like, she's a small, lively, warm, and friendly woman with short gray hair, a round childish face, and merry brown eyes)*

ELISABETH   Jenny! Well, this is a nice time to show up!

JENNY *(Confused)*   Wasn't it five o'clock?

ELISABETH   No, it was two o'clock, and nearly everyone has gone. But come in. How nice to see you. What a smart outfit. Is it new? And how pretty you are! My God, if only I looked like you! Darling, I *am* pleased to see you. *(Kiss)* Where's your husband? Oh yes, of course, he's in America. How nice.

(Laughing both from friendliness and from having had a lot to drink, she takes JENNY *by the arm and leads her into the studio, which is on two floors and full of fashionable furniture and objects. The walls are crowded with her paintings, which express a mild joie de vivre. Over all this the early summer sun. The doors onto the roof terrace are wide open, letting in a breeze from the harbor.*

One or two guests have lingered and ELISABETH *hastens to introduce them)*

ELISABETH   This is Mikael. I'm madly in love with him actually, and he's so sweet to me it's just unreal, and this is his best friend and his name's Ludvig. He does *not* like to be called Ludde. The three of us are off to the Bahamas in a few weeks. This is Tomas, you must have heard of him, he's the one who travels around the developing countries teaching the girls how to use contraceptives, it's all frightfully interest-

ing, besides he's the sweetest doctor in the world if
you have any trouble with love, you know what I
mean. And this is—no, I have no idea, Mikke my
poppet, do you know who this is, oh well, let's not
disturb him, he's taking a nap, and I should think so
too, after the way he abused us all just now, he's *very*
committed, you know. These are a couple of charming girls, and *so* clever, who have just opened a bou-
tique around the corner. *(Whispers)* There *is* something about those young girls in their low-cut
blouses. Imagine if we were to—fancy if you and I—

(She bursts out in a snorting giggle and hugs JENNY *to her
as she draws her over to the bar, which extends along the whole
end of the lower floor)*

JENNY   And now you're happy?

ELISABETH   I say it only to you, Jenny, because you understand that sort of thing. Naturally we have problems.

JENNY   Oh?

ELISABETH   Cheers, Jenny!

JENNY   Cheers, Elisabeth.

ELISABETH   He's so *complicated*, Mikael. Sometimes I'm
almost afraid of him. You know, that Ludvig is a bad
lot, really. But you have to take the rough with the
smooth. And on the whole I suppose—we—are—what
you'd call—happy.

JENNY   How is that, Elisabeth?

ELISABETH   I've come to the conclusion that I'm grateful. *Humbly* grateful, if you know what I mean. Not only for this with Mikael but because I still have myself. I *know* that it's *my* feelings and sensations, since there's no gap between myself and what I experience. Heavens, how badly I'm putting it.

JENNY   I almost envy you.

(ELISABETH *is about to answer when the two awfully clever girls in their décolleté blouses come up to take their leave and she busies herself seeing them to the door.* JENNY *is left alone for a moment. She sits down in a secluded corner and closes her eyes.*
   Suddenly she feels that someone is watching her. She turns around. Obliquely behind her DR. TOMAS JACOBI *has ensconced himself in a deep armchair. He smiles encouragingly.* JENNY *returns his smile)*

TOMAS   How are you?

JENNY   Fine, thanks. And how might *you* be?

TOMAS   I'm always well.

JENNY   So what shall we talk about now?

TOMAS   We have an excellent topic.

JENNY   Oh?

TOMAS   You have a patient who happens to be my half-sister.

JENNY   Maria?

TOMAS   Yes.

JENNY   It seems improper somehow to discuss a patient in this setting.

TOMAS   *(Cheerfully)*   We don't have to.

JENNY   Meaning?

TOMAS   We can have dinner together. There's a nice little fish restaurant just around the corner.

JENNY   Well, I *was* going to—

TOMAS   Of course. Some other time then. I'm in town till the middle of August. Good-bye, Jenny.

(He gets up with a smile and leaves her. She now sees that his left leg is lame; it seems stiff and hard to maneuver. He exchanges a few words with ELISABETH, *kisses her on the cheek, and limps to the hall, where he looks around for his cane. On an impulse* JENNY *gets up quickly and hurries over to him)*

JENNY   Wait for me down at the restaurant. I'll just make a phone call. If the offer's still open, that is?

*(*TOMAS *looks at her with a smile, then nods in confirmation and opens the front door.* JENNY *goes to look for* ELISABETH, *who is in the kitchen attended by her two boys. She is busy clearing up, neat person that she is)*

JENNY   May I use your phone?

ELISABETH   Why of course, darling. Use the one in the bedroom and you won't be disturbed. I'm afraid it looks like rather a mess, the boys started trying on all my underwear just before the guests arrived. *(Laughs)* They gave me quite a fright—they threatened to appear in drag—in my evening dresses!

*(*JENNY *goes into the bedroom. It is certainly messy. She finds the telephone on the floor, half shoved under the sofa)*

JENNY   Hello, Martin! What luck I caught you. Sorry, but this evening's off. What? Yes, it's a patient. What? Have I met someone who's more fun? Don't be silly now, Martin. Jealousy is most out of place between us. *(Laughs)* Yes, I know you were joking. Bye-bye, darling! *(Puts down the receiver)* Dear God! Dear God in heaven!

(At that moment ELISABETH *opens the door a crack and peeps in, smiling delightedly. Then she enters)*

ELISABETH   Are you having dinner with Tomas?

JENNY   Were you listening?

ELISABETH   Darling, you look so frightfully *guilty*, it's *too* exciting!

JENNY   *(Laughing)*   Do I?

ELISABETH   Tomas is crazy about women. But *terribly* mixed up!

JENNY   That sounds nice.

ELISABETH   In the days when I was married to Carl, Tomas was young and ill-mannered and very temperamental. And so sensitive! So sensitive that I . . . well, never mind. Good-bye darling, take care of yourself. I'll call you next week to see how it went.

(They embrace warmly and kiss each other.
    ELISABETH *sees* JENNY *to the door.* MIKAEL STRÖMBERG, *the young lover, floats up to his mistress's side. He puts his arms around her and gives her a smacking kiss on her snub nose, saying that he must pop down and buy cigarettes before the store at the corner closes.* ELISABETH *puts her hands on his hips and shakes him gently, with great tenderness, asking if he has money. Yes, he has.*
    JENNY *and* MIKAEL *go quickly downstairs)*

MIKAEL   You're a shrink, aren't you?

JENNY   Yes, why?

MIKAEL   I've got a friend who could use some advice.

JENNY   I'm afraid that will be difficult. I have no private practice.

MIKAEL   Too bad for my friend. I've been watching you. You seem nice.

JENNY   Do I? Thank you!

MIKAEL   Do you have time to talk?

JENNY   Five minutes.

MIKAEL   Let's go into the courtyard. We can sit there.

(The courtyard is planted with trees and shrubs, and has a little fountain which has already gone to sleep for the evening. The old apartment houses rise around them. There stands a little white bench. MIKAEL *offers* JENNY *his last cigarette. She declines. He takes it himself and smokes for a while in silence.* JENNY *steals a glance at her watch)*

JENNY   Well?

MIKAEL   I'm worried about something.

JENNY   Does it concern your friend Ludvig?

MIKAEL   No! I've never known anyone less afraid of death than Ludde.

JENNY   So your friend is afraid to die.

MIKAEL   Exactly.

JENNY   And it worries you.

MIKAEL   Do you think someone can commit suicide out of fear of death? It sounds crazy, but do you think it's possible?

JENNY   It's not unusual.

MIKAEL   Anyone who's constantly afraid of dying can't get much pleasure out of living.

JENNY   No.

MIKAEL   It's like a disease.

JENNY   Shouldn't your friend see a doctor?

MIKAEL   Christ, yes. He runs from one clever quack to the next, babbling about his fear of death.

JENNY   Well?

MIKAEL   Oh, they listen ever so kindly and prescribe tranquillizers. (*Looks at her*) Seriously, Jenny. Isn't there any cure for this hellish suffering?

JENNY   So the friend is you.

MIKAEL   Yes, my darling. You're pretty shrewd after all.

(*He smiles with his beautiful mouth and the big blue eyes grow dark with fear*)

JENNY   You can call me on Monday at the hospital. Here, I'll write down the number. You'd better call just after eight in the morning. Then I'll see what I can do.

MIKAEL　But what am I supposed to do in the meantime?

JENNY　Is it that bad?

MIKAEL　Yes. Suddenly time stops, the seconds are endless. It's like sitting in an airplane when the engines fail. Every step I take—every word I say—every moment . . . Funny, isn't it? I'm the luckiest person in the world. It's summer. Elisabeth is the kindest little mother imaginable. I'm extremely talented. Tomas, the old dinosaur—you saw him upstairs—we were friends for a time, he's sort of a humanistic desperado and actually he has also tried to . . . Well, he says that the only way to get rid of your fear of death is to love life and live as if you were never going to die. All very well for him to talk. That's how it is, Jenny! I'm afraid to go to sleep in case I never wake up again. And I know it's inevitable. I, I, I, Mikael Strömberg, will die at any moment, somehow or other. It's no use crying or running and hiding. If I believed in something great it would be different. Sometimes I know just how it smells.

JENNY　Smells?

MIKAEL　The smell of death. The stench of a corpse. I look at my hand, I put it to my nose, and I can smell it, sickly sweet and nauseating.

(The anguished blue eyes, the handsome actor's face, the well-trained voice)

JENNY   Call me on Monday.

MIKAEL   Jenny!

JENNY   Yes?

MIKAEL   Are you never afraid of death?

JENNY   No, I don't think so. I'm like most people, I suppose, who regard death as something that happens to others but never to yourself.

MIKAEL   Do you have to go now?

JENNY   Yes, I must.

MIKAEL   So long then, Jenny. Thanks for the talk.

JENNY   You'll call me on Monday. For sure.

MIKAEL   For sure.

(*He gives his most enchanting smile and quells the anguish in his big blue eyes.* JENNY *is suddenly unsure*)

JENNY   You won't do anything foolish?

MIKAEL   Foolish? Oh, I see! No, no, don't worry, darling. At the moment it's one mad whirl. I won't be alone for a second.

JENNY (*Getting up*)   Weren't you going to buy cigarettes?

MIKAEL   Yes, but I'll sit here for a while and rest. Rest my ears from that delightful monkey-chatter up there on the fifth floor. I love it—oh, I love it all right—but sometimes it makes me sick, if you know what I mean.

JENNY Bye-bye.

MIKAEL Beware of Tomas!

JENNY Oh, why?

MIKAEL He's a real Alice in Wonderland. Though duller, if you get what I mean.

JENNY No.

MIKAEL Give him a kiss from me!

JENNY *(Laughing)* Give it to him yourself! Bye-bye.

(They both laugh and JENNY *leaves the actor to rest after his big scene.*

Now she is standing in the street. It is narrow and winding, lined by tall old houses. The air is still warm from the sun, despite the gathering dusk. The clock of the neighboring church strikes eight. People stroll past her. She takes a few steps, then stops. She has half a mind to turn and disappear around the corner.

But TOMAS *has already seen her. He has been waiting outside the restaurant, half hidden behind the low awning)*

TOMAS Shall we go in or are you going to stick to your impulse to run away? You can do as you like. I'll be disappointed, of course, but I won't crack up. They do a delicious fillet of sole.

JENNY   I'm ravenous.

TOMAS   Well then, let's eat, and see what happens. All
right?

*(With so many people away for the summer, the little fish
restaurant is nearly empty.* TOMAS *and* JENNY, *in good
spirits, have dined on the famous sole and a vintage
wine. They are having coffee.* TOMAS *is smoking an expensive cheroot.* JENNY *is indulging in a small glass of
brandy)*

TOMAS   And what would you like to do now? Shall I take
you home or would you care for a little drive out of
town? My house is nicely situated but rather dilapidated. We can sit on the veranda in the twilight and
listen to music. I can even promise complete silence if
you find that more agreeable.

JENNY   You talk like a book.

TOMAS   It's just a way of speaking. I'm rather shy, you
see.

JENNY *(Smiling)   You* shy?

TOMAS   Believe it or not, but I *am* rather shy. I live so
much alone, you see. And what about yourself?

JENNY   I'm not given to talking. The reason is that I too
am rather shy. Besides, I'm not used to being in this
situation.

TOMAS   What situation?

JENNY Dining with a strange man. I feel rather daring, to be quite honest. What's more, I haven't made up my mind whether to have a bad conscience or not.

TOMAS *(Gaily)* Some people regard a bad conscience as an extra spice to the enjoyment.

JENNY *(Protecting herself)* Won't you tell me about Maria?

TOMAS *(Sighing)* Where shall I start? She was generally considered very gifted. She dabbled in writing and acting and had one or two dramatic love affairs and equally dramatic breakdowns when the young men tired of her. Just between the two of us, I must say I don't blame them.

JENNY Oh?

TOMAS Maria's mother died in tragic circumstances— she killed herself. Maria, who was very young at the time, came to live with us. We have the same father, as you may have gathered. Then it got to be absolutely hellish.

JENNY I see.

TOMAS Oh, I can't complain. I was mostly away from home, first at college and then abroad, but Maria provoked my parents and my younger brother until they almost lost their minds.

JENNY What do you mean by provoked?

TOMAS   Love as elephantiasis. Kindness as cruelty, self-sacrifice as selfishness. Concern that becomes an octopus. I don't know. Sometimes I wonder if I'm the one with something wrong and Maria's normal. That bothers me even more, of course.

JENNY   Do you feel sorry for her?

TOMAS   I don't know. As a child I saw a dog being killed. They shot it. Several times. It didn't die. It kept howling and looking at us. Finally someone poured gasoline over it and set it on fire. *(Smiles)* Shall we go?

(TOMAS *lives in an old-fashioned, tumble-down house surrounded by an overgrown, neglected orchard*)

TOMAS   The house is falling down with age and disrepair. Now and then I think about moving to something more modern, but that's as far as it gets. What would you like to drink?

JENNY   Nothing, thanks.

TOMAS   Some coffee, perhaps?

JENNY   No, no. Later maybe.

TOMAS   Do sit down. That's the most comfortable chair. That one's mine. Just ignore it. I'm the only one in the whole world who thinks it's comfortable.

JENNY   Do you play?

(Indicating the grand piano)

TOMAS   No, it was my wife who played.

JENNY   Is she dead?

TOMAS   Hmm? Oh. No. We got divorced some years ago.

JENNY   And that was as much of a success as everything else?

TOMAS   The actual divorce was the most successful part.

JENNY   My husband is away for three months.

TOMAS   So you implied at dinner.

JENNY   Actually I miss him very much.

TOMAS   Oh, I'm quite sure you do.

JENNY   All the same I've taken a lover who isn't half as nice. Can you understand that?

TOMAS   Yes, up to a point.

JENNY   To put it bluntly, he's a bore.

TOMAS   Well then, get rid of him.

JENNY   No, he'll do—until the middle of August. Then Erik will be home.

TOMAS   Do you have any other remedy for your anguish? Here—and there.

(Indicates breast and abdomen)

JENNY   We're moving into a new house in the fall.

TOMAS   How nice.

   (Confused pause)

JENNY *(Smiling)*   You're so very polite. Are you bored?

TOMAS   Not at all. I'm just wondering about your breasts. I imagine they're very beautiful.

JENNY   To satisfy your curiosity I can tell you that they *are.* And with that you'll have to be content.

TOMAS *(Sadly)*   You misunderstand me, but never mind.

   (There is a long, awkward silence. They toast each other. JENNY goes over to the window and looks at the garden in the twilight)

TOMAS   Would you care for a cigarette?

JENNY   No, thank you. I don't smoke.

TOMAS   Sensible. Very sensible.

JENNY   Sensible or not, I'm going home.

TOMAS   Jenny! Wait!

JENNY   I'm very tired.

TOMAS   May I drive you?

JENNY   That wasn't the idea. Please call me a taxi.

TOMAS Will you listen to me? Just for a moment.

JENNY (*Wearily, with a smile*) Well, what is it?

TOMAS Couldn't you and I be friends? No, don't sneer. I'm serious, I mean it. Jenny! Are you listening?

(TOMAS *is still smiling, but his face is tormented.* JENNY *is very angry, tired and angry. She returns his gaze. She is smiling also*)

JENNY Oh yes! I just want to know how we get from here to your bedroom. I also want to know what fantastic method you have for getting over the absurdity of undressing. Then of course I want to be told what technique you'll use to satisfy me—and yourself. And what you expect *me* to do—just how progressive and creative you will let me be, so that in my sudden passion I don't frighten you.

TOMAS You're very amusing.

JENNY A pity, because I'm being serious. Oh yes! Please tell me also how we are to wind it all up when the sex act is over. Is it to be tenderness and silence—a cigarette glowing in the gray morning light—or will it be nervous small talk about the next time as we exchange phone numbers?

TOMAS You really won't let me drive you home?

JENNY No, thank you. I *want* to take a taxi. Besides, you've been drinking.

TOMAS Good-bye, Jenny, my dear. And thanks for a pleasant evening. I hope to see you again sometime.

JENNY We could go to a movie.

TOMAS Or a concert. There are some very good concerts in the summer.

JENNY That would be nice.

TOMAS I'll be in touch.

JENNY *I* might call *you* up.

TOMAS That *would* surprise me.

JENNY Then perhaps I'll call you for just that reason.

TOMAS The taxi's here.

(They go out onto the steps. It is already daylight, but the sun has not yet risen)

The sun makes an intricate pattern on the gently ageing wallpaper of the drawing room. The clocks tick; the time is a quarter past three. It is very quiet in the big room, which is so full of strange and unreal things. The birds are singing loudly and defiantly in the park.

JENNY has sat down in GRANDPA's chair without taking off her coat. She has simply found herself there, and gone on sitting. She is not sleepy in the least, only tired. Her eyes ache slightly, but she cannot close them. Her hands are clenched on top of the smooth surface of her pocketbook.

The door to GRANDPA*'s room is opened without a sound, as if by a ghost. After a few moments* GRANDPA *shuffles slowly in. He is in his bathrobe and slippers and his fluffy gray hair makes a cloud around his old head.*

JENNY *does not make her presence known, and is well hidden in the big chair.* GRANDPA *stops by the window and stands there for some time, looking out onto the street. The orange rays of the sun outline his profile and his skinny neck against the dark wall.*

Then he rouses himself, as though leaving his sad thoughts behind. He makes his way to the grandfather clock out in the dining room and fumbles for the key. Then he begins slowly to wind it up. At that moment the door of GRANDMA*'s room opens and she comes padding out.*

GRANDMA *(Crossly)*   What are you doing up at this hour?

GRANDPA   The clock—

GRANDMA   My dear, we wound it properly last night. It's not good for it to wind it too often.

GRANDPA   It keeps stopping.

GRANDMA   No, it doesn't. We had a watchmaker here who overhauled it and said it was one of the best grandfather clocks he had ever seen.

GRANDPA   It loses time.

GRANDMA   It keeps the same time as the other clocks, but if you insist on tampering with it, then it's sure to stop.

(He sits down stiffly and cautiously on a dining chair, his head bent in shamefaced submission. GRANDMA *sits beside*

him and waits. After GRANDPA *has sighed for a while and vented his anxiety in various ways, she takes his hand gently in hers)*

GRANDMA   I'm not going to put you in a home. It's all your imagination, do you hear?

GRANDPA   But we can't afford . . .

GRANDMA   What nonsense. Don't you remember that the lawyer was here last week and told you that our finances are very good?

GRANDPA   He's even more senile than I am.

GRANDMA   Oh no, he isn't.

GRANDPA   Isn't he?

GRANDMA   No, he isn't.

GRANDPA   So he's clearheaded, you mean.

GRANDMA   Yes.

GRANDPA   *(Sighing heavily)*   I'm so damned ashamed.

GRANDMA   You have nothing to be ashamed of.

GRANDPA   Not with you. But with all the guests.

GRANDMA   Now you're being silly. Jenny isn't a guest.

GRANDPA   There's so much worry in the house.

GRANDMA You're anxious just because you've been sick, that's all. It's summer now and in August we'll go down to the country. That will do you good.

GRANDPA Old age is hell.

(GRANDPA *has begun to weep; he weeps despairingly like a child, at the same time trying to control his outburst, ashamed of his tears.* GRANDMA *sits still, holding his hand between hers*)

GRANDMA There, there, never mind now. There, there, now, you have me. I'm always with you, you know that. There's nothing to worry about.

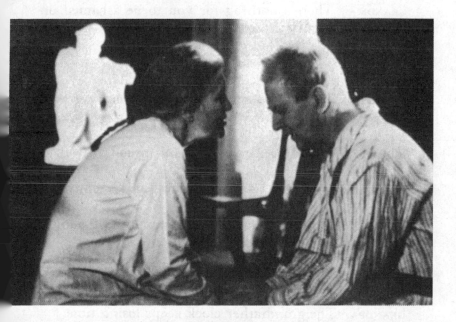

(GRANDPA *keeps crying for some time. Then he stops, tired out, and leans his head against* GRANDMA*'s shoulder. She strokes his head and cheek*)

GRANDPA   Forgive me.

GRANDMA   Come in and lie in my bed, you'll feel easier and get to sleep better.

GRANDPA   I'll just snore and keep you awake.

GRANDMA   I've had quite enough sleep already. Come along now, and I'll make you nice and comfy.

GRANDPA   I get so angry.

GRANDMA   There's nothing for you to be ashamed of. Have you taken a pee?

GRANDPA   I don't need to.

GRANDMA   You'd better go all the same. Otherwise you'll have to get up the minute you're asleep.

GRANDPA   Can't I decide *anything* for myself!

GRANDMA   Well, don't shout so. You'll wake Jenny.

GRANDPA   I'll go and take a pee anyway. And I'll do it to please you. As always.

GRANDMA   Careful how you stand up. Off we go now.

GRANDPA   The grandfather clock keeps losing time.

GRANDMA I'll call the watchmaker tomorrow.

GRANDPA There's no need to *rush*. I don't walk as well as I used to.

(They disappear into GRANDMA *'s room, murmuring together. After a while there is the sound of the toilet being flushed. Gradually all becomes quiet.*

The sun rises higher and higher. The pattern on the wall changes and deepens, moving sideways. The birds in the park have fallen silent. It is in fact very quiet.

JENNY *has dozed off, sitting in the chair. Suddenly she wakes up in alarm. The telephone is ringing. She looks at the clock and sees that it is almost six. When she lifts the receiver all she can hear at first is someone breathing. She says hello, but there is still no answer from the other end. Music can be heard in the background. Suddenly someone giggles faintly. A man's voice says something to her, then the receiver is put down.*

JENNY *stands for a moment or two at a loss, aware of a nasty, creepy feeling. Her eyes are aching with fatigue. Then she makes up her mind.*

At this hour of the morning the streets are still empty. It is already very warm. The sunlight quivers over the town. JENNY *drives her little car quickly and determinedly. She reaches the deserted house within twenty minutes. She puts the key in the lock, opens the door, and enters.*

First she searches the ground floor. It is empty and silent; a few flies are buzzing against the dirty windows. Outside, the summer foliage is dense and protective. She hurries upstairs. She finds MARIA *on the floor of what used to be the bedroom. She is lying on her side, curled up like a fetus. Her eyes are half open and show no sign of reason. After a quick examination* JENNY *gets up and goes into the next room, where the telephone rests on a chair that has been left behind.*

She sits down on the chair, puts the phone in her lap, and dials the number of the hospital.

It is then that she discovers she is not alone. A man of about fifty is standing in the doorway. Another man can be glimpsed in the background. He is much younger, almost a boy)

THE MAN   Who are you calling?

JENNY   I must get Maria to the hospital as soon as possible.

THE MAN   What's the hurry?

JENNY   She's unconscious. What have you done to her?

THE MAN   So you're sure we're the ones who gave her a fix?

JENNY   Whoever it was, she must be gotten out of here.

THE MAN   We can help you. You don't need an ambulance.

JENNY   I'd prefer to handle this my own way.

(THE MAN *goes up to her, takes the telephone, and puts down the receiver*)

THE MAN   Don't be scared, I won't hurt you.

JENNY   I have a suggestion. You get out of here at once and I'll take Maria with me. I won't report you for housebreaking, I won't even let on that I've seen you.

(THE MAN *squats in front of her. He smiles.* THE BOY *has come into the room and shut the door behind him*)

THE MAN   Listen to me for a minute.

JENNY   I don't know that I'm interested.

(THE MAN *reaches out and draws his hand across her face in a rather brutal gesture*)

THE MAN   No, you're not interested. But anyway, it's like this, whether you want to know or not. Maria came to our place late last night. During the night she got sick and began calling for you and said we had to take her to you at once, wherever you were. So we looked you up in the phonebook and brought her here. No one opened the door, so the guy over there crawled in through a cellar window. When we found out the house was empty I called up the hospital, and after a hell of a hassle I got the number of where you're living now.

(*Suddenly the younger man pushes* JENNY *down on the floor. She tries to get up but he lies down on top of her. She begins to struggle but the older man holds her firmly.* THE BOY *pulls up her skirt and rips her pants.* THE MAN *begins to laugh, finding* THE BOY*'s frantic efforts amusing. He keeps pressing her arms and shoulders hard against the floor. Suddenly* JENNY *stops resisting and lies still. Above her is* THE BOY*'s red, frenzied face. He reeks of sweat, nicotine, and dirt. He has seized her left breast and now begins to suck at it with a desperate sort of hunger, making abortive attempts time and again to thrust into her.* JENNY *looks at the wild, distorted face pressed against her breast, the thick, mousy hair, the forehead, the smooth cheek, and the* *childish mouth. She gazes at his face for a long, unreal moment)*

THE BOY   No, she's too tight.

(He gets up and zips his fly. JENNY *remains lying on the floor. The two men go into the next room. They mumble together for a few moments. Then the older man comes back, carrying her pocketbook. He opens it and rummages inside. He finds some bills which he stuffs in his pocket, then drops the bag on the floor)*

THE MAN   Some women have to pay for a lay. You didn't know that, did you? *(He bends over her and gives*

her a long, hard look) Now you can call your ambu-lance.

(He moves the telephone within reach, then goes into the next room. A door bangs, and after a few moments the kitchen door also is slammed. A car starts behind the house and noses its way on the crunching gravel down toward the road.

JENNY *reaches for the phone and calls the ambulance. She goes into the next room to* MARIA, *who has not moved and is still lying curled up on her side.*

Then JENNY *goes into the bathroom and rinses her face, drying it on a handkerchief which she finds in her bag. She stands for a while leaning forward, her arms propped against the sink. It is very stuffy in there; the sun glitters through the misted panes, where a few flies are buzzing helplessly. She has a splitting headache.*

When the ambulance has driven off she sits down on the solitary chair beside the telephone. She takes a little red book out of her bag and hunts through it. Then she finds the phone number)

JENNY   Hello. May I speak to Dr. Jacobi? Tell him, please, that it's Dr. Isaksson. Jenny Isaksson. Yes.

(She is kept waiting. She is kept waiting a long time. She fights a violent agitation as she feels a gray panic surging up from her bowels. It tightens and rages, and she is assaulted by a terrible need to scream. She rocks slightly on the chair, brushes her face with her hand several times, sits on the floor, closes her eyes, opens them, fetches heavy sighs as she breathes.

Despite all this emotion she manages to steady her voice when TOMAS *finally comes to the phone)*

JENNY   I thought I ought to call you at once. Maria is in a very bad way. I don't know. Probably an overdose of drugs but I'm not sure. She had run away from the hospital. I found her at my place. Yes, in the house. Couldn't I see you? Then I could tell you more. What? Are we going to a concert this evening? Yes, that'd be fine. You can pick me up at the hospital. Oh no, thanks anyway.

The concert hall is located in a mansion built at the turn of the century, now used as an art gallery. The rooms are crammed with paintings and sculptures from the period. The lawns and trees of the park can be seen through the big windows, and a calm stretch of water gleams in the twilight of the summer evening.

The audience fills not only the concert hall itself but also the adjacent rooms, corridors, and stairs. JENNY *and* TOMAS *have arrived late and therefore find themselves on the broad mahogany staircase leading to the second floor. They are sitting on a short bench on the landing, their backs to the wall. They are pressed close together, as other latecomers have squeezed into the available space.*

(The pianist plays Mozart's Fantasia in E Minor.) The twilight mixes with the pale light from the big chandelier softly illuminating the many faces around JENNY. *She is surprised that so many people are listening restlessly and without concentration; they dart glances here and there, touch their faces, fidget, fiddle with invisible objects, as though still captive in the day's impulses and movements. It is better to look at those who have their eyes shut, who have turned into themselves, who are listening, who are in repose, resting in happy thoughts or none at all. There are two young people absorbed in each other, there is an old man by himself, bent and deformed, but dignified in his listening. There is a middle-aged woman with a great loneliness around her and a calm sadness in her face, there is a dark-skinned boy in thick glasses with his eyes turned to the twilight*

from the big window, his face full of longing. A little girl has fallen asleep propped against a youngish woman who is perhaps her mother. She in turn leans her head against a man's shoulder. They are wrapped in intimate harmony, content with each other, themselves, and the constant flow of music. There is an elderly woman heavily made-up and with blue-tinted hair, obviously an American tourist, sitting stiffly, pressed into a corner, and far from comfortable, but she smiles constantly to herself and her large gray eyes stray quietly from one person to the next.

JENNY *has to close her eyes, she must go into herself. But she discovers at once that that is not the place to be. Something is going on there that frightens her and makes her giddy. No, not there. She can't go there. As long as she keeps still, watching* TOMAS*'s hand with half-closed eyes, all is well. As long as she has the self-discipline not to turn inward, all is well. It's a matter now of minute by minute, hour by hour.*

She knows instinctively that the longer she can put off what is going to happen at any moment, the better chance she has of clinging to the reality that is gradually disintegrating. She knows that this is the most important thing in the world right now.

Then they are driving along in TOMAS*'s car. It is still light; the sky is white and red, and a thin bluish veil-like mist hangs over the trees and the road and the gleaming water. Before they enter the house* JENNY *checks him with a movement against the hand that is opening the front door.*

JENNY Let's not talk much.

TOMAS Just as you like.

JENNY You understand, don't you?

TOMAS (*Kindly*) No, not really.

JENNY It's like this: One has to get through certain hours of life.

(*She regards him appealingly, as though expecting him to understand, but he gives a friendly, questioning smile*)

TOMAS Well, and what of that?

JENNY There are certain hours or perhaps only certain minutes.

TOMAS Is it like that? Now?

JENNY It may be. At any rate I'm thankful we're together.

(*They enter the hall.* JENNY *gives a little shiver. Tomas takes her by the shoulders*)

TOMAS You need a drink, no doubt about that.

(*He pours one out and gives it to her. She stands beside him, watching*)

JENNY Last time we met we were rather absurd. Don't you think so?

TOMAS I hardly ever think I'm absurd.

(JENNY *moves about the room, touching various objects. Now and then she stops and looks at him, as though making sure he is still there and hasn't vanished into thin air*)

JENNY   Do you have some good sleeping pills?

TOMAS   Yes, quite good. Do you want one?

JENNY   I'll tell you what I'd like most of all.

TOMAS   We weren't going to talk, you said.

JENNY   Give me the pill, or even two if you think I'll sleep twice as well.

TOMAS   And then?

JENNY   Then let me sleep here with you in your bed. Without making love. But you must hold my hand if necessary. Would you consider something like that?

(TOMAS *goes straight out to the bathroom and returns with a glass of water and some sleeping pills balanced on the palm of his hand. He takes her brandy glass*)

TOMAS   If you're going to take such a strong dose you'd better not drink.

JENNY   No, that's true.

TOMAS   Here are a half a milligram of Valium and two Mogadon. It's usually a good combination. I take it myself and it has no aftereffects. If you drink some strong coffee in the morning you'll pick right up.

JENNY   Yes.

TOMAS   There you are.

JENNY   Thanks.

TOMAS What time shall I wake you?

JENNY Just before seven. I have to be at the hospital by eight thirty.

TOMAS Can't you phone and say you're ill?

JENNY *(Shaking her head)* If you force everything to be as usual then it *will* be as usual. Don't you agree? *(Looks at him)* That's how it is with me anyway.

TOMAS Is that how you cure your patients?

JENNY No. But they're sick. I'm not.

(They are lying one on either side of the double bed. TOMAS *puts out the reading lamp. At first it is quite dark, but after a few moments the dusky light outside shows against the blind and soon* JENNY *can make out the objects in the room. She lies silent for some time with her eyes closed)*

JENNY Something odd happened to me today. *(She turns on her side with her arm under her cheek and fixes her eyes on the bright rectangle of the window)* When I went to get Maria there were two men in the house. One of them tried to rape me. At first I was frightened, then I thought it was ridiculous, and then . . .

TOMAS *(Turning his head)* And then?

JENNY He was all red in the face. He lay pressing his mouth to my breast and trying to thrust into me.

TOMAS And?

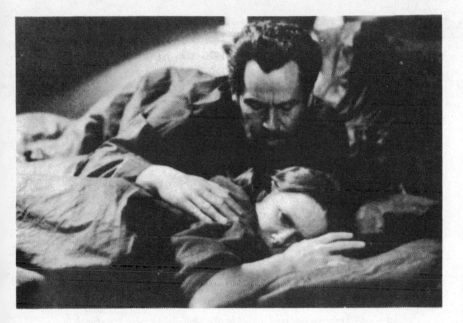

JENNY Suddenly I wanted him so desperately to do it.

TOMAS Do you think that was so strange?

JENNY No. The strange thing was that I couldn't take him, much as I wanted to. I was all tight and cramped and dry.

(Suddenly she begins to laugh. It bursts out as if she had long been trying to stifle it, a completely dead laugh. She shakes with laughter, tries to control it, for a moment it is checked then breaks out again. TOMAS is bewildered. At first he smiles to keep her company. When it dawns on him that she is not laughing at the comic side of the situation nor for the sheer joy of living but that this is something frightening,

he switches on the light and sits up in bed. JENNY *is lying on her back, with the backs of her hands pressed to her face; her long hair is tousled over the sheet, the pillow has fallen onto the floor, her body is racked with suppressed fits of laughter)*

JENNY   I'm sorry. I don't know . . . I can't help . . . What's the matter with me . . .

TOMAS   Try to sit up.

(JENNY *sits up, her back bent, her shoulders sagging, her arms stiff)*

JENNY   I can't think what . . .

TOMAS   Try to breathe calmly now. Take a deep breath.

(JENNY *tries obediently to do as she's told. But a fresh gale of laughter bursts through the deep breathing. Then the wild laughter changes to retching sobs)*

JENNY   No. No. I don't want to. I don't want to.

(TOMAS *tries to hold her in his arms, but she fights to get free, stares at him in alarm, and shakes her head. The whole time she is racked by convulsive sobs)*

JENNY   I want to go home. Please call a taxi. No, you're not to come with me. I can manage by myself. It will pass.

(*She gets out of bed, shivering as though with fever. Just as suddenly as she burst out crying, she now begins to laugh again)*

TOMAS   Should I call a doctor?

JENNY   What! With all the expertise here already. I'm just tired, there's nothing wrong with me. I'll get home and into bed. There's absolutely nothing wrong with me.

(With a violent effort she straightens her body, then stands quietly for a moment or two as though musing, listening inward)

TOMAS   How do you feel now?

JENNY   Better.

TOMAS   Say what you like, but I'm going to drive you home.

(During the drive they say little. When they pull up outside JENNY*'s door* TOMAS *is about to get out and help her, but she stops him)*

JENNY   I'm much better now. Thank you. I'm sorry I . . . Forgive me. Forgive me for being so silly. Now I'll snatch a few hours' sleep and tomorrow I'll be fine and then I have two days off. *(She leans forward and kisses his cheek)* Next time we'll talk only about you.

(She undresses quickly and sets the alarm clock. She is in full control of herself, almost in a good mood. She switches on the little transistor radio by the bed, which plays something soft. Daylight shines outside the window. She snuggles down into bed and sinks into a dreamless sleep. Con-

sciousness slips away, is smudged out. She breathes deeply.
She wakes up to find GRANDMA *sitting on the edge of the*
bed with a breakfast tray beside her. JENNY *stares at her,*
bewildered and still dazed with sleep)

JENNY   What is it?

GRANDMA   You slept all day yesterday and evidently all
last night. I was getting worried.

JENNY   What day is it?

GRANDMA   Saturday. It's nine o'clock. I phoned the hospital and said your tummy was upset.

JENNY   Heavens, I've slept right round the clock.

GRANDMA   I've brought you some breakfast.

JENNY   That's sweet of you, but I don't want anything.

GRANDMA   Have some coffee and a piece of toast. It will
do you good.

JENNY   My head's aching.

GRANDMA   You probably have a temperature.

JENNY   If I stay in bed today and tomorrow it will go
away.

GRANDMA   I'm afraid I can't be at home to look after you.
Grandpa and I have been asked to go and stay with the
Egermans at Högsätra, and we can't refuse them.

Grandpa is looking forward enormously to being in the country for a few days.

JENNY   But Grandma dear, I'll be quite all right by myself.

GRANDMA   Will you? Are you sure?

JENNY   I'll enjoy it.

GRANDMA   Everything you need is in the freezer—there's steak and a chicken casserole. And I've bought milk and bread and—

JENNY *(With an effort)*   Grandma dear! Have a nice time at Högsätra and for goodness' sake don't go around feeling guilty because of me. I enjoy looking after myself when I'm not feeling well.

GRANDMA   You promise to call me up if you get worse?

JENNY *(With an effort)*   I promise. Cross my heart.

(GRANDMA *kisses her on the cheek, pats her head, and looks at her with sharp, clear eyes)*

GRANDMA   There's nothing else?

JENNY   No.

GRANDMA   Are you sure?

JENNY   Quite sure.

GRANDMA   Shall I ask Aunt Erika to drop in and see how you are?

JENNY   Anything, but not Aunt Erika.

GRANDMA   All right, then.

(GRANDMA *leaves.*
After a few minutes JENNY *has sunk into a coma.*
She is awakened by a golden light pouring into the room, which is almost dazzling. It is Sunday morning and the church bells echo over the empty streets, calling people to matins. She sits up, feeling light in body and head. The room is shimmering with light and her eyes hurt slightly)

JENNY   It must be Sunday—morning—obviously—the church bells—I ought to get up and perhaps eat something, I feel rather peculiar but the anxiety is gone and that's the main thing. One step at a time, then I'll be all well by tomorrow. A little food. A walk. A nice book. Perhaps go to a movie.

(She gets out of bed, managing better than she had imagined. She goes into the kitchen and puts the kettle on, gets out eggs, cheese, and bread, finds the coffee tin—it all goes much better than she dared to hope.
The bells clang, the bright sunlight hovers over curtains, carpets, chandeliers, pictures, and statuettes; the greenery on the other side of the street billows darkly. There is not a soul in sight, not a car, not a living creature. She fishes out a thin blouse, a pair of threadbare slacks, and some comfortable sandals. It is getting rather warm, the edge of her scalp is perspiring, while at the same time her hands and shoulders feel cold. Otherwise she feels very well, even slightly exhilarated. She laughs to herself and stretches)

JENNY   I'll call Tomas. I don't see why he shouldn't take me to a movie tonight. *(She hurries out to the kitchen and takes the boiled eggs off the stove, makes the coffee, sets the table, phones* TOMAS. *He answers almost at once)* Hello, Tomas, it's Jenny. I just wanted to apologize for being so disagreeable last time. I feel splendid. I thought you might like to ask me to a movie this evening. What's that? Oh, how nice.

*(*JENNY *looks up. In the mirror she sees the drawing room bathed in light. The tall woman is standing where the sun pours in, gazing at* JENNY *with her one eye. Her right eye socket is a black hole.*

JENNY *puts down the receiver slowly and turns toward the drawing room. The figure between the windows is still there. She goes into her room and sits down on the bed, trying to move calmly and composedly. Then she goes back to the drawing room, which is now empty. She looks around her, goes into* GRANDMA's *room, which is also empty. There is no hideous figure with an empty eye socket in* GRANDPA's *room either. Stillness, bright sunlight, her heart pounding, she stands at the kitchen table, her hands on the checked oilcloth. The kitchen clock ticks busily, cheerful radio music comes from an apartment facing the courtyard, two little girls are playing hopscotch down on the black asphalt. The sky is white with light.*

Back in her room, she sits down on a chair by the window and takes out her little pocket tape recorder from under a pile of books with foreign titles. She is quite calm now. From time to time she takes a deep breath. She starts the recorder)

JENNY   Dear Erik, my dear one. It's easier to speak like this to a tape recorder than to write a letter. It has always been the way with me that whenever I go to put something in writing, the words escape me. In a

little while I'm going to take fifty Nembutal. Then I'll get into bed and go to sleep. I'm afraid you'll be angry with me for this. As far as I know we have never discussed the possibility that one or the other of us might commit suicide—there has never been any call to. All the same, I realize suddenly that what I'm going to do in a little while has been lurking inside me for several years. Not that I've consciously planned to take my life, don't think that. I'm not so deceitful. It's more that I've been living in an isolation that has got worse and worse—the dividing line between my outer behavior and my inner impoverishment has become more distinct. I remember last Whitsun, for instance.

You and I and Anna went for a ramble in the forest. You and Anna thoroughly enjoyed yourselves. I made out it was wonderful too, and said how happy I was, but it wasn't true. I wasn't taking in anything of all the beauty surrounding us. My senses reported it, but the connections were broken. This upset me and I thought I'd try to cry but the tears wouldn't come.

This is only one example picked at random, but the more I think back, the more I remember. I stopped listening to music, as I felt sealed up and apathetic. Our sex life—I felt nothing, nothing at all. I pretended I did, so that you wouldn't be anxious or start asking questions. But I think the worst of all was that I lost touch with our little girl. A prison grew up all around me, with no doors or windows. With walls so thick that not a sound got through, walls that it was useless to attack, since they were built from materials I supplied myself.

I think you should explain all this to our daughter. You should explain it very thoroughly, you must be unflinchingly truthful. We live, and while we live we're gradually suffocated without knowing what is happening. At last there's only a puppet left, reacting more or less to external demands and stimuli. Inside there is nothing but a great horror.

Erik my dear, I don't feel afraid or sad or lonely. Please don't feel sorry for me—I'm quite content, almost excited, like when I was little and going on a trip. It may even be that this is a recovery from a lifelong illness. I give you my word . . .

(What JENNY *was going to promise she can't recall, so after a moment's thought she switches off the recorder, removes the cassette, and puts it into an envelope, which she seals. On the front she writes "To Erik" and lays it on the bedside table.*

Then she goes quickly into the lavatory and gets the sleeping pills and a glass of water. She makes the bed, pulls the blind down three-quarters of the way, shuts the door, straightens up her things, looks around—it is all very neat. She sits on the edge of the bed, after having laid her bathrobe on the chair at the head.

She begins methodically to swallow the sleeping pills, first one by one then several at a time. She is breathless and has to rest for a few moments. She looks at herself in the misty mirror of the big wardrobe: her face is calm, almost smiling, her pupils enlarged, her body hunched and shivery.

Now she takes the rest of the pills. Half an hour has passed. She sits for a while with her eyes closed and her palms pressed to her thighs)

JENNY I'm not afraid. I don't feel lonely. I'm not even sad. It feels rather nice in fact.

(Then she lies down and pulls the quilt over herself. She sinks quickly down in a dark swirl of dreams and visions)

JENNY *is in a hurry, is late, and rushes down a long corridor with high walls extending up to the ceiling, where a wan light filters down through broken panes. The floor is of rough boards and very dirty: scraps from meals, old newspapers, cans, patches of sticky oil, piles of garbage. She's in a great hurry, but at the same time must be careful where she sets her foot, and has to hold up her long, dark, red dress, which wraps her in a rustle of flounces and lace.*

She sees herself in a large mottled mirror: she is dressed for a banquet but her face is pale, almost sallow, and her eyes are feverish. Her hair is tucked into an embroidered medieval hood, which fits closely around her ears and cheeks. Her forehead shines with sweat. Nevertheless it is cold. She sees that the surfaces of the room paneling, carvings, floors, are covered with hoarfrost and dirty white snow that has been carelessly swept out of the way.

She opens a door she seems to remember and finds herself in a large room that is vaguely familiar: it is GRANDMA *and* GRANDPA*'s drawing room. Yet it is very different. Everything is filthy, dilapidated, decayed; a murky half-light seeps in through the tattered sacking hanging in front of the windows.*

In the middle of the room an old man is sitting in a large battered chair. He is wearing an old-fashioned, ill-fitting tail-coat and his head keeps shaking. At his knee stands a little girl in a long red dress; she looks now at him, now at a candle which flickers in a short holder on a small table to the right of the man (who grows more and more like JENNY*'s grandfather). The candle gutters and is almost burnt out: this obviously frightens the little girl and her grandfather.*

A musty, damp cold pervades the room. White patches, as of snow or frost, can be seen on the floor and walls.

As JENNY*'s eyes grow used to the gloom, she sees that quite a lot of people are assembled. On the sofas, behind the mirror in the corner by the tiled stove, half-hidden in doorways, she catches glimpses of faces and bodies: men in ancient tailcoats, women in peculiar, faded, ill-fitting ball gowns. Behind one of the richly carved, half snow-covered lintels she can even make out a gaunt, ravaged face with two huge eyes shaded by a top hat.*

JENNY *turns around; behind her* HELMUTH WANKEL *is standing. He seems very nervous and worried: he keeps biting at a nail. He also has a bad cold and a cough.*

JENNY I'm sorry I'm late, but it's such terrible weather. Some streets are blocked by snow.

WANKEL Not at all. The best people are always late.

JENNY   It's chilly here, isn't it.

WANKEL   Many people complain that it's far too warm.

JENNY   Excuse me, but what is the nasty smell?

WANKEL   It's the *accelerating necrosis*. All these people
. . . *(Checking himself)* Exactly.

JENNY   So I've come too late.

WANKEL   Unfortunately. The ball is over. But you
haven't missed anything much. I can't really see why
people persist with masquerades like this.

JENNY   Is it a masquerade?

WANKEL   *(Menacing)*   Didn't you know?

JENNY   *(Anxious)*   Yes, of course.

WANKEL   And what are you going to do now?

JENNY   I don't know. *(Anxious)* Do you realize this is a
dream?

WANKEL   *(Coughing)*   Are you sure?

JENNY   Yes, this is a dream. The whole of this ridiculous
spectacle is a result of my illness. You mustn't forget
I'm a pretty experienced doctor. It's a dream.

WANKEL   One wakens out of dreams, surely?

JENNY   That's just what I intend to do.

WANKEL You can try.

JENNY I wake up when *I* want to.

(*A door opens and out of the darkness behind it steps a large man in a peculiar get-up. He has a long, scarred face, a huge nose, and a big mouth. One of his eyes has been gouged out. On his head he has a checked Napoleon hat. The thickset, almost hunchbacked figure is wrapped in a kind of clown costume. He walks into the room on crooked legs. Everyone greets him with horror-filled respect. He turns toward the grandfather and the little girl, who clings in terror to the old man.*
  The candle flickers, about to go out. It grows very still.
  The big clown smiles at the girl in the red dress, but his smile seems only to add to her terror. The grandfather makes a feeble gesture as if to ward him off)

JENNY (*Whispering*) What is happening?

WANKEL That which you can do nothing about.

JENNY I don't want to see.

WANKEL You don't have to. In a few moments that light will go out. Nothing will happen as long as the candle is burning.

(*At that instant the light goes out. In an endlessly prolonged second* JENNY *sees the clown with the gouged-out eye make a gesture toward the little girl, who presses herself in vain against her grandfather.*
  JENNY *hears herself call out. She turns away, runs a few steps along the corridor, and stops in front of a small door.* WANKEL *is still with her*)

WANKEL   I'd advise you not to open that door.

JENNY   You keep trying to scare me.

WANKEL   Well, it's your own fault.

JENNY   If I open that door, I'll wake up.

WANKEL   You can't wake up.

JENNY   I can if I try.

WANKEL   Try.

JENNY   I suddenly remember something. *(Pause)* I bungled my suicide.

WANKEL   Not entirely.

JENNY   What do you mean?

WANKEL   Brain damage due to lack of oxygen. Have you never heard of that calamity?

(He sits down on a chair and, taking off his glasses, stares sadly at JENNY*)*

JENNY   It can't be so horrible.

WANKEL   Oh yes, it can! An absolute mercilessness that is also self-inflicted.

JENNY   Will I always live like this?

WANKEL   It seems likely.

JENNY Will I never wake up?

WANKEL Don't worry, they'll keep you alive by every means they have. Whether you're awake or unconscious.

JENNY How long?

WANKEL Until you die. Properly.

JENNY And how long before that?

WANKEL Seconds, minutes, years. How do I know?

JENNY It mustn't be.

WANKEL Yes. It must.

JENNY Then it doesn't matter if I open that door.

WANKEL *(With a weary, sarcastic smile)* Logically, your argument is unassailable.

JENNY By the way, do *you* know what's in there?

WANKEL No, how should I?

JENNY Then why do you warn me?

WANKEL We're thankful for the horrors we're used to. The unknown ones are worse.

JENNY But it may be something better.

WANKEL Not here.

JENNY How can you be so sure?

WANKEL *(Smiling)* This isn't only *your* dream, Jenny. *We're sharing it.*

JENNY I'm going to open it, anyway.

WANKEL By all means. You always have your free will.

JENNY You're leaving?

WANKEL *(Smiles)* I don't want to get into a worse mess than I'm in already. So if you'll excuse me. *(Suddenly he turns around and walks up to her. His face is distorted, his pale eyes glare at her malignantly, his breath has an evil smell. He shakes his finger at her)* I've been pretty patient with you, my dear Jenny. I've answered your foolish questions, I've shown you around, I've been kind and obliging. But have you *for one moment* been interested in how I am? Have you said *a single word* to show that you were pleased to see me? Have you *in any way* thanked me for my kind warnings? By the way, your face is yellow, which is a bad sign. Now I'll go out of *your* dream and into my own. Good-bye.

(JENNY *opens the door and steps into* GRANDMA *and* GRANDPA *'s apartment. It looks the same as usual except for the light, which is gray and shadowless (like the light on a rainy day in autumn). She calls* GRANDMA, *enormously relieved; her eyes fill with tears of joy. She calls again, going from room to room.*

Finally she sinks down at the shiny black dining table, her sallow complexion and dark red dress reflected faintly in the table top as though in deep stagnant water)

JENNY   If only I could wake up.

(She looks around her; everything is familiar but remote and shadowy. She turns her head toward the drawing room opening up beyond the French doors. It is a little lighter in there.
   In the middle of the room, clearly outlined and tangible in the fluid light, stands the big one-eyed woman, looking at her)

THE WOMAN   You're cold.

JENNY   Yes.

THE WOMAN   You can have my cardigan.

JENNY   Thank you.

(THE WOMAN goes up to her and wraps her in a large dark cardigan, which covers the red dress and her bare shoulders. JENNY draws it around her. THE WOMAN sits down on a chair near her)

THE WOMAN   So *now* you're not afraid.

JENNY   I don't think so.

(THE WOMAN reaches out her arm and draws JENNY to her in a motherly gesture. JENNY makes no resistance, her head sinks onto the old woman's breast.
   The long dark cardigan covers her completely. At the same moment someone takes her roughly by the arms and shakes her, calling her name. An agonizing, wavering light that gets brighter and brighter bores through her closed eyelids)

JENNY   Leave me alone. I don't want to. I don't want to. Can't you leave me in peace. I don't want to.

*(Now she can see a window; the sunlight strikes her face
and burns her eyes. A familiar seeming face appears. It is
TOMAS.*

*She is wet with sweat and can smell a sour stench, the
hospital nightshirt is damp and stained, she can see her bare
feet somewhere far away.*

JENNY *(Trying to smile)*   I think my legs have come off.
Can't someone get them from the corner over there
and fasten them on?

TOMAS   Hello.

JENNY   What are you doing here?

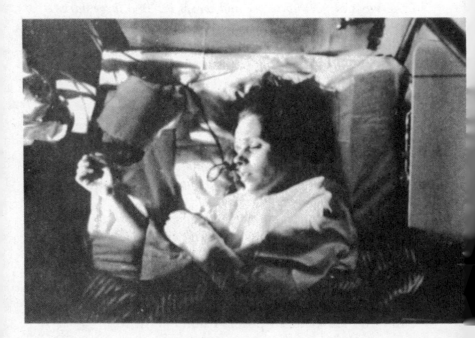

TOMAS   We were going to a movie together. Remember?

JENNY *(Shaking her head)*   No.

TOMAS   Suddenly you were silent and put the receiver down. I didn't know what to think, though it did seem odd.

JENNY   Oh. *(Wearily)* Oh, I see.

TOMAS   So I kept phoning off and on, but there was no answer. I thought you might have been attacked by a burglar or something—I just didn't know what to think. It was very unpleasant. Are you thirsty? Wouldn't you like something to drink?

JENNY   Yes, please.

TOMAS   Take this. I'll help you. Wait a moment, you can't do it by yourself. Careful now.

JENNY *(Drinks)*   Thank you. *(Dully)* I am very grateful.

TOMAS   Finally I was so worried that I went and rang your doorbell. When no one answered I got the janitor to open the door.

JENNY   God, what a bore. I'm so sleepy.

(She succumbs to the temptation, unable to go on any longer. The deadly tedium washes over her. "Oh Christ," she mutters hoarsely and vanishes from the world of the living, leaving TOMAS *on the sunlit shore. She returns to the land where the light is like thin ashes and the air is musty, raw, and chill.*

She is again in GRANDMA *and* GRANDPA's *apartment, again wearing the red dress. She goes from room to room calling her parents in a clear, anxious voice)*

JENNY   Mama! Where are you? Daddy! I'm home now. Why are you hiding? If it's a game it's not a nice one. Come out now and don't frighten me like that . . .

(A middle-aged man in a gray overcoat comes toward her, followed by a somewhat younger woman. They appear suddenly, unexpectedly, and seem intent on running into her and knocking her down.

The man is tall but stooped. He has clear blue eyes and thin gray hair; his expression is tense. The woman with him is very beautiful, with regular features and large dark eyes. She also has an anxiously questioning expression.

They stop just short of JENNY *and look back, as if in search of someone or as if they had lost their way)*

JENNY   Mama, it's me. Daddy, it's *me!* Don't you recognize me?

*(*JENNY *calls to them, but their anxiety is far too great, they don't hear her whisper. She knows it is very urgent and that she must say the right words)*

JENNY   I'm so very fond of you both, you were always so good to me. It was so odd when you suddenly just disappeared. I saw you when you were dead, lying in the funeral parlor. I didn't know you. Mama dear, why are you so anxious? There's nothing to worry about, I'm not nine years old any more. I'm grown up and have taken sleeping pills, it doesn't seem to have come off, they're hard at work on me at the hospital.

You couldn't help being so anxious about everything. Dear little Mama, everything had to be exactly
right and proper and so drearily neat and tidy. And
Daddy who was so affectionate and liked to be
hugged and who was so sad and nervous. We used to
hurt each other without meaning to. Just think, all
our lives, all the days and all the words and little
things. We had nice times too, didn't we? I was a
child, I didn't know what it was all about. *(Furious)*
No, you . . . you just slammed the door and there we
were with the guilt. Always a bad conscience, always
to blame! *(Weeping)* Go away and never come back.
I'm going to forget you so completely that I'll never

have to see your anxious eyes again and never have to hear your timid voices.

(Her parents are ashamed and humiliated. They begin whispering furtively to each other and at last reach some kind of agreement. Her mother buttons her coat and tightens the belt around her slender waist; her father puts on his hat, which he has been holding all this time in his left hand; under his right arm he carries a brief case)

JENNY *(Wearily and in despair)*   It's always the same! First I say I love you, then I say I hate you, and then you turn into two scared children, ashamed of yourselves. Then I feel sorry for you and love you again. I can't go on any longer.

(She strikes at them at the same time as she tries to embrace and kiss them. They defend themselves lamely and with unreal gestures. Their clothes tear with a brittle, rasping sound. JENNY tries to hold on to them though they are now retreating hastily into the darkening twilight.
  Finally she trips over her red dress and falls)

TOMAS   Jenny!

(She opens her eyes and looks around. It is evening. The ceiling light is on and the night lamp, with its indirect glow, is also burning)

JENNY   What a horrid smell in here, and I'm so nasty and dirty. Can't you ask them to let me have a wash?

TOMAS   Your husband is here.

JENNY *(Plaintively)*   Not now!

(But it's too late. The door opens with a faint sigh and a nurse appears but goes out again at once, making room for ERIK, JENNY*'s husband.*

TOMAS *withdraws tactfully and husband and wife are alone. They look at each other in embarrassment.* ERIK*'s eyes are slightly bloodshot—whether from fatigue after the long plane trip or from sorrow is hard to say. But he is carefully dressed in a lightweight, fashionable summer suit and his hair is well groomed. His weak mouth trembles a little and his face is very pale. He is holding the cassette with* JENNY*'s letter)*

ERIK *(Smiling)*   Well, you do have a knack for springing surprises.

JENNY   Yes, don't I.

ERIK   I've come straight from the airport.

JENNY   Poor Erik. You must be awfully tired.

ERIK   No, not in the least.

JENNY   Won't you sit down?

ERIK   Oh yes. Yes, of course.

(When he has sat down, coming quite close to her, their shyness is, if possible, even more of a barrier)

JENNY   I smell nasty. I'm so sorry.

ERIK   No, no, my dear, it doesn't matter.

JENNY   Can't you come back tomorrow? By then we'll both have recovered a little.

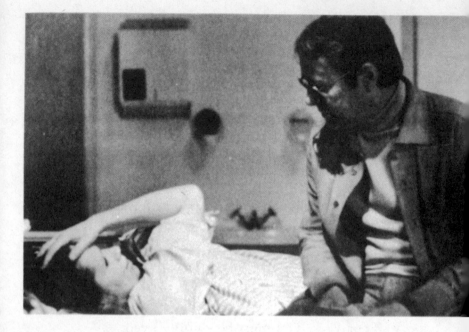

ERIK   Yes, of course. Though tomorrow I must fly back. It's hopeless! I'm to be the chairman of—

JENNY   Poor you!

ERIK   Oh, I'm all right.

JENNY   The trouble I cause.

ERIK   It would have been awful if you . . . I'd never have . . . In all my life I've never been so . . .

JENNY   Forgive me!

ERIK   Why did you do it?

JENNY   Forgive me. Forgive me.

(The same tone of voice. The wide dark eyes, the hair, matted with perspiration, straggling over the white brow, the lips sore —a child trapped in the bitter anguish of death. It is too much for ERIK. *He lowers his eyes and looks at his white hand with the Doctor's ring and the well-tended nails)*

ERIK   *(Quietly)*   I realize I'm largely to blame for this. Though I don't know how. I've tried to think it out—

JENNY   Another time, Erik?

ERIK   Do you think you can rest now?

JENNY   Yes, I think so. Please don't worry. there's no need.

ERIK   That Tomas seems to be a decent fellow.

JENNY   Yes.

ERIK   Have you known each other long?

JENNY   No.

ERIK   Apparently he's a doctor but not here at the hospital. A gynecologist, isn't he?

JENNY   Yes.

ERIK   What do you want me to say to Grandma? She's bound to ask.

JENNY   Tell her the truth.

ERIK   And to Anna?

JENNY   I'll have to talk to her myself. You can just call her up and ask how she's getting along at the camp.

ERIK   Yes, I will.

(The silence between them grows into a solid transparent wall. They are both pretty worn out with emotion and grief)

JENNY   Bye-bye, my dear. We'll keep in touch! Eh?

ERIK   Bye for now!

(And he is gone.
JENNY turns her head to the side and closes her eyes. She suddenly finds herself in a low, arched room. Outside the windows it is winter and snow lies thick. The room is lighted by big globes hanging from the ceiling. They give out a dirty yellow half-light which pitilessly exposes the peeling plaster on the walls, the filthy floor, and the stained, colorless cloth on the conference table. A naked woman is sitting in a gynecological chair, covered with a soiled sheet. She is dead, and several doctors in white coats have gathered around her, consulting in whispers.

At one end of the table JENNY is sitting in her red dress, but with a doctor's coat thrown over her bare shoulders. She now sees that the dead woman in the gynecological chair is MARIA.

The doctors sit down at the table. They look through their papers, light cigarettes, drink mineral water, whisper among themselves. DR. WANKEL looks at JENNY with an interested expression and nods to her encouragingly)

JENNY   She said she loved me. I admit I didn't understand the significance of that statement. Besides, she
herself did her best to confuse the issue. Please listen!
I have a right to defend myself before the matter is
remitted.

*(The men stare at her in sudden surprise, as though her re-
proach were most uncalled for)*

JENNY *(Vehemently)*   I don't see the point of all this.
If I have broken any of the rules, scientific or ethi-
cal, that we have pledged ourselves to respect, then
charge me.

(No one moves or reacts. No glances or secret understandings.
WANKEL *props his head in his hand and doodles on a pad. The
glasses of the man next to him catch the light.*

JENNY *gets upset. She starts to her feet, the chair top-
ples over, the white coat spreads out over the red dress. She
stands for a moment with clenched fists, looking down at
the table)*

JENNY   That soft body, those soft arms, those large soft
breasts. And then that mouth, which was always so
soft and moist and half open. I felt a physical disgust
which I tried to overcome, and when she touched me
I had to fight to control myself, to stop myself from
striking her. *(She is silent, then bends down, picks up the
chair, and sits down)* I'm sure there *is* something called
love. I even think I've met people who love or have
loved. *(She shuts her eyes and slowly puts her hands to her
face. After a few moments of tense silence she lowers them and
speaks harshly)* I've tried to live like everyone else. And
I've failed. Do you think I don't see that myself? *(Cries
out)* I have no words to say what I mean. It's hopeless.

(Pause) This is too hard, I'm not equal to it. *(Pause)* Once only in my life have I *understood* another human being. For one short moment. Understood a human being! Do you see . . .

(The faces turned toward her face. The eyes, the mouths, the hands. The naked white body gleaming there behind the men's polite smiles, the closed dead face. Outside the arched windows, the gray dusk and the snow. All this)

WANKEL   Have you anything more to say?

JENNY   No.

WANKEL   Then the hearing is over.

JENNY   What happens next?

WANKEL   The case will be passed on to the Committee on Medical Ethics.

JENNY   And then?

WANKEL   Then? Nothing.

JENNY   Nothing?

WANKEL   No, of course not. That's the most usual.

JENNY   Nothing?

WANKEL   What did you expect?

JENNY   A punishment.

WANKEL   You do presume. Even if we despise each other behind our backs, we must stick together outwardly. You know that as well as I do.

JENNY   Nothing . . . Nothing . . . Nothing . . .

(When JENNY *wakes up from her dream it is night. She sees someone sitting in the visitor's chair and puts on the bedside light to see who it is—perhaps it's a ghost. It is* TOMAS. *He is wearing an old sweater and has a blanket wrapped around his legs and his feet up on the other chair. Beside him he has a thermos of coffee and some cheese and sausage sandwiches. When* JENNY *switches on the light he blinks rather sleepily)*

JENNY   What time is it?

TOMAS   I'll have a look. One thirty.

JENNY   What day is it?

TOMAS   Tuesday. It'll be light soon. Tuesday, June twelfth.

JENNY   Oh.

(Slowly, slowly it dawns on JENNY *that it's odd after all that* TOMAS *should be in her sickroom at one thirty in the early hours of Tuesday, June twelfth)*

TOMAS   How do you feel?

JENNY   I don't know. *(Pause)* Tomas!

TOMAS   Yes?

JENNY   Why are you sitting here keeping watch?

TOMAS   I have my reasons.

JENNY   Oh?

TOMAS   Anyway, I'm your doctor.

JENNY   I didn't know that.

TOMAS   No. But now you do.

(*Both become lost in their own thoughts.* JENNY *is sinking back into her other state, which awaits her just behind the wall. She makes an effort to stop herself*)

JENNY   Do you have coffee in that thermos?

TOMAS   Yes.

JENNY   Do you think I could have some?

TOMAS   No, I think you'd feel pretty sick if you started gulping down a lot of strong coffee. But you can have fruit juice.

JENNY   No thanks.

TOMAS   It's good for you to drink something.

(*He helps her to drink, turns the pillow, goes back to his chair. Silence*)

JENNY   How can you do your work if you sit here day and night?

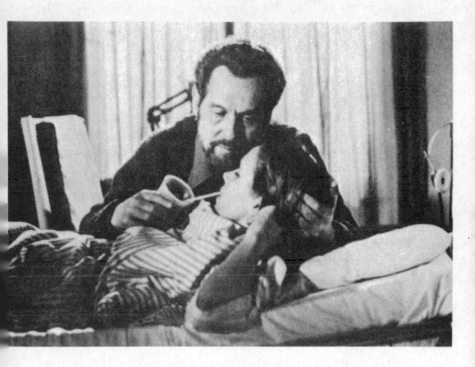

TOMAS I'm on vacation.

JENNY Oh. Couldn't you find a nicer way of spending it than watching over a mixed-up suicide?

TOMAS No.

JENNY Tell me about yourself.

TOMAS When I was nine I learned to belch. My older brother taught me. One day at dinner I thought it was a good opportunity to demonstrate my newly acquired skill to the assembled family. I watched for my chance between the meat balls and the apple pie.

JENNY *(Interested)*   Well?

TOMAS   It was not a success. From sheer stage fright I happened to fart at the same moment I belched. More-over, the fart was much louder than the belch, which I rather bungled technically.

JENNY *(Smiling)*   Poor Tomas!

TOMAS   I made a stir but was a failure. I was sent away from the table and not allowed any apple pie and cus-tard. My upbringing was very strict, not to say dog-matic.

JENNY   Tell me more. I like to hear.

TOMAS   I don't know that there's much to tell. My life has been pretty uneventful. And the little I *have* ex-perienced, I've tried to forget.

JENNY   Anything will do. Perhaps you've just read something or met someone interesting or been to a movie or on a trip.

TOMAS   Frankly, it's over a year since anything hap-pened to me.

JENNY   And what happened then?

TOMAS   Someone walked out on me.

JENNY   Oh yes, of course. You're divorced.

TOMAS   No, it had nothing to do with a wife.

JENNY   Oh?

TOMAS   It was a friend who walked out.

JENNY   Oh!

TOMAS   I was very fond of him. *(Pause)* No, that's not true. I loved him. We lived together for five years. You met him at that ridiculous party given by Wankel's wife. I take it you know who I mean.

JENNY   The actor?

TOMAS   Yes. Nowadays we are "just friends."

JENNY   Why did it break up?

TOMAS   In our cruel market, my dear Jenny, disloyalty is total and competition ruthless. Mrs. Wankel offered better terms: she accepted his new friend and offered to support them both. As you know, she has resources.

JENNY   Wasn't he fond of you at all?

TOMAS   Oh yes, I think so. But he's good-looking and unintelligent and pretty spoiled, and I suppose he thought: anything for a change. My emotions and my jealousy were too much for him. (TOMAS *pours himself some coffee out of the thermos, selects two lumps of sugar with great care, and keeps stirring on and on. He is smiling the whole time)* Would you like to sleep?

(She turns her head to the wall. TOMAS *puts out the bedside light. It is broad daylight out in the hospital park and the birds are singing. They are making an awful noise.*

JENNY is standing in her office at the General Hospital, wearing her red dress. There is a crowd of people there. JENNY *taps her pen on the desk to make herself heard. The murmuring stops at once and everyone's eyes are turned expectantly, anxiously, toward her face. She asks in a faint voice who is the day's first patient, and a man in the crowd puts up a timid hand. She pushes her way over to him and asks how he is. He doesn't answer, but puts his hand to his face and begins to pull at the skin, which comes off. He has been wearing a mask— very skillfully made—but under the mask his face is disfigured by bleeding sores and festering ulcers. He looks imploringly at* JENNY, *who can hardly hide her disgust. When he realizes that his sores nauseate her, he meekly takes a large handkerchief out of his pocket and drapes it in front of his face)*

JENNY   You may come back in a month. Ask the nurse for an appointment. Don't forget to take your medicine.

*(*JENNY *turns immediately to the next patient, a woman with heavy breasts and rounded shoulders; her eyes are dilated with horror and her cheeks are abnormally taut. A strip of paper is sticking out of her mouth.* JENNY *takes hold of the end of the strip and pulls cautiously; something is written on the paper.* JENNY *pulls more and more of it out of the woman's mouth)*

JENNY *(Reading)*   Help me! They've made an incision in my head and cut away my anguish, but when they sewed my head up again they left the daily dread behind.

(Suddenly JENNY *is standing face to face with* GRANDPA. *He looks at her with a hurt expression, then whispers something. She can't hear what he is saying and has to bend closer)*

GRANDPA   I'm afraid of dying.

JENNY   So am I.

GRANDPA   What can I do?

JENNY   Count to ten. If you're still alive when you get to ten, then start again.

GRANDPA   And after that?

JENNY   Just keep on. You just have to count.

GRANDPA   You think it will help?

JENNY   You have to put something important between yourself and death all the time. Otherwise you'll never stand it.

GRANDPA   One two three four five six—*(Breaks off)* I'm still afraid.

JENNY   *(Whispering)*   I must see to the other patients. We're rushed off our feet with Christmas coming on. I don't know what gets into people.

GRANDPA   Yes, I quite understand. Forgive me.

*(*JENNY *turns away. Then she sees her daughter* ANNA *standing over by the wall, dressed in a soiled gray shirt, weeping quietly, her shoulders hunched. At last* JENNY *reaches her and*

stretches out her arms to warm, protect, and embrace her, but ANNA *avoids her.* TOMAS *looks at her gravely. She grasps at his hand, which is gloved)*

JENNY   If only for *once* I had the right words. Just for once.

TOMAS   Exactly, Jenny. They're sitting there in the dark, your patients, longing for *the right word*. But it must be *their* word, *their* feeling, not your word and your feeling.

JENNY   I know that loneliness—people's loneliness— that they are brave in their loneliness. Like children in the dark who are determined not to call out lest they grow even more afraid if no one should come. They weep quietly and restrainedly in their loneliness. *(Pause)* A human head is so fragile. To hold someone's head between your hands and to feel that frailty between your hands . . . and inside it all the loneliness and capability and joy and boredom and intelligence and the will to live and . . . *(Pause)* An old person's hand . . . the day has been long and trying but evening comes, the hand that opens. *(Pause)* I can't go on, no.

TOMAS   Once upon a time there was a mighty prince who was tormented by a raging desire for affection. He went out and caught his subjects in big hunting nets and then took them on strings of pack mules to his palace. There he had them tortured, and when they groaned with pain he tried to comfort them with tokens of affection and gifts. What's the matter?

JENNY   I can't take any more.

(She turns her head and sees the white wall of the hospital room. She is lying in her bed and it is broad daylight outside the window)

JENNY What day is it?

TOMAS It is still Tuesday.

JENNY And what's the time?

TOMAS You've slept for two minutes.

JENNY *(Weeping)* Why are children frightened and killed? How can we pretend it doesn't happen?

TOMAS What do you mean?

JENNY That children die. That children are ill-treated. That children starve to death. There's no living with all that. What is it we do to each other? How can I pretend it isn't happening?

TOMAS I think you're paying for that indifference with an utterly abstract anguish.

JENNY What's going to happen?

TOMAS I don't know. When my friend left me, I got into my car and drove it into a deep ravine. I sat there trapped for several hours with water up to my nose. Then I was fished out of the wreck with a crushed foot.

JENNY That was no answer.

TOMAS   You complain that man is a wolf to man. Objectively, you can't do anything about it. Pity is only coquetry anyway, and mostly ends in a neurotic fiasco. Or political hysteria. It's a matter of taste which you choose. (TOMAS *stops speaking and looks out of the window. In the bright daylight he looks pale and wretched, his eyes are tired and bloodshot and he is unshaven*) Has it never struck you that you are surrounded by overgrown children? They don't starve physically, but mentally. They die. Not that they're shot, but they are slowly and methodically harassed to death in a society which on the whole is just as cruel as in the Middle Ages. On all sides grown-up children and little children being tormented and suffering and dying. Unfortunately there's nothing you can do about it.

(*He has taken off his glasses and keeps blinking.* JENNY *watches him out of the corner of her eye*)

TOMAS   That's how it is.

JENNY   Are your eyes hurting?

TOMAS   Once when I was young and drunk I took a swim in one of the canals in Venice. I should have known better. I caught a chronic virus infection of the cornea. Sometimes it smarts and then I blink.

JENNY   In any case, I don't know what to do.

TOMAS   A million years ago a few spinal marrow cells ran amok in a baboon's head and started dividing like cancers. And all of a sudden there it was!

JENNY   Who, what?

TOMAS   The human brain. A crazy gadget without any counterpart in the rest of zoology. There it was, like a big, damp woolen cap hung up on the simple needs and instincts of the old brain. There it was, sending out messages left and right and every which way. A computer-operated army headquarters with hundreds of thousands of programmed generals, who are supposed to guide a small native tribe through the perils of life and the jungle. The results had to be staggering. And they are.

JENNY   Come and sit here. On the edge of the bed.

TOMAS   Well, here I am. What do you want?

JENNY   Nothing in particular. It's just nice.

TOMAS   (*After a long pause*)   I do see that life has its moments of splendor. With a certain objectivity I admit that it is even extraordinarily beautiful. And generous. Intellectually I can grasp that it offers all sorts of things. I'm only sorry to say that I personally think it's a pile of shit.

(*He stops talking and looks at the wall. Then he looks at* JENNY *with his blinking, red-rimmed, rather dilated eyes.* JENNY *meets his gaze, deciding to look into his right eye, which appears more hopeful than the left.*
   Then she notices that he is crying. Noiselessly, without his face moving, the tears are flowing one by one, very hesitantly, down his cheeks. He takes out a neat handkerchief and blows his nose and dries his eyes)

JENNY   (*Astonished*)   Are you crying, Tomas?

TOMAS   No, no for Christ's sake. It's just that eye inflammation. Excuse me if I go to the men's room for a moment.

JENNY   Tomas!

TOMAS   No, no, don't be silly now. It's stinging like hell. I'll go out and have a cigarette and get some more coffee. (*With an apologetic gesture he moves toward the door*) I'll be right back.

(*In a moment he has managed to withdraw from the room.*
    Outside the window the morning is overcast. It is raining tentatively. JENNY *falls asleep almost at once.*
    She sees herself lying in a white coffin. It has been set up

in GRANDMA's *drawing room. The windows and walls
are covered with sheets, the furniture also is covered over.
Bunches of white flowers are everywhere. In all this white-
ness there is a group of people dressed in black. The dead
woman is dressed in red; in a very wide gown, so volumi-
nous that it swells out over the edge of the coffin in an almost
obscene way. On her feet she is wearing red stockings and
shoes, her arms are bare and pressed to her sides, the palms
turned outward. Her head lies flat, the hair, loose and
flowing, is adorned with white flowers. Her eyes are wide
open and she follows the proceedings with horrified amaze-
ment.*

JENNY *sees now that a* CLERGYMAN *has stepped forward to
the coffin. He is wearing an ample cassock and a large silver
cross on a chain. He bends over* JENNY *in the coffin. Terrified,
she meets his eyes)*

CLERGYMAN   It's possible that she was alive a while ago,
but now I can guarantee she's dead. Let us therefore
proceed to the ceremony.

(Everyone approaches the coffin, looking self-important.
JENNY *goes up to* TOMAS, *who is standing in a corner)*

JENNY   This is nothing to grieve over.

TOMAS   It's not for this that I'm crying.

(The CLERGYMAN *has brought forth a small box of sand from
under his wide cassock. He takes a few fistfuls and tosses them
into the coffin)*

CLERGYMAN   Bring the lid, she stinks already. I think
they've botched the embalming, as usual.

(Everyone turns toward a corner, where JENNY *'s parents are struggling with the lid, which seems too heavy for them. They stagger as they approach with it.*

JENNY *in the coffin makes a panic-stricken movement as though to sit up, but falls back with a faint cry of protest. The lid is lowered. Fussy hands are poked in to stuff the swelling red dress down inside the edges of the coffin. Nevertheless, when the lid is at last in place, a lot of material is still sticking out. There are worried whispers. The* CLERGYMAN *goes over to* GRANDMA *'s work table by the window. Out of a drawer he takes a large pair of scissors, which he hands to one of the mourners, who immediately sets about cutting away the protruding cloth.*

A faint knocking is heard from inside the coffin but no one takes any notice. They begin to screw down the lid. The CLERGYMAN *and some of the mourners sing something that is supposed to be a hymn. Suddenly the coffin begins to burn.* JENNY *has crept up and set fire to it! We catch a momentary glimpse of the red dress, a pair of frantically waving arms, a gaping mouth. Then everything is one huge flame.* JENNY *wakes up.*

TOMAS *comes back, bringing a fresh thermos of coffee. He sits down, trying to stifle a wide yawn but not succeeding very well. He smiles apologetically)*

JENNY *(After a long pause)* As a child I was afraid of death. It seemed to be all around me. My poodle was run over, that was almost worse than anything. Mama and Daddy were killed in a car crash. I told you that, didn't I? *(Pause)* Then a cousin died of polio. I was fourteen then. We had sat under the dining table kissing on the Saturday, the next Friday he was dead. Grandma made me go to the funeral. I begged and pleaded to be let off, but Grandma wouldn't relent. He lay in an open coffin and there were lots of people and his mother kept crying and he looked so funny. Grandma told me to go up to him and look at him and "bid farewell," as she put it, I imagined he was breathing and that his eyelids were twitching. I said so to Grandma. She said it was a common optical illusion and that I should control myself. When they screwed down the lid I knew for sure that Johan would wake up in there in the dark, way under the earth. When we got home after the funeral I told Grandma I hated her. She boxed my ears, hard, and told me not to be hysterical. She was sorry afterwards and apologized. But I never forgave her.

TOMAS   You've always been regarded as a miracle of sanity, haven't you.

JENNY   I've followed the principle that now I'll make up my mind to feel like this and I feel like this. I decided I'd never be afraid of death and the dead. I decided to ignore the fact that people died every day, every moment. Death didn't exist any more except as a vague idea, and that was that. *(Pause)* Before I got married I lived for some time with a crazy artist. Once when he was angry with me he said, You know, your frigidity is so complete that it's interesting. I was angry too and said, It's only with you that I'm frigid. With other men I get an orgasm. Then he said, It's only in boxing that you can have a technical knockout. *(Pause)* One evening at a party not long ago someone read aloud a poem about love and death and how love and death merge. And include each other.

TOMAS   Well?

JENNY   I remember being pretty sarcastic about that poem. Stupid of me. Don't you think?

TOMAS   Yes, perhaps.

JENNY   We act the play. We learn our lines. We know what people want us to say. We lie. In the end it's not even deliberate.

Self-discipline. *(Pause)* Bewilderment. Pride. Humiliation. Self-confidence, the lack of it. Wisdom that is stupidity and the other way around. Arrogance and vulnerability. Easily hurt, *that's* it, terribly easily hurt. Touchy and bad-tempered but inhibited, everywhere inhibited, reticent, paralyzed. Capable. And conscientious. You can rely on Jenny. Just as if she were something real! An airplane engine or a rowboat. Daddy was very kind, and he drank. He liked to be cuddled, we got on well together, he and I. Then Mama would say as she went past, That's enough of that soppiness. And Grandma would go past and say, Your father may be a dear but he's a lazybones, and Mama agreed with Grandma. They backed each other up in despising Daddy and in the end I sided with them. It was as simple as that. And suddenly I was embarrassed by Daddy's hugs and kisses—Grandma thought he was silly and lazy and I was anxious to please her. Then I got a child of my own. Anna had a funny cry, it wasn't like other babies', she didn't cry with rage or because she was hungry and wet. It was more like real sobbing. It was heart-rending and sometimes I wanted to hit her for crying like that and sometimes I was beside myself with tenderness. But all the time with myself in the way. A most peculiar selfish fear: I would not let myself go. And then the joy went out of everything. *(Long pause)* I remember the first time I heard Mama cry. I was in the nursery and I heard Grandma and Mama talking and Grandma had a curt, funny tone. Then Mama screamed. I have no idea what it was about. I felt terribly afraid, mostly because Grandma's voice sounded so nasty. I rushed into the living room. Mama was sitting in a low chair by the window, crying. Grandma was standing in the middle of the room. When I came in she turned her face and looked at me. And it was Grandma's face and yet *not* Grandma's face. *She looked like a mad dog that was about to bite!* I was even more afraid and rushed into the nursery and prayed to God that Grandma would get her real face back and that Mama would stop crying. It's horrible with faces that change so that you don't recognize them. Sometimes it sticks in my throat. Sometimes I think it's disgusting.

TOMAS   What is?

JENNY   The world's going to the dogs and I doctor my mental ailments. It's disgraceful.

TOMAS   Your logic is hardly dazzling.

JENNY   Oh?

TOMAS   First you try to take your life because of terror, confinement, and isolation. Then you despise our efforts to break out of the same confinement, terror, and isolation.

JENNY   While the world comes to an end?

TOMAS   The world begins and ends with yourself. That's all there is to it.

JENNY *(Bursting out)*   I can't talk about that!

TOMAS   You must try.

JENNY   I can't, I won't!

TOMAS   There's no avoiding it. You must try.

JENNY   Leave me alone. Let me be. My head's aching.
Can't you give me a shot or something? *(Bangs her head
against the wall)* It's more than I can bear. I can't go on.

TOMAS   You must. *Nothing is more important!*

JENNY   Let me be. You're hurting me. *(Weeping)* Leave
me in peace. Let me go, for Christ's sake! You have
nothing to do with me. Go away.

TOMAS   Jenny, *please*. Jenny, it's important for me too.
You can't just slink away.

JENNY   I feel so sick.

TOMAS   Lie down. Breathe deeply.

JENNY   I can't live with this.

TOMAS   Slow, deep breaths.

JENNY   You can't wear that dress today. It's your Sunday best. You'll never manage that, my dear. Let me
help you. Using lipstick, are you? Most unseemly
while you're living in our home. Eat up what you have
on your plate. You're late again. Will you never learn
to be punctual? You're lazy and spoiled. If you go on

like this Grandpa and I will send you to boarding school, you'll soon learn to mend your ways there, my girl.

In this house, Jenny, live decent people, people who have tried to live in cleanliness and truth. You'll have to behave properly if you intend to go on living here with Grandpa and me. You should be grateful. If only for *once* you could show a little gratitude. *(Screams heart-rendingly)* Don't hit me like that. You're not to hit my face. I can't stand it. *(A different voice)* I'll teach you to behave. What's all this nonsense? Stop crying. I don't believe in those tears.

(Shouts) I'll do as I like. You're not going to order me around. You're a goddamn stupid bitch. I hate you and I could kill you. *(Whispering)* You'd better decide after all. Yes, I know you love me. I think you mean well. I know that I must do as you say. Why, *(complainingly)* *why* must I always have a *bad conscience?* *(With hatred)* I will beg your forgiveness. Forgive me. I apologize. I know I've done wrong. I always do wrong. I will be Grandma's good little girl. I'm Grandma's little pet. We can talk about everything, you and I. With you it's always nice and calm and safe. *(Turns pale, her eyes go inward)* I can see all the furniture, all the pictures, I can see the plate of porridge and the reflection from the window in the shiny glazing. Mama smelled so nice and she had small round hands with flat fingertips and her hands were always warm. *(Whispering)* If you lock me in the closet I'll die. *(Still fainter)* I'll be good if only you don't lock me in the closet. Please, please Grandma, forgive me for everything, but I can't live if I have to be locked in the closet. *(Lame gestures with her hands. Pause. Then in a clear voice)* Can you imagine shutting up a child who's afraid of the dark in a closet? Isn't it astonishing?

TOMAS   Yes, it's astonishing.

JENNY   Do you think I'm crippled for the rest of my life? Do you think we're a vast army of emotionally crippled wretches wandering about calling to each other with words which we don't understand and which only make us even more afraid?

TOMAS   *(Mumbling)*   I don't know.

(JENNY *bends her head and sits for a long time silent and sad.* TOMAS *leans forward hesitantly, puts out his left hand, and rather shyly begins to stroke her head)*

TOMAS   There's an incantation for us who don't believe.

JENNY   What do you mean?

TOMAS   Now and then I say it over silently to myself.

JENNY   Can't you tell me what it is?

TOMAS   I wish that someone or something would affect me *so that I can become real.* I repeat over and over: Let me become real one day.

JENNY   What do you mean by real?

TOMAS   To hear a human voice and be sure that it comes from someone who is made just like I am. To touch a pair of lips and in the same thousandth of a second know that this is a pair of lips. Not to have to live through the hideous moment needed for my experience to check that I've really felt a pair of lips. Reality would be to know that a joy is a joy and above all that a pain has to be a pain.

(He is silent)

JENNY　Please go on.

TOMAS　Reality is perhaps not at all what I imagine. Perhaps it doesn't exist, in fact. Perhaps it only exists as a longing.

(The door is thrown open and the floor nurse, VERONICA, stares—with controlled astonishment, of course—at the two figures over by the window)

VERONICA　Sorry to disturb you.

TOMAS　You here in the middle of the night, Nurse?

VERONICA *(Cheerfully)*　The middle of the night?

TOMAS　My watch says only five past four.

VERONICA　Well, I don't know, but outside it's five past ten.

JENNY　But it *is* Tuesday, isn't it?

VERONICA　Oh yes. I just wanted to tell you that your daughter is sitting out there and would like to see you.

JENNY　Oh!

(JENNY is seized with panic for a moment and looks around as if for a means of escape. TOMAS has stood up and is folding

his blanket. He turns to her and is about to say something when JENNY *anticipates him)*

JENNY   I'd like to talk to her. But not in here. Perhaps we could sit in the visitors' room?

VERONICA   By all means. The old lady who has appropriated it is out walking in the park.

JENNY   I must fix myself up.

TOMAS   Of course, my dear Jenny. I'll go.

VERONICA   Dr. Isaksson, what about a breakfast tray in the visitors' room? Wouldn't you like a cup of coffee? And perhaps your daughter would too.

JENNY   *(From the bathroom)*   Yes, please.

TOMAS   I think we can let Mrs. Isaksson go home today. That is, if she wants to.

VERONICA   Shouldn't I ask Dr Wankel?

TOMAS   I don't think that's necessary.

*(*JENNY *pokes her head out from behind the curtain. She has just washed her face and is holding a towel)*

JENNY   Will I be seeing you?

TOMAS   That would be nice, but it may be some time.

JENNY   Some time, how do you mean?

TOMAS   I'm off to Jamaica tomorrow.

JENNY   You didn't tell me.

TOMAS   I suppose I forgot.

JENNY   So you mean I'll have to manage on my own?

TOMAS   *I'm* the one who'll have to manage on his own.

JENNY   Supposing I come with you to Jamaica?

TOMAS   No thanks.

JENNY   What are you going to do there?

TOMAS   I've heard that one can lead such a wonderful life of vice in Jamaica.

JENNY   But you'll come back?

TOMAS   I won't promise.

JENNY   Bye-bye, Tomas.

TOMAS   Bye-bye. Take care of yourself and those who are fond of you.

(*He goes out quickly.* JENNY *sits on the edge of the bed, feeling faint from getting up so fast and affected by the sudden farewell. Then, pulling herself together, she completes her morning toilet, puts on a hospital gown and a pair of bath slippers, and shuffles out into the corridor in search of her daughter.*

ANNA *is standing with her back to the door, looking out the window. She is tall and lean. She has long red hair, big gray eyes, and a broad forehead, but otherwise soft features, a childish mouth and chin, astonished eyebrows. When she hears her mother's steps she turns around)*

ANNA Hello, Mama.

JENNY Hello.

ANNA *(Rapidly)* Daddy phoned and said you were sick. Since he came rushing home like that all the way from America I thought it was something serious and I'd better come and see you, though Daddy said I shouldn't.

JENNY Heavens above.

ANNA You know how Daddy always exaggerates.

JENNY Did he tell you why I was here?

ANNA He said you'd been taken ill suddenly and they'd brought you to the hospital in an ambulance.

JENNY He didn't tell you the reason?

ANNA No, he didn't.

(ANNA looks at her mother reproachfully. JENNY sits down in a rather shabby chair. Just then a nurse comes in with the breakfast tray, which she puts on a table beside JENNY, and then disappears)

JENNY Like some?

ANNA   No. *(Pause)* No, thank you.

JENNY   Can't you sit down?

ANNA   Yes.

JENNY   This is not going to be easy, Anna.

ANNA   Oh?

JENNY   For either you or me.

ANNA   Oh.

JENNY   I did something very stupid a few days ago.

ANNA   *(Looking at her)*   Did you?

JENNY   I tried to commit suicide.

ANNA   *(Looking at her)*   Did you?

JENNY   It's hard to explain how it could happen. You might get the idea I didn't like you and Daddy, trying to sneak off like that. But you must never think that. *(Pause)* I'm more fond of you than of anyone else. You and Grandma. And Daddy. *(Pause)* Have you never just done something on the spur of the moment, without stopping to think?

ANNA   *(Looking at her)*   Yes. Perhaps.

(The vulnerable open face, the lean straight shoulders, the soft uncertain mouth, the beautiful broad hands with their dirty blunt nails)

JENNY You must try to forgive me.

ANNA I don't know what you mean.

(The distance, the insurmountable distance. JENNY *is mute and beaten)*

JENNY Are you going back to camp today?

ANNA There's a train in an hour.

JENNY Do you have enough money?

ANNA   Yes thanks.

JENNY   Are you all having a nice time?

ANNA   Oh, not bad.

JENNY   Give my love to Lena and Karin.

ANNA   Yes.

JENNY   Is it on Friday that camp's over?

ANNA *(With a sigh)*   Yes.

JENNY   Couldn't we have dinner together, you and I, on your way through to Skåne? You get to town in the afternoon and your train doesn't leave until nine thirty in the evening. We could have dinner and then go to a movie. Wouldn't that be nice?

ANNA   Yes. Very nice.

JENNY   Well, you'd better go now, so that you don't miss the train.

(ANNA *gets up obediently.* JENNY *goes up to her, takes her face in both hands, and kisses her. The girl submits but looks embarrassed. Then she goes to the door, stops, turns around*)

JENNY *(Still hopeful)*   Yes?

(ANNA *gives her a long, hard look, and there is a glint of anguish in her gray eyes*)

ANNA   Will you do that again?

JENNY   No.

ANNA   How can I be sure?

JENNY   You must count on me to tell the truth.

ANNA   But do you know what you're saying?

JENNY   I think so.

ANNA   But you're not sure.

JENNY *(Vehemently)*   Just what are you getting at? Can't you understand *anything?*

ANNA   You've never liked me anyway.

(JENNY *stands with her arms hanging and looks at the girl over by the door, the fingers with the dirty bitten-down nails that won't stop fiddling with the little picture in a gold frame she wears around her neck. A long silence)*

ANNA   You haven't, you know. *(Pause)* Well, I must go now. *(Pause)* Don't worry. I'm good at managing on my own. Bye-bye.

(*And* ANNA *goes out, closing the door quietly behind her. A nurse looks in and asks if she can take the tray)*

JENNY   Yes, do. Thank you.

That same afternoon JENNY *returns to the house on the silent street.* GRANDMA *meets her in the hall. They embrace.*

GRANDMA   Are you better now?

JENNY   Much better.

GRANDMA   Why didn't you say something?

JENNY   There was nothing to say.

GRANDMA   I asked that Dr. Jacobi who called me up and he said you were under too much strain.

JENNY   Yes.

GRANDMA   And Erik rushing home like that.

JENNY   He's gone back, hasn't he?

GRANDMA   Oh yes. When he realized it wasn't so serious. That it was just strain.

JENNY   Did you have a talk?

GRANDMA   He was up for a little while, yes.

(They are in JENNY *'s room, and* GRANDMA *is helping her to unpack. The afternoon sun is very hot. The windows are wide open and the blinds are half down.* JENNY *sits on the bed.* GRANDMA *breaks off what she is doing)*

GRANDMA   You're tired. Shall I make the bed? Then you can lie down.

JENNY   No, thank you. There's no need.

GRANDMA   If you've been overdoing things you should go away for a few weeks and rest.

JENNY   It's impossible just now. Erneman won't be back for another two months. After that perhaps Erik and I will take a vacation. We had in fact planned a trip to Italy.

(JENNY *checks herself and looks at* GRANDMA. *It's as if she saw her for the first time. The old woman has sat down on a chair by the wall and the sunlight is shining in her face.* JENNY *discovers now that her grandmother is very old, that the clear blue-gray eyes are sad, that the firm mouth is not so firm, that she is not holding herself as straight as usual, that in some way* GRANDMA *has become smaller, not very much, but quite noticeably. And when she turns her face to* JENNY *and gives a little questioning smile, her head shakes almost imperceptibly but it shakes nevertheless, and the strong broad hands, the capable active hands, lie tired and idle in her lap*)

JENNY *(With sudden affection)*   What is it, Grandma?

GRANDMA   Grandpa wouldn't get up today. I nagged and scolded him but he just looked unhappy. It's probably a slight stroke, but you never know with Grandpa. The doctor has been—old Samuelson, you know. He just said for me to let Grandpa rest for a few days.

JENNY   And what do *you* think?

GRANDMA   I have a feeling in my bones that Grandpa will never get up again. He seems so terribly tired. (GRANDMA *can't say anything more for a while. She looks helplessly at* JENNY, *at her hands, out the window*) Well, that's the way it is. *(Pause)* I've been expecting this for several years. But it still feels funny when it comes. *(Pause)* Well, that's how it is.

(GRANDMA *gives a deep sigh and a tired little smile*)

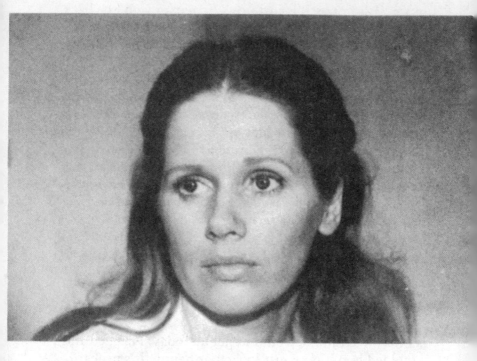

JENNY   I'll go in and say hello to him.

GRANDMA   Wouldn't you like something?

JENNY   No thanks. I had something to eat before leaving the hospital.

(GRANDMA *holds open the door.* GRANDPA *is lying in the big double bed, looking very small. As* GRANDMA *and* JENNY *approach he opens his eyes and looks at them anxiously)*

GRANDMA   Don't be nervous. I'll sit with you. I'm here all the time.

(The anxious eyes grow calmer and he gives a little nod, then takes GRANDMA*'s hand. She sits down beside the bed and pats him. Again and again she pats his hand.*

JENNY stands for a long time at the door looking at the two old people and the way they belong together, moving slowly in toward the mysterious and awful point where they must part. She sees their humility and dignity and for a short moment she perceives—but forgets just as quickly—that love embraces all, even death)

JENNY *(Softly)*   I think I'll go for a little walk.

GRANDMA   When you come back we'll have those chops that are in the refrigerator. There's some cold potato left too that you can fry. If the shop down at the corner is open, you might buy a lettuce.

(JENNY nods and tiptoes out)

She has done her shopping at the store on the big tree-lined avenue. The traffic is busy, the offices have shut for the day, and there are a lot of people about. The sun shines brightly in the hot afternoon and the water glints in the canal. The huge treetops are rustling and the headlines of the evening papers are black and screaming.

She has stopped at a crosswalk with five or six others. She sees a tall woman, dressed in a white coat and white hat; her gray hair sticks out under the brim. She is holding a white cane and feeling her way with it against the curb. She is wearing sun-glasses.

JENNY   May I help you across the street perhaps?

(THE WOMAN *turns, and in a moment of surprise* JENNY *recognizes the passionate, pale face, the sarcastic smile. The dead, gouged-out eye*)

THE WOMAN   That's very kind of you, my dear. Thank you.

(JENNY *takes her by the arm and says, "Well, let's go then." They begin to walk slowly over the white markings of the crosswalk, while the other people hurry past without even glancing at them*)

Autumn Sonata

PROLOGUE

VIKTOR Sometimes I stand looking at my wife, without her knowing I'm here. She's fond of sitting over there by the corner window; at the moment, I think she's writing a letter to her mother. The first time she entered that room she said: "Oh, how nice. I feel at home here." We had only known each other a few days; there was a bishops' conference in Trondheim, and she was there as the representative of some church paper or other. We met at a lunch, and I told her about the parsonage out here. She was so interested that I ventured to suggest our coming out here one morning when the conference was over. On the way I asked her if she would marry me. She didn't answer, but when we entered the room she turned to me and said: "Oh, how nice. I feel at home here." Since then we've lived a quiet, happy life here at the parsonage. Eva has, of course, told me about her earlier life. After graduating from high school she went on to college, got engaged to a doctor and lived with him for several years, wrote two small books, fell ill with tuberculosis, broke off the engagement, and moved from Oslo to a small town in the south of Norway, where she began to work as a

journalist. *(Turns the pages of a little book)* This is the first of her books. I like it so much. This is what she wrote: "One must learn to live; I practice every day. The biggest obstacle is that I don't know who I am. I grope blindly. If anyone loves me as I am, I may dare at last to look at myself." *(Stops reading)* I'd like to tell her just for once that she is loved wholeheartedly, but I can't say it in such a way that she'd believe me. I can't find the right words.

1

EVA   I've written a letter to Mother. May I read it to you, or am I interrupting?

VIKTOR   No, no, come in and sit down. Let's have some light. Autumn really seems to be here, the way the days are drawing in. I'll just turn off the radio; it's an afternoon concert.

EVA   If you'd like to finish listening to it, I'll come back later.

VIKTOR   I'd much rather you read me the letter.

EVA   *(Reading)* "I was in town yesterday and ran into Agnes, who was on a short visit to her parents with her husband and children. She told me that Leonardo had died. Dearest little Mother! I know what a terrible blow this must be to you. Agnes also said you were at Ascona on a short vacation between two concert tours. I called up Paul and got the address from him. *(Pause)* I'm wondering now if you'd care to come here to us at Bindal for a few days or weeks, just as you yourself wish and can. So that you won't take fright and say no outright, I must tell you that the parsonage is very spacious. You'll have your own room, entirely separate and with all conveniences. It's already autumn here. We've had one or two nights of frost, the birches are turning yellow and red, we're picking the last cloudberries on the bog. But as yet there are no gales, and many clear, mild days still remain. We have a fine grand piano, and you can practice as much as you want to. Wouldn't you be glad not to have to stay at a hotel for a few weeks? Mother dearest, do say you'll come! We'll make a fuss over you and spoil you in every way we can. It's simply been ages since we last met—seven years in October! Much love from Viktor and your daughter Eva."

2

CHARLOTTE *arrives earlier than expected. It is eleven o'clock in the forenoon when she drives up in front of the long yellow parsonage.* EVA *is halfway up the stairs. Through the window, herself unseen, she watches her mother slowly get out of the car and stop undecidedly at the trunk. A moment of immobility.*

EVA *(In front of the house)* Mother darling! Welcome! Oh, I'm so glad you're here, I can hardly believe it's true! You'll stay for a long time, won't you? Heavens, what heavy bags! Did you bring all your music? How lovely! Now you can give me some lessons. You will, won't you? Oh, you do look tired! But no wonder, after such a long car trip. Viktor's not home at the moment; we didn't think you'd come so early.

3

CHARLOTTE   I sat with Leonardo the last day and night. He was in bad pain, although he'd been given shots every other hour. Now and then he wept, but he wasn't afraid of dying, just wept because it hurt. The day dragged on. Outside the hospital there was building work going on; they drilled and hammered and clattered. The sun blazed down; there were no Venetian blinds or awnings. Poor Leonardo was so embarrassed because he smelled nasty. We tried to get another room, but several wards were shut for repairs. In the evening the noise from the building site stopped, and when the sun had set I could open the window. The heat was like a wall outside—there wasn't a breath of wind. The professor came; he's an old friend of Leonardo's. He sat down on the chair at the head of the bed and told Leonardo that it wouldn't be long now, that he'd be given a shot every half-hour so that he could die without pain. The professor stroked his cheek and said he was going to a Brahms concert that evening and would look in afterwards. Leonardo asked what was being played; and when he heard it was the double concerto with Schneiderhahn and Starker, he asked the professor to tell Janos that he wanted to give him his Coltermann cello, that he'd been thinking of it for some time. Then the professor left, and the ward sister came in and gave Leonardo a shot. She thought I should eat something but I wasn't hungry; I felt sick with the smell. Leonardo slept for a few minutes, then woke up and asked me to go out of the room, and rang for the night nurse. She came in at once with a shot. A minute or two later she came out to me in the corridor and said Leonardo was dead. I sat with him all night. *(Pause)* I kept thinking of Leonardo, that he had been my friend for eighteen years, that we had lived together for thirteen, that we had never had an angry word. For two years he had known he was going to die, that there was no hope. As often as I could I went to see him at his villa outside Naples. He was kind and thoughtful and happy about my success. We talked and joked and played a little chamber music. He hardly ever spoke of his illness and I didn't like to ask —it would have displeased him. One day he gave me a long look, then laughed and said: "This time next year I'll be gone, but I'll always be with you just the same. I'll always think of you." It was sweet of him to say so, but he was apt to be rather theatrical. *(Pause)* I can't say I go around grieving. Leonardo's death was both expected and longed-for. Oh yes, of course, he's left a gap, but it's no good fretting. *(Laughs)* Do you think I've changed much in these seven years we haven't seen each other? Well, I dye my hair, of course —Leonardo didn't want to see me with grey hair—but otherwise I'm the same as ever, don't you think? I bought this outfit in Zürich. I wanted something comfy for the long car trip. I saw it in a window on Bahnhofstrasse. I went in and tried it on and it fitted perfectly and was amazingly cheap. Don't you think it's rather nice?

EVA Yes, Mother dear, awfully nice.

CHARLOTTE Well, I must unpack. Give me a hand with this suitcase, there's a dear. It's dreadfully heavy, and my back's giving me hell after the journey. Do you think we could find a board to put under the mattress? I must have a hard bed, as you know.

EVA There's a board under the mattress already. We put it there yesterday.

CHARLOTTE Wonderful. *(Checks herself)* Eva, my dear, what is it? You're crying! No, let me see. What's wrong? My pet lamb, you're upset. Have I said something silly? You know how I chatter!

EVA I'm only crying because I'm so glad to see you.

CHARLOTTE Give me a nice squeezy hug, just as you did when you were little. I've done nothing but talk about myself. Now you must tell me about you. Let me look at you, Eva dear. How awfully thin you've grown these last years, I can see now. You're not happy either. You must tell me what's wrong. Come along, let's sit here. Do you mind if I have a cigarette? Just how are things, Eva, my dear?

EVA Oh, fine. Couldn't be better.

CHARLOTTE   Don't you lead a very isolated life?

EVA   We have parish work, both Viktor and I.

CHARLOTTE   Yes, of course.

EVA   I often play in church. Last month I had a whole musical evening. I played and talked about each piece. It was a great success.

CHARLOTTE   You mustn't forget to play for me. That's if you'd like to.

EVA   I'd love to.

CHARLOTTE   I had five school concerts in Los Angeles in their music hall. Three thousand children each time. I played and talked to them. You've no idea what a success it was. But terribly tiring.

EVA   Mother, there's something I must tell you.

CHARLOTTE   Yes?

EVA   Helena is here. *(Pause)*

CHARLOTTE   *(Angry)* You should have written to me that she was here. It's not fair confronting me with a *fait accompli*.

EVA   If I'd told you she was living here, you wouldn't have come.

CHARLOTTE   I'm sure I'd have come just the same.

EVA   And I'm sure you wouldn't have.

CHARLOTTE   Isn't Leonardo's death enough? Did you have to drag poor Lena here too?

EVA   Lena has been living here for the last two years. I wrote to you that Viktor and I had decided to ask her if she'd like to live here with us. I wrote to you.

CHARLOTTE   I never got the letter.

EVA   Or else you never bothered to read it.

CHARLOTTE   *(Suddenly calm)* Aren't you being rather unfair?

EVA   Yes.

CHARLOTTE   I'm not up to seeing her. At any rate, not today.

EVA   Mother dear! Lena is a wonderful person. It's just that she has great difficulty in speaking, but I've learned to understand what she says. I can be there and translate. She's longing terribly to see you.

CHARLOTTE   Oh dear, and it all seemed so nice for her at that nursing home.

EVA   But I missed her.

CHARLOTTE   Are you sure she's better off here with you?

EVA   Yes. And I have someone to look after.

CHARLOTTE   Has she gotten any worse? I mean is she . . . ? Is she . . . ? I mean, worse?

EVA   Oh yes, she's worse. It's part of the disease.

CHARLOTTE   Come along then, and we'll go and see her.

EVA   Are you sure you want to?

CHARLOTTE   (*Smiles*) I think it's horrible, but I've no choice.

EVA   Mother!

CHARLOTTE   I've never really got on with people who are unaware of their motives.

EVA   Do you mean me?

CHARLOTTE   If the shoe fits . . . Let's go.

4

CHARLOTTE   Lena darling! I'll give you a hug and a kiss. I'll take your arms like this and put them on my shoulders. I've thought of you often, every day.

(HELENA *says something*)

EVA   Helena says she has a sore throat and doesn't want to give you a cold.

CHARLOTTE   *(Kissing her again)* Oh, I've never been afraid of germs. It's twenty years since I had a cold. What a nice room you have. And what a view! It's the same view I have from my room.

(HELENA   *says something)*

EVA   Lena says for me to take off her glasses so that you can see her properly.

CHARLOTTE   I can see you all right.

(HELENA   *says something)*

EVA   She wants you to take her head in your hands and to look at her.

CHARLOTTE   Like that?

HELENA   Yes.

CHARLOTTE   I'm so glad Eva's looking after you. I had no idea. I thought you were still at that home. I'd thought of coming to see you before I left. But it's much better like this, isn't it?

HELENA   Yes.

CHARLOTTE   Now we can be together every day.

HELENA   *(Happy)* Yes.

CHARLOTTE   Are you in pain?

HELENA   No.

CHARLOTTE   How nicely you've done your hair.

(HELENA *says something*)

EVA   It's in your honor, Mother.

CHARLOTTE   I'm reading an awfully good book about the French Revolution. Supposing I read aloud to you? We can sit on the veranda together and I'll read to you. Would you like that?

HELENA   Yes.

CHARLOTTE   And we can go for a drive. I've never been in these parts before.

HELENA   Yes.

CHARLOTTE   I've thought about you so much.

(HELENA *says something and laughs*)

CHARLOTTE   What did she say?

EVA   Lena says you must be awfully tired, and not to make any more effort today. She thinks you've done very well.

CHARLOTTE   Doesn't Lena have a watch?

EVA   Oh yes. She has a clock by the bed.

CHARLOTTE   Here, Lena, I'll give you my wrist watch. It was given to me by an admirer who thought I was always late. Will Lena have dinner with us?

EVA   No, I usually give her the main meal in the middle of the day. She's on a diet, anyway. She ate far too much at the hospital.

(HELENA *says something*)

EVA   Lena says that—

CHARLOTTE   Wait! I know what Lena wanted to say: "There's a butterfly in the window!" Was that right?

5

CHARLOTTE   *(Alone)* Why do I feel as if I have a temperature? Why do I want to cry? So idiotically stupid! I'm to be put to shame, that's the idea. And then a guilty conscience. Always, always a guilty conscience! I was in such a hurry to get here. What was I imagining? What was I longing for so desperately, although I didn't dare to admit it to myself? I'll have a shower and then sleep for a while, or at any rate lie down and close my eyes. Then I'll put on something nice for dinner, so that Eva will have to admit that her old mum is well preserved. It's no good starting to weep. It's after four already. Damn it! There she sat gazing at me with her big eyes. I held her face between my hands and could feel the disease twitching at her poor throat muscles. Damn it, to think I can't lift her up and carry her to my bed and comfort her like when she was three years old. That soft, torn body, that's my Lena! Don't cry now, for Christ's sake. It's a quarter past four already. I'll have a shower, and it'll put me in a better frame of mind. I'll shorten my visit. But four days will be all right, I can manage that. Then I'll go to Africa as I originally planned. It hurts. Hurts. Hurts. Let me see now. Does it hurt in the same way in the Bartók sonata, second movement? *(Hums to herself)* Yes, it does. I've been taking those bars much too fast, of course I have. It should go like this: the upbeat pam-pam and then comes a little snake of pain. Slowly but with no tears, because there aren't any more tears or there have never been any. That's it. If this is right, my visit to the parsonage has been of some value after all. Now, I'll put on my red dress just to spite Eva, who I'm sure thinks I ought to wear something more suit-able so soon after Leonardo's death. There's nothing wrong with my body anyway. It may not be so darned elegant, but it's a good and kind body. When I get to Africa I'll . . . or supposing I go to Crete to see Harold? *(Laughs)* Hog though he is, Master Harold, he's a good cook and he knows how to live. I'll call him up this evening, that's what I'll do. It'll be a relief after four hours of sanctimoniousness. *(Suddenly)* Why am I being so unkind? I'm angry the whole time. Eva has been sweet to me and shown that she's glad to have me here. Come to that, Viktor's a decent sort of fellow. Lucky for Eva, the crybaby, having such a nice hus-band. I bet you now that the shower doesn't work. Well, I never! It does!

6

EVA   This extraordinary mother, I can't make her out!
You should have seen her when I told her that Lena
was living here with us. You should have seen her
smile. Just imagine, she managed to produce a smile,
despite her surprise and alarm. And then, as we stood
outside the door to Lena's room: an actress before her
entrance, terribly frightened but self-possessed. The
performance was superb. Do you think my mother is
completely heartless? Why on earth did she come?
What did she expect of a meeting after seven years?
What did she expect? And what did *I* expect? Does one
never stop hoping?

VIKTOR   I don't think so.

EVA   Does one never stop being mother and daughter?

VIKTOR   Some do, I suppose.

EVA   It's like a heavy ghost that suddenly falls on top of
you when you open the door to the nursery, having
long since forgotten that it *is* the nursery door after all.
Do you think I'm grown-up?

VIKTOR   I don't know what is meant by being grown-up.

EVA Neither do I.

VIKTOR Being grown-up is being able to cope with your dreams and hopes. You have no longings.

EVA Do you think so?

VIKTOR Perhaps you stop being surprised.

EVA How sensible you look sitting there with your old pipe. You're *quite* grown-up, I'm sure.

VIKTOR I don't think I am. I'm surprised every day.

EVA At what?

VIKTOR At you, for instance. Besides, I have the most unreasonable dreams and hopes. And a sort of longing too, come to that.

EVA Longing?

VIKTOR I long for you.

EVA Those are very pretty words, aren't they? I mean, words that have no real sense. I was brought up with beautiful words. The word "pain," for instance. Mother is never furious or disappointed or unhappy; she is "pained." You have a lot of words like that too. With you, I suppose, it's a kind of occupational disease. If you say you long for me when I'm standing here in front of you, I begin to be suspicious.

VIKTOR You know quite well what I mean.

EVA   No. If I knew, it would never enter your head to say you long for me.

VIKTOR   *(Smiles)* That's true.

EVA   Which goes to show I'm just as wise as you are, maybe wiser, not that that's saying much. Well, I must go out to the kitchen and see to the roast veal. Mother has always thought I'm hopeless as a cook. She's a real glutton. I once heard her spend the entire evening discussing with an American impresario how to make sauces. They were in ecstasy, both of them.

VIKTOR   I think you're a—

EVA   —wonderful cook. Thank you, darling. By the way, I mustn't forget to make caffeine-free coffee for my dear mama. I've often wondered why she sleeps badly. I think I know the reason. If that woman slept normally, her vitality would crush everyone around her. Her insomnia is nature's own regulator to bring her down to more or less tolerable proportions. *(Out, in again)* You just see how carefully she dresses for dinner. Note the perfect getup, intended to serve as a reminder that she's a lonely and mourning widow after all.

7

EVA   Why, Mother, what a lovely dress!

CHARLOTTE   Do you think it suits me? For a long time I
thought I couldn't wear red, but one day I ran into my
old friend Samuel Parkenhurst and he said: "Charlotte, I've just come from Dior's autumn collection and
there was a divine red dress which is absolutely *you.*"
I asked him to get it for me and . . . well, it does suit
me. I'm ravenous.

EVA   I hope you'll approve. I've done you some roast
veal. You used to like it.

CHARLOTTE   Splendid. Some plain home cooking after
all the hotel food.

VIKTOR   Well, your health, dear Charlotte. We're happy
to have you with us. Heartily welcome! May you feel
at home and stay for a long time.

8

CHARLOTTE   *(In English, on the phone)* Hallo. Oh, it's you, Paul. Well, you *are* disturbing, actually. We're at table. No, we're having dinner. Well, we are. In this country they have dinner at five o'clock. Speak up, will you. More distinctly. There's an awful crackling on the wire. Where are you, anyway? In Nice! What are you doing in Nice? Mind you don't gamble my money away. What did you say? *(Businesslike)* Yes, I did, but they needn't think they'll get off as lightly as last time. Tell them from me that my fee is to be the same, apart from your commission and traveling expenses. In addition, they're to pay my expenses. It cost the earth; I was practically ruined. What's more, they must arrange their rehearsal to fit in better. *(Looks at her appointment book)* I'll be coming from Munich. They'll have to rehearse on Saturday and Sunday morning if Varvisio insists on two rehearsals. I'm not going to rush and tear. The connections are shockingly bad, and I'll have to spend the entire day sitting about at airports. Wait, I must have my glasses. Where the devil did I put them? Eva, be a dear and see if I left my specs on the table over by the window. Thank you, Eva darling! Let's see . . . The old girl has glasses on her nose now. No, I can't possibly. It's my time off then, you know that quite well. No, it's no good, I wouldn't dream of it. I've written here Free, Free, Free. How much will they pay, did you say? Well, I'm damned. Oh well, if they can make their wretched concert Wednesday, I don't really mind. And tell them from me that they're to fix up a proper toilet behind the platform next time, so I don't have to piss in a flower vase. I don't care how baroque the castle is. God bless you, Paul. Thirty-three degrees! Take care of yourself and don't overdo things. Remember, we're no longer as young as we were. I love you, you know that. *(Puts the phone down)* That was my agent, he's so sweet. Nowadays he's the only friend I have in this world. No thanks, no brandy, but I'd love a drop of whisky later in the evening. Let me help clear away.

VIKTOR   We said we were going to spoil you.

CHARLOTTE   *(Sits down at the piano)* What a fine old instrument, and what a lovely tone. And just been tuned! *(Plays a little)* Now I'm really in a good mood. I needn't have worried.

EVA   What do you mean, Mother?

CHARLOTTE   *(With tears in her eyes)* Well, what do you think, my girl? Don't you realize I felt anxious about seeing you again after seven years? I was scared stiff and didn't sleep a wink all night. This morning I very nearly phoned to say I couldn't come, let me tell you.

EVA   Why, Mother!

CHARLOTTE   Do you think I'm made of flint? Two lumps of sugar, please. This caffeine-free coffee is a bore, but what am I to do when I can't sleep? I see you're working on the Chopin preludes. Won't you play something?

EVA   Not now, Mother.

CHARLOTTE   Eva! Don't be childish. You'd give me great pleasure if you'd play to me.

VIKTOR   Eva dear, only the day before yesterday you said you hoped your mother would listen to you. Have you forgotten?

EVA   Well, if you insist. But I'm far from . . . I mean, it's all bluff, I've no technique. I've ignored the fingering in this edition, it's beyond me.

CHARLOTTE   Darling! No more excuses. Come on now, play.

(EVA *plays Chopin's Prelude No. 2 in A-minor*)

CHARLOTTE   Eva, my dearest.

EVA   Is that all you have to say?

CHARLOTTE   No, no. I was just so moved.

EVA   *(Brightening)* Did you like it?

CHARLOTTE   I liked *you*.

EVA   I don't know what you mean.

CHARLOTTE   Won't you play one of the others? Now that we're all nice and cozy.

EVA   I want to know what I did wrong.

CHARLOTTE   You didn't do anything wrong.

EVA   But you didn't care for the way I played this particular prelude.

CHARLOTTE   Everyone must have his own interpretation.

EVA   Yes. Exactly. And now I want to know yours.

CHARLOTTE   What's the good of that?

EVA   *(Hostile)* Because I'm *asking* you.

CHARLOTTE   You're cross already.

EVA   I'm upset because you evidently don't think it worth the trouble to tell me *your* idea of this prelude.

CHARLOTTE   All right, if you insist. *(Calmly)* Let's disregard the purely technical side, which wasn't at all bad, although you might have taken a little more interest in Cortot's fingering—it helps with the interpretation. However, let's not bother about that, we'll just talk about the actual conception.

EVA   Well?

CHARLOTTE   Chopin isn't sentimental, Eva. He's very emotional but not mawkish. There's a huge gulf between feeling and sentimentality. The prelude you played tells of suppressed pain, not of reveries. You must be calm, clear, and harsh. The temperature is feverishly high, but the expression is manly and controlled. Take the first bars now. *(Plays to show what she means)* It hurts but I don't show it. Then a short relief. But it evaporates almost at once and the pain is *the same*, no greater, no less. Total restraint the whole time. Chopin was proud, sarcastic, passionate, tormented, furious, and very manly. In other words, he wasn't a mawkish old woman. This second prelude must be made to sound almost *ugly*. It must never become ingratiating. *It should sound wrong.* You must battle your way through it and emerge triumphant. Like this. *(Plays the whole prelude)*

EVA I see.

CHARLOTTE *(Almost humbly)* Don't be cross with me, Eva.

EVA Why should I be cross? On the contrary.

CHARLOTTE For forty-five years of my life I've worked at these terrible preludes. They still contain a lot of secrets, things I don't understand. But I won't give up.

EVA When I was little I admired you enormously. Then I was pretty tired of you and your pianos for several years. Now I think I'm beginning to admire you again, though in a different way.

CHARLOTTE *(Sarcastically)* Then there's *some* hope.

EVA *(Gravely)* Yes, I suppose so.

VIKTOR I think Charlotte's analysis is seductive, but Eva's interpretation is more moving.

CHARLOTTE   *(Laughing happily)* Viktor, for that remark you deserve a kiss!

VIKTOR   *(Embarrassed)* I only say what I think.

9

EVA   I come here to the grave every Saturday. If it's mild like this evening I sit for a while here on the bench and let my thoughts wander. *(Pause)* Erik was drowned the day before his fourth birthday. We have an old well in the yard and the lid is nailed down, but somehow he'd gotten it off and fallen in. We found him almost at once but he was already dead. It was too much for Viktor —there was something special between Erik and his father. I grieved a lot outwardly. Right inside I felt from the outset that he was still alive, that we were living close beside each other. I've only to concentrate, however little, and he's there. Sometimes, just as I'm falling asleep, I can feel him breathing against my face and touching me with his hand. Do you think it sounds neurotic? I can perhaps understand if you do. For me it's quite natural. He's living another life, but at any moment we can reach each other, there's no dividing line, no insurmountable wall. Sometimes, of course, I wonder what it looks like—the reality where my little boy is living and breathing. At the same time I know it can't be described, as it's a world of liberated feelings. It's much harder for Viktor than it is for me.

He says he can't believe in God any more because God lets children die—be burned alive or shot or starved or go mad. I try to explain to him that there's no difference between children and grown-ups, since the grown-ups are still children who have to live disguised as grown-ups. To me, man is a tremendous creation, an inconceivable thought; and in man there is everything, from the highest to the lowest, just as in life; and man is God's image; and in God there is everything, vast forces, and then the devils are created and the saints and the prophets and the obscurantists and the artists and the iconoclasts. Everything exists side by side, one thing penetrating the other. It's like huge patterns changing all the time, do you know what I mean? In that way there must also be countless realities, not only the reality we perceive with our blunt senses but a tumult of realities arching above and around each other, inside and outside. It's merely fear and priggishness to believe in any limits. *There are no limits.* Neither to thoughts nor to feelings. It's anxiety that sets the limits, don't you think so too? When you play the slow movement of Beethoven's Hammerklavier Sonata, you must surely feel you're moving in a world without limitations, inside an immense motion that you can never see through or explore. It's the same with Jesus. He burst asunder the laws and the limitations with an entirely new feeling that no one had heard of before—love. No wonder people were afraid and angry, just as they nearly always try to sneak off in alarm when some big emotion overwhelms them, though they eat their hearts out pining for their withered and deadened feelings.

10

CHARLOTTE   I'm appalled when I hear her holding forth. It's so neurotic—so beyond all reason. And all such a matter of course! She's in touch with your little boy, she has solved the mystery of the universe, there are answers to all questions.

VIKTOR   *(Smiles)* Yes, yes.

CHARLOTTE   You can't let her go around like this.

VIKTOR   What do you mean?

CHARLOTTE   I think actually she's terribly unhappy, and that one day she'll suddenly realize how bad things are and do something desperate.

VIKTOR   Do you really think so?

CHARLOTTE   Yes, I do.

VIKTOR   Is she upstairs with Lena?

CHARLOTTE   Yes, she went up to get her ready for the night.

VIKTOR   If you'll sit down for a moment, my dear Charlotte, I'll try to explain how I view my wife.

CHARLOTTE   Well? I'm sitting . . .

VIKTOR   When I asked Eva to marry me, she said straight out that she didn't love me. I asked if she loved someone else. She replied that she had never loved anyone, that she was incapable of loving. *(Pause)* Eva and I lived here for several years. We were kind to each other, worked hard, went abroad for my vacations. Then Erik was born. We'd already given up hope of a child of our own and talked of adopting one. . . . *(Pause)* Well. With her pregnancy Eva underwent a complete change. She became cheerful, gentle, and outgoing. She grew lazy and couldn't be bothered with her parish work or her piano playing. She could sit in that chair with her feet up on another chair, gazing at the play of light over the fell and the fjord. We were suddenly very happy. If you'll forgive my saying so, we were very happy in bed actually. I'm twenty years older than Eva. I felt as if a grey film was settling over existence, if you know what I mean. I felt as if I could look back and say, Well, well, so that was my life, that's how it all turned out. But suddenly things were different, there were some wonderfully . . . *(Pause)* There were some wonderfully . . . *(Pause)* Please forgive me, Charlotte, but it's still rather hard to . . . *(Pause)* Yes. We had some years that were very rich. You should have seen Eva. You really should have seen her.

CHARLOTTE   I remember those years around Erik's birth. I was busy recording all the Mozart sonatas and piano concertos. I hadn't a single day free.

VIKTOR   No. We invited you over and over again, but unfortunately you never had time.

CHARLOTTE No.

VIKTOR When Erik was drowned, the grey film became even greyer and more opaque. For Eva it was different.

CHARLOTTE Different? In what way?

VIKTOR Her feeling lives uncorroded, or so it seems anyway. She has grown thin and angular, and her temper is more unbalanced; for instance, she will suddenly fly into a violent rage. But I don't think she's neurotic or peculiar. And if she feels that her son is alive and near her, well, perhaps that's how it is. She doesn't often speak of it. I expect she's afraid it might upset me, as indeed it would. But what she says sounds true enough. I believe her.

CHARLOTTE Of course. You're a parson.

VIKTOR The little faith I have lives on her conditions.

CHARLOTTE I'm sorry if I hurt you.

VIKTOR It doesn't matter, Charlotte. Unlike you and Eva, I'm a diffuse and uncertain sort of person. It's my own fault.

11

CHARLOTTE   I think I'll take a good dose of sleeping pills tonight. Yes, I think I will. It's so quiet and peaceful here, only the soft hiss of the rain on the roof. Two Mogadons and two Valiums are usually about right.

EVA   Have you everything you need?

CHARLOTTE   Couldn't be better. The right kind of biscuits and mineral water and a tape recorder and cassettes and two detective novels and earplugs and a bandage for my eyes and an extra pillow and my little traveling rug. Like to taste my delicious Swiss chocolate, fresh from Zürich? Here you are, you can have two pieces.

EVA   Thank you, Mother dear, but I don't care for chocolate.

CHARLOTTE   How odd. I seem to remember you were mad about sweets as a child.

EVA   Helena liked candy. I didn't.

CHARLOTTE   Good, all the more for me.

EVA   Good night, Mother dear.

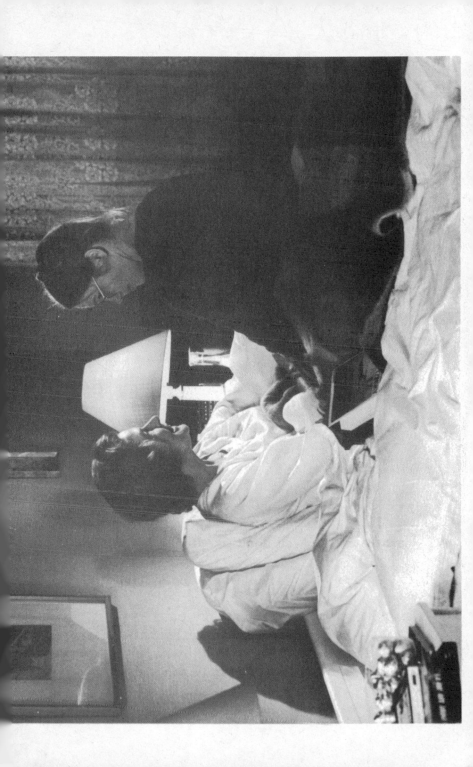

CHARLOTTE   Good night, my pet. I did enjoy this evening. Viktor is a delightful person. You must take care of him.

EVA   I do.

CHARLOTTE   Are you happy together? Do you get on well?

EVA   *(Patiently)* Viktor is my best friend. I can't imagine life without him.

CHARLOTTE   He said you didn't love him.

EVA   Did he say that?

CHARLOTTE   Yes. Why?

EVA   Oh, just rather surprising.

CHARLOTTE   Was it a secret?

EVA   No.

CHARLOTTE   But you don't like his having said it?

EVA   Viktor's not in the habit of confiding in people.

CHARLOTTE   We were talking of you.

EVA   If you want to know anything, you can ask *me*. I promise to be as truthful as I can.

CHARLOTTE   My dear, you're making a mountain out of a molehill. It's not unnatural for an old mother to want to know how her daughter is getting on. We spoke of you with the greatest affection, I can assure you.

EVA   If only you'd leave people alone!

CHARLOTTE   I think I've left you alone far too long.

EVA   *(Smiles)* You're quite right there.

CHARLOTTE   Let's not talk about such unpleasant feelings, or I won't sleep a wink tonight either, in spite of the sleeping pills.

EVA   We can have a talk some other time.

CHARLOTTE   Yes. Give me a hug and promise you're not angry with your old mother.

EVA   I promise.

CHARLOTTE   I love you, don't you see?

EVA   *(Politely)* I love you too.

CHARLOTTE   It's not much fun being alone always, let me tell you. In fact, I envy you and Viktor. Now that Leonardo's dead, I'm so damned lonely. Can you understand?

EVA   Yes, I can.

CHARLOTTE   No, no, no. I'll begin to weep with self-pity in a minute, and we'd decided there was to be no spate of emotion this evening. This whodunit isn't at all bad.

It's by a new writer, Adam Kretzinsky. Have you heard of him?

EVA   No.

CHARLOTTE   I met him in Madrid. He was as mad as a hatter. I could hardly defend myself. That's to say I didn't defend myself at all. Good night, Eva dear.

EVA   Good night, Mother.

CHARLOTTE   He admired me madly and said I was the most beautiful woman in his life. What's to be done about that?

EVA   Let me know when you want breakfast.

CHARLOTTE   No trouble on my account.

EVA   But I *want* to spoil you.

CHARLOTTE   Very well, if you insist.

EVA   Strong coffee, hot milk, two slices of dark German bread with Emmenthal cheese, one slice of toast with honey. Isn't that right?

CHARLOTTE   And a glass of orange juice.

EVA   Fancy, I nearly forgot.

CHARLOTTE   I can really—

EVA   You shall have your juice. Good night, Mother!

CHARLOTTE   Good night, darling.

12

CHARLOTTE *(Alone)* I think I'll have a look at my accounts. *(Takes out a red notebook)* I mustn't forget to have Brammer invest the money from Leonardo. The house is worth quite a bit too. You never bothered your head about such things as assets and liabilities, you were above mundane worries, you left all problems to Charlotte. "Charlotte, you're so wise about money. Charlotte, you're my minister of finance." Once when you were angry with me you said I was mean. Perhaps I *am* mean. Careful with money, of course. Grandpa's peasant blood and horse sense. Three million seven hundred and thirty-five thousand eight hundred and sixty-six francs. To think you had so much money, Leonardo. Who could believe it? And you leave it all to your old Charlotte. I've a little nest egg too. Together it makes over five million. What am I to do with so much money? I'll buy a nice car for Viktor and Eva. They can't drive around in that old rattletrap down in the courtyard. It looks dangerous. On Monday we'll go into town and look at a car. It'll cheer them up. Me too, for that matter. *(Yawns)* At last I'm beginning to feel relaxed and sleepy. I'll dip into Adam's book and then I'll put the light out. How quiet it is here. The rain has stopped. Aah . . . *(Reads)* "She offered him the red flower of her virginity with mute dignity. He accepted it without enthusiasm, in spite of

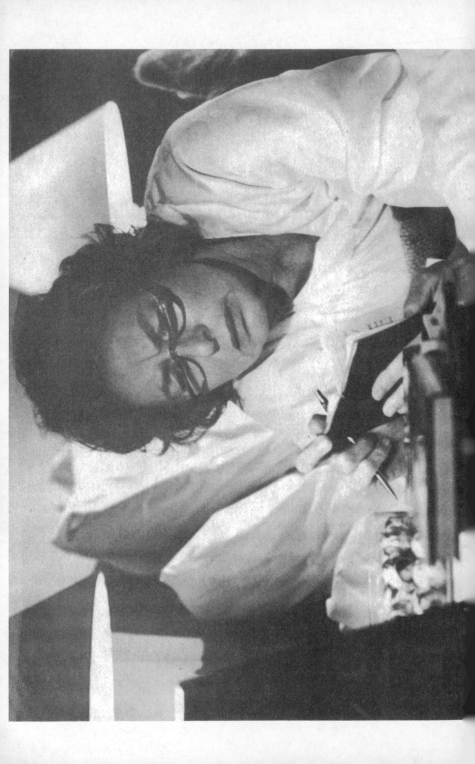

having stared the whole morning at her small, firm breasts and the bushy golden pubic hair visible above the waistband of the bikini." God, what drivel! He was really rather an idiot, Adam was, if he did nearly commit suicide because of me. *(Smiles)* Supposing I buy a new car for myself and give Eva and Viktor the Mercedes? Then I can fly back to Paris and buy a car there, and I won't have to drive all that way. *(Yawns)* Tomorrow I'll really get down to Ravel. It's disgraceful how lazy I've been the last few weeks. *(Closes her eyes)* He's a bore, Viktor. Uncannily like Josef, though more insignificant. I suppose they bore each other.

(The door opens. CHARLOTTE *is very frightened. Suddenly* HELENA *rushes into the room and throws herself over her mother. She is heavy and strong. After a short struggle* CHARLOTTE *wakes up)*

13

EVA   Why, Mother, what's happened? I heard you call out, and when I went into your room you weren't there.

CHARLOTTE   I'm sorry if I woke you, but I had such a horrid dream. I dreamed that . . .

EVA   Yes?

CHARLOTTE   No, I can't remember what it was.

EVA   I'll gladly keep you company if you'd like to talk.

CHARLOTTE   No, thank you, my dear. I'll just sit for a moment and calm down. You go back to bed.

EVA   Very well.

CHARLOTTE   Eva!

EVA   Yes, Mother?

CHARLOTTE   You do like me, don't you?

EVA   Why, of course. You're my mother.

CHARLOTTE   That wasn't a plain answer.

EVA   Then I'll ask *you* a question. Do you like me?

CHARLOTTE   I love you.

EVA   It's not true. *(Smiles)*

CHARLOTTE   You're accusing me of a lack of love.

(EVA *doesn't answer; looks at her*)

CHARLOTTE   Don't you see how absurd that is?

EVA   *(Looks at her)* It wasn't an accusation.

CHARLOTTE   Do you accuse yourself of not loving Viktor?

EVA   I told Viktor I didn't love him. You're *pretending* to love. That's different.

CHARLOTTE   Supposing I was in good faith?

EVA   I don't know what you mean.

CHARLOTTE   What if I was genuinely convinced that I loved you and Helena?

EVA   It's not possible.

CHARLOTTE   Do you remember when I broke off my career and decided to stay home?

EVA   I don't know which was the worst: the time you were at home acting wife and mother or the time you were on tour. But the more I think of it, the more I realize that you made life hell for us, both for Father and me.

CHARLOTTE   You know *nothing* of my relationship with your father.

EVA   He was just as cowed and compliant as I was, and everyone else.

CHARLOTTE   It's not true. Your father and I were happy together. Josef was the finest, kindest, most affectionate man in the world. He loved me, and I'd have done anything for him.

EVA   Oh yes. You were unfaithful to him.

CHARLOTTE   I was *not*. I fell in love with Martin and went away with him for eight months. Do you imagine it was a bed of roses during that time?

EVA   Anyway, it was I who had to sit with Father of an evening, and it was I who had to comfort him, and it was I who had to keep repeating that you did love him in spite of everything and that you were sure to come back, and it was I who had to read him your letters. Your long, tender, loving, amusing, humorous letters in which you told us choice bits from your interesting travels. We sat there like idiots, reading your letters two and three times and thinking that a more wonderful person than you didn't exist.

CHARLOTTE   *(Quiet, astonished)* Eva, you hate me.

EVA   I don't know. I'm so confused. Suddenly you come here after seven years, and I look forward to your coming. I don't know what I imagined. Maybe I thought you were lonely and sad. I don't know. Maybe I thought I was grown-up and could look dispassionately at you and myself and Helena's illness and our childhood. I see now that it's all a terrible muddle. *(Pause)* Good night, Mother. It's no good talking about the past. It hurts too much; and besides, it's pointless.

CHARLOTTE   You pour out a lot of accusations and then go!

EVA   Because it's too late anyway.

CHARLOTTE   What's too late?

EVA   Nothing can be changed.

(A long-drawn-out wail, hardly human, is heard through the silence. CHARLOTTE *looks at her daughter in alarm)*

EVA   It's Helena, she's woken up. I'll go up to her for a while and see if she needs anything.

*(*EVA *hurries through the dark house. She knows the way without putting the light on. Outside the window everything is quite still in the moonlight, no wind, no birds.* EVA *cautiously opens the door of* HELENA's *room. The wail stops almost at once. She puts on the table lamp. Helena is lying propped up high in the bed with its guard rails. Her throat and shoulders are twitching, and she is biting her lips. Her eyes are tight shut; she is asleep.* EVA *wakens her gently. Slowly she opens her eyes, slowly she becomes aware of her reality. She tries to say something but refrains almost at once.* EVA *asks her if she is thirsty. She shakes her head, closes her eyes, and falls asleep immediately. The twitching abates, her face grows calm.* EVA *sits with her, looking at her. She puts the light out and looks again at her)*

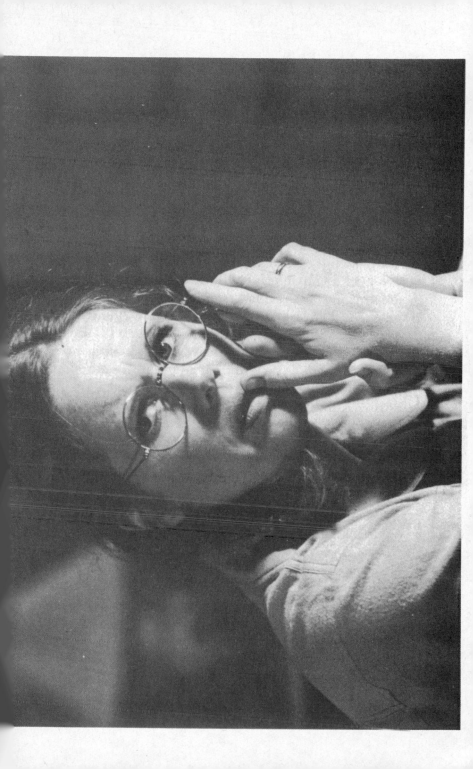

14

EVA   To you I was a doll that you played with when you had time. If I was sick or naughty, you handed me over to the nanny or to Father. You shut yourself in and worked, and no one was allowed to disturb you. I used to stand outside the door listening. When you stopped for coffee, I'd steal in to see if you really did exist. You were kind, but your mind was elsewhere. If I asked you anything, you hardly answered. I'd sit on the floor looking at you. You were tall and beautiful, the room was cool and airy, the awnings were lowered. Outside a breeze stirred the leaves and everything was swathed in an unreal green light. Sometimes you'd let me row you out on the inlet. You had a long, white, low-cut summer dress which showed your breasts. They were so beautiful. You were barefoot and had plaited your hair in a thick braid. You liked to look down into the water. It was clear and cold, and you could see the big stones far down on the bottom, the plants and the fish. Your hair got wet and your hands too. Because you always looked so nice, I wanted to be nice too. I grew meticulous with my clothing. I was always anxious that you wouldn't like my appearance. I thought I was so ugly, you see, lean and angular with big cow's eyes and big ugly lips and no eyebrows or lashes, and my arms were far too long and my feet were too big and my toes too flat and . . . no, I thought I looked almost repulsive. But you hardly ever showed that you were worried over my appearance. Once you said: "You should have been a boy," and then you laughed so that I wouldn't be upset. I was, of course. I cried for a whole week in secret, because you detested tears—other people's tears.

Then suddenly one day your suitcases would be standing downstairs and you'd be talking on the phone in a foreign language. I used to go into the nursery and pray to God that something would happen to stop you from going, that Grandma would die or that there'd be an earthquake or that all the airplanes would have engine trouble. But you always went. All the doors were open and the wind blew through the house and everyone talked at once, and you came up to me and put your arms around me and kissed me and hugged me and kissed me again and looked at me and smiled at me and you smelled nice but strange and you yourself were a stranger, you were already on the way, you didn't see me. I used to think: Now my heart will stop, I'm dying, it hurts so much, I'll never be happy again. Only five minutes have passed, how can I bear such pain for two months? And I cried in Father's lap, and he sat quite still with his soft little hand on my head. He went on and on sitting there, smoking his old pipe, puffing away till the smoke was all around us. Sometimes he'd say something: "Let's go to a movie this evening," or "What about ice cream for dinner today?" But I couldn't have cared less about movies or ice cream because I was dying. So the days and the weeks passed. Father and I shared the loneliness quite well. We hadn't much to say to each other, but it was so peaceful with him, and I never disturbed him. Sometimes he looked rather worried. I didn't know he was always short of money, but whenever I came clumping along his face would brighten and we'd have a talk or he'd just pat me with his pale little hand. Or else he'd be sitting on the leather sofa with Uncle Otto, drinking brandy, and both of them mumbling to each other. I wonder if they heard what they said. Or else Uncle Harry was there, and when they played chess it was extra quiet. I could hear three different clocks ticking in the house. Several days before you were due home I'd get feverish with excitement, and at the same time I was worried in case I got really ill because I knew you were afraid of sick people.

And then when you did come I could hardly bear it, I was so happy, and I couldn't say anything either, so sometimes you were impatient and said: "Eva doesn't seem to be very pleased to have her mother at home again." Then my cheeks flamed and I broke out in a sweat but couldn't say anything—I hadn't any words because you had taken charge of all the words at home. I loved you, it was a matter of life and death—I thought so anyway—but I distrusted your words. I knew instinctively that you hardly ever meant what you said. You have such a beautiful voice, Mother. When I was little I could feel it all over my body when you spoke to me, and often you were cross with me for not hearing what you said. It was because I was listening to your voice, but also because I didn't understand what you said. I didn't understand your words—they didn't match your intonation or the expression in your eyes. The worst of all was that you smiled when you were angry. When you hated Father you called him "my dearest friend," when you were tired of me you said: "darling little girl." Nothing fitted. No, wait, Mother, I must finish speaking. I know I'm tipsy, but if I hadn't had a drink I wouldn't have said what I have. Later, when my courage fails and I don't dare to say any more, or keep quiet because I'm ashamed of what I've said, you can talk and explain, and I'll listen and understand, just as I've always listened and understood. In spite of everything, it wasn't so bad being your little child. There was nothing wrong in my loving you. You tolerated me pretty well, as you had your travels. But one thing I've never understood is your relationship to Father. I've thought of you both so much lately, but your life together is a riddle. Sometimes I think you were totally dependent on Father, although he was so much weaker than you were. In some way you were considerate to him, as you never were to me and Helena. You spoiled him and talked of him as if he were made of finer material. Yet poor Father was very mediocre really—kind of meek and unoffending. I gathered that you paid Father's debts on several occasions. Wasn't that so?

CHARLOTTE Yes.

EVA I think Father had little affairs. At any rate, I remember three strange women who came to see us and sat in the living room when you were on your travels. I think one of them was called Maria van Eyck. She was your pupil, wasn't she?

CHARLOTTE Father did have an affair with Maria. A mild one, and brief at that.

EVA Didn't you bother about his love affairs?

CHARLOTTE No, indeed, I was never angry with your father for his little affairs. Besides, he had good taste. You said he was mediocre. That's both a cruel and unfair judgment. It shows that you didn't know your father. In other circumstances Josef would have been one of the great European architects, but he was far too considerate and far too decent. He had to play second fiddle to his elder brother, who wasn't half so gifted, and it was unfortunate that their father left his firm to them jointly. Josef never liked making a fuss or asserting himself. But he had brilliant ideas. For instance, he designed a concert hall for Copenhagen, or was it Oslo? No, it was Lyons, as a matter of fact, and everyone agreed that it was one of the most beautiful buildings that had been created during the thirties. Then came the war, and the project came to nothing. Poor Josef, he was unlucky in everything he undertook. He was a *really great* man and not at all mediocre. You look so skeptical, Eva. Don't you believe me?

EVA   What does it matter? Your words apply to your reality, my words to mine. If we exchange words, they're worthless.

15

CHARLOTTE   You spoke before of my self-deception. I think you're wrong. I never lied to myself. The actual state of affairs was rather frightening. I had backaches and couldn't practice properly. My concerts got worse, I lost important engagements. I began to think my life was meaningless. At the same time I had a bad conscience about you and Josef. It seemed idiotic trail-

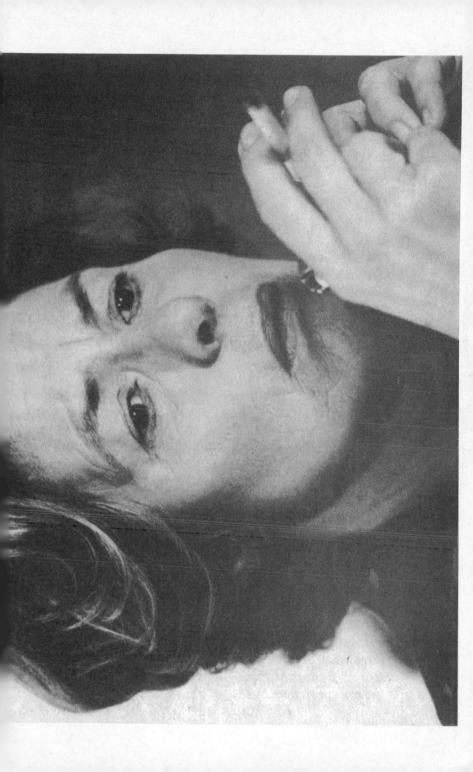

ing around from city to city, slated and disgraced, when I could be at home with you two instead. You smile sarcastically. I'm trying to speak truthfully, I'm merely telling you how I felt. I don't care what you think then. But it's as well to have this out for once, then we won't refer to it again.

EVA   I'm trying to understand.

CHARLOTTE   I was in Hamburg; I played the Beethoven First. It's not particularly difficult, and everything had gone well. Afterwards I went out to supper with old Schmiess, you know, the conductor (he's dead now). We always did. When we'd been eating and drinking for quite a long time and I was content and relaxed and my back was hardly aching at all, Schmiess said: "Why don't you stay at home with your husband and child and lead a respectable life instead of laying yourself open to constant humiliation?" I stared at him and then burst out laughing. "Do you think I played *so* badly this evening?" "No, I don't," he said with a smile. "But I can't help thinking of the eighteenth of August, nineteen thirty-four. You were twenty years old and we played the Beethoven First together in Linz. Do you remember that evening? There was a heat wave, the hall was packed, we played like gods, the orchestra was inspired. After the concerto the audience stood up and shouted and stamped and the orchestra gave a fanfare. You had a very simple red summer dress and long hair to your waist. You were gay and unconcerned, for your part we could have played the concerto five more times the same evening, it would have been just as enjoyable." "How do you remember all that?" I asked. "I wrote it down in my score," Schmiess said. "I usually make a note of my great experiences."

When I got back to the hotel, I couldn't sleep. At three o'clock in the morning I called up Josef at home and told him I'd made up my mind: I'd stop touring and stay at home with him and you, we'd be a real family. Josef was awfully happy. We wept with emotion, both of us, and talked for nearly two hours. And that was that. It was not deception at any rate. Perhaps a childish notion that life could offer a merciful way out even for Charlotte Andergast. Silly, of course. After a month I realized that I was an awful burden to you and Josef, that I longed to get away. After a year or so I calmed down. I began to give lessons and devoted myself to you and your upbringing, and shared Josef's worries. We spent the summers in a cottage out in the archipelago—you remember, don't you? (EVA *nods and smiles without smiling*) We were fairly happy, I think. Or were we? Weren't you happy?

EVA   (*Shakes her head*) No, I wasn't happy.

CHARLOTTE   (*Sighs*) You said that things had never been so good.

EVA   I didn't want to disappoint you.

CHARLOTTE   That just goes to show. (*Laughs*) What did I do wrong?

EVA   You did nothing wrong. As always, you were magnificent. I thought you were dreadful. I was fourteen and for lack of something better you directed the whole of your pent-up energy against me. You had taken it into your head that you had neglected me, and now you were damn well going to make up for it. I did my best to defend myself, but I hadn't a chance. Added to everything else, I loved you and was quite convinced the whole time that you were right and I was wrong. Do you know what you did? You never criticized outright, you merely insinuated. But every hour of the day you were there with your smiles, your little jests, your tender thoughtfulness, or your slightly worried tone of voice. There wasn't one detail that didn't come in for your loving energy. I had a stoop, having grown too fast. You got to work with gymnastics, and of course we did exercises together, you pleading your own bad back as an excuse. I had pimples, having reached puberty, and hey-presto, along comes a skin specialist who was a friend of the family's. He prescribed ointments and tinctures, which gave me nausea and made my skin still redder. You thought I couldn't be bothered looking after my long hair properly, so you had it cut short. I was hideous, I thought I looked a sight. And worst of all, you got the idea that my teeth had grown crooked, so you saw to it that a bridge was made. I looked a perfect fright. You told me I was a big girl now and wasn't to go about in slacks and sweaters but in dresses, which you had made or made yourself without asking what I thought, and I couldn't say no because I didn't want to upset you. You gave me books to read that I didn't like—they were far too advanced for me. I read and read and then you and I were to discuss what I'd read. You explained and held forth, and I hadn't the vaguest idea what you were talking about. I was scared that one day you'd show me up, me and my boundless stupidity.

I felt paralyzed, but one thing I did understand quite clearly: there wasn't a shred of the real me that could be loved or even accepted. You were obsessed, and I became more and more afraid, more and more crushed. I didn't know who I was any more, because at every moment I had to please you. I turned into a clumsy puppet that you worked. I said what you wanted me to say, I made your gestures and movements so that you would approve of me. I didn't dare to be myself for one second, not even when I was alone, because I violently disliked what was my own. It was horrible, Mother, and I still shake all over when I talk of those years. It was horrible, but it was to become worse. You see, I didn't realize I hated you because I was quite convinced we loved each other and that you knew best. So I couldn't hate you, and the hatred turned into an insane fear. I had ghastly dreams, I bit my nails and pulled out tufts of hair. I tried to cry but couldn't. I couldn't get a sound out. I tried to scream but only made stifled grunts that frightened me still more. One day you took me in your arms, sat down beside me on the sofa, and wept a little. You said you were worried about my development and that we'd better see a kind doctor. I gathered you really meant that I was going out of my mind, and that possibility gave me a kind of melancholy satisfaction. So I was sent to a psychiatrist, a tired old fogey in a white coat who kept poking his fat belly with a big paperknife the whole time we were talking. He began to ask me about my sex life but I didn't know what he was talking about—I hadn't even had my first period —so I had to make it all up. I think my advanced tastes and perverted fancies surprised him. Or else he saw through me and didn't want to hurt me. He was kind and well-meaning and said I was to remember that my mother loved me and thought only of my own good, but I knew that already.

CHARLOTTE   And I went off with Martin. You've never forgiven me, have you?

EVA   I've never thought those words.

CHARLOTTE   But you thought I let you down.

EVA   Yes.

CHARLOTTE   Have you never—*(Checks herself. Pause)*

(EVA *is silent.* CHARLOTTE *is silent)*

EVA   Do you remember Stefan?

CHARLOTTE   Indeed I do! You and Stefan would never have coped with a child.

EVA   Mother! I was eighteen. Stefan was grown-up. We were fond of each other, we'd have made out.

CHARLOTTE   You'd never have coped.

EVA   Oh yes, we would. *We wanted to have the baby*, but you destroyed our relationship.

CHARLOTTE   It's not true. It's damn well not true! On the contrary, I said to your father that we must make allowances, that we should wait and see. Didn't you realize that your Stefan was a nitwit, a semi-criminal little wastrel who fooled you from first to last?

EVA   *(With hatred)* You hated him from the first moment because you saw that I loved him, that I was drifting away from you. You did your utmost to wreck our relationship, pretending all the time to be understand-ing and sympathetic.

CHARLOTTE   And the child?

EVA   Stefan was a different man when he heard I was pregnant.

CHARLOTTE   Your Stefan got stoned, took my car, drove it into the ditch, and was arrested for drunken driving. *That* was his reaction to your pregnancy.

EVA   *(In a fury)* Do you think you know everything? Were you present at our discussions? Were you lurking under the bed when Stefan and I were together? Have you *any* idea what you're talking about? Have you ever bothered to find out what someone else was thinking and feeling? Come to that, do you give a damn about any living soul except yourself?

CHARLOTTE   I've heard those accusations before.

EVA   Stefan wasn't like the others but much better and more honest.

CHARLOTTE   I suppose that's why he stole that little Rembrandt etching and pawned it, that's why he lied to you about his childhood and youth and the tragedy of his family, that's why he broke into our summer cottage with his fine friends and drank up all the liquor and left the place in a filthy mess?

EVA   All that happened *afterwards*. Have you forgotten? Have you forgotten that you managed to get me put away in a psychiatric clinic after the abortion and that you reported Stefan to the police when he made his way into the house to talk to you?

CHARLOTTE   If you'd really wanted a child, I could never have forced you into having an abortion.

EVA   How could I defy you? You had brainwashed me from childhood, I had always given in to you. I was afraid and uncertain and needed help and support.

CHARLOTTE   *(In distress)* I thought I *was* helping you. I was convinced that the abortion was the only solution. I've been convinced of that up to this moment. It's terrible that you've been nursing this hatred all these years. Why have you never said anything?

EVA   Because you never listen. Because you're a notorious escapist, because you're emotionally crippled, because in actual fact you detest me and Helena, because you're hopelessly shut up inside yourself, because you always stand in your own light, because you have carried me in your cold womb and expelled me with loathing, because I loved you, because you thought I was disgusting and unintelligent and a failure. And you managed to injure me for life just as you yourself are injured. All that was sensitive and delicate you bruised, everything alive you tried to smother. You talk of my hatred. Your hatred was no less. *Your hatred is no less.* I was little and malleable and loving. You bound me, you wanted my love, just as you want everyone else to love you. I was utterly at your mercy. It was all done in the name of love. You kept saying that you loved me and Father and Helena. And you were an expert at love's intonations and gestures. People like you—people like you are a menace, you should be locked away and rendered harmless. A mother and a daughter—what a terrible combination of feelings and confusion and destruction! Everything is possible and everything is done in the name of love and solicitude. The mother's injuries are to be handed down to the daughter, the mother's disappointments are to be paid for by the daughter, the mother's unhappiness is to be the daughter's unhappiness. It's as if the umbilical cord had never been cut. The daughter's misfortune is the mother's triumph, the daughter's grief is the mother's secret pleasure.

(HELENA *is awakened by* EVA's *voice. The intonation and pitch of voice frighten her. She works her way up out of bed, climbing over the high rail and slithering to the floor. She drags herself to the door on elbows and knees, falls on her side, lies panting and shaking)*

EVA *(Voice)* We lived on your conditions, on your mean little marks of favor. We thought life was meant to be that way. A child is always vulnerable, can't understand, is helpless. It can't understand, doesn't know, nobody says anything. Dependent on others, humiliated, and then the distance, the insurmountable wall. The child calls out, no one answers, no one comes. Can't you see?

16

CHARLOTTE In your awful hatred you've formed a picture of me, but is it true? Do you seriously think it's the whole truth?

(EVA *hides her face in her hands, shakes her head*)

CHARLOTTE   Do you remember your grandmother? No, of course not, you were only seven or so when she died. Grandpa you remember better; in fact, I think you got on quite well with him.

EVA   I was afraid of Grandma, she was so overwhelming both physically and mentally. Grandpa was kind.

CHARLOTTE   Yes. That's how it was for you.

EVA   But not for you.

CHARLOTTE   No, hardly. Mother and Father were distinguished mathematicians. They were obsessed by their science and by each other. They were dominating, irresponsible, and good-humored. They regarded us children with surprised benevolence, but without any warmth or real interest. I can't remember either of them ever having touched me or my brothers, whether with caresses or punishments. Actually I was completely ignorant of everything to do with love: tenderness, contact, intimacy, warmth. Only through music did I have a chance to show my feelings. Sometimes when I lie awake at night I wonder whether I have lived at all. "What a wonderful life you do lead, Mrs. Andergast!" someone will say, wanting to be kind. "Just think, being able to make people so happy!" But what I think is: *I'm not alive. I've never been born. I was squeezed out of my mother's body. It closed and turned at once to Father. I didn't exist.* At times I've wondered if it's the same for everybody or if some people have a greater talent for living than others. If some people never live but just exist.

EVA   How long have you known all this?

CHARLOTTE   Three years ago I was ill, maybe you didn't know. I got blood poisoning and was in a hospital in Paris for two months. Leonardo canceled his concerts and stayed with me the whole time. I nearly . . . well, I suppose I almost died. Then it took me a long time to . . . I had some sort of depression, or whatever you like to call it.

EVA   But, Mother, I had no idea.

CHARLOTTE   There was no point in worrying you. Well, anyway, Leonardo and I began to talk to each other, as we had plenty of time for once. That's to say, Leonardo did the talking. I listened and tried to understand. It was quite hard at first. Oh, I can be soulful if necessary, but the soul itself I've never bothered about. *(Sighs)* It was like lessons in the first grade, and I wasn't a very apt pupil. I mostly thought that Leonardo talked nonsense, but it was nice having him sitting on the bed. *(Smiles)* He had infinite patience, though at times he did say I was a great goose, and it was beyond him how I could be the tolerably good musician I was. *(Pause)* At last I formed a picture of myself: *I've never grown up—my face and my body age, I acquire memories and experiences, but inside the shell I'm, as it were, unborn. (Pause)* I can't remember faces, not even my own. Sometimes I try to recall my mother's face, but I can't. I know she was big and dark and had blue eyes and a large nose and full lips and a broad forehead, but I can't fit the various bits together, I can't see her. In the same way it's impossible for me to recall your face or Helena's or Leonardo's. The only thing I remember about giving birth to you and your sister

is that it hurt, but just what the pain was like I don't remember. *(Pause)* Leonardo once said that . . . how did he put it now? . . . "A sense of reality is a matter of talent," he said. "Most people lack that talent and maybe it's just as well." Do you know what he meant?

EVA   I think so.

CHARLOTTE   How very . . . *(Is silent)*

EVA   *(After a pause)* What?

CHARLOTTE   How very strange.

EVA   Strange?

CHARLOTTE   I've always been afraid of you. *(Surprised)*

EVA   I can't understand that.

CHARLOTTE   *(Quiet astonishment)* I think I wanted you to take care of me. I wanted you to put your arms around me and comfort me.

EVA   I was a child.

CHARLOTTE   Does that matter?

EVA   No.

CHARLOTTE   I saw that you loved me and I wanted to love you, but I couldn't because I was afraid of your demands.

EVA   I didn't have any demands.

CHARLOTTE   I *thought* you had demands that I couldn't meet. I felt awkward and crippled. I didn't want to be your mother. I wanted you to know that I was just as helpless as you, but poorer, more frightened.

EVA   Is that true?

CHARLOTTE   I hear myself saying things I've never said before. Am I lying, am I acting, am I telling the truth? I don't know, Eva. I don't know. I feel upset and bewildered. Maybe it's Leonardo's death. Maybe Helena's illness. Maybe your terrible hatred. *(In great distress)* Eva, be kind to me! It hurts so!

EVA   I know it hurts.

CHARLOTTE   Why are you looking at me like that?

EVA   I'll tell you.

(With great difficulty HELENA *has opened the door and crawled out into the hall upstairs. She has dragged herself to the top of the stairs, where she lies in the dark, listening to the two women talking)*

CHARLOTTE   Tell me what you're thinking of.

EVA   I'm thinking of Helena and Leonardo.

CHARLOTTE   I don't understand.

EVA   Don't you?

CHARLOTTE   They hardly knew each other.

EVA Mother!

CHARLOTTE We were together at Bornholm one Easter.

EVA You went off and left us after three days.

CHARLOTTE I remember that it rained. I think there was even some snow.

EVA Mother!

CHARLOTTE I was to play the Bartók First with Ansermet in Geneva. *(Pause)* I was anxious to get there in time. I wanted to go through the concerto with the old boy in peace and quiet. So it's possible I left earlier. The weather was appalling. *(Long pause)* Leonardo was in a bad mood. You were pretty glum too.

EVA Mother!

CHARLOTTE I don't know why you want to make me remember that idiotic Easter. I can tell from your tone that I ought to be ashamed of something. Well, I'd have you know that—

EVA You and Leonardo arrived on Thursday. We spent a wonderful evening together. We laughed and sang and drank wine and played some old game we found in a closet. Helena was with us, she wasn't so ill then. She cheered up and was warm and happy. Leonardo was happy because *she* was. He talked and joked with her. She fell head over heels in love and they sat together until late at night. Next morning Helena told me in strict confidence that Leonardo had kissed her.

After breakfast Leonardo and Helena went for a drive.
It was Good Friday, the weather was warm and still,
a real spring day. Fancy your forgetting, Mother.
When they came home they were cheerful and sun-
burned. You were making a phone call, you'd been
telephoning all morning. When they entered the hall
and Leonardo put Helena down on a chair, you broke
off your call and said: "Now thank Leonardo properly
for having been so kind to you." Helena laughed and
said: "You speak to me as if I were a little girl of eight.
How touching!" Then you said in quite a different
tone: "I'm glad you haven't lost your sense of humor."
Then you went on telephoning as if nothing had happened. In the afternoon Leonardo fished a book out of
his suitcase. It was a biography of Mozart. He read
aloud to Helena and they looked at the pictures together. You practiced your Bartók concerto for several
hours. About four o'clock you came out to me in the
kitchen to make some tea. You said: "Have you *seen*
Helena! Isn't it touching?" We had guests to dinner.
Leonardo drank too much and played all Bach's solo
suites. He was quite unlike himself—as though enlarged, heavy and gentle and as drunk as a lord. He
played badly but beautifully. Helena sat there in the
dusk, beaming. I've never seen anything like it. The
guests made off, exhausted and rather gloomy. You
and I went for a walk in the dark. You chattered away
about some fantastic trip you'd made in Kenya or
wherever it was, I didn't really listen. I was thinking
of those two people. When we got home they were still
sitting where we had left them, one at each end of the
room. The fire and the candles had almost burned
down. I saw that Leonardo had been crying. He didn't
make the slightest effort to conceal his distress. Helena
hid her feelings better, talking to us about this and that

in a quiet, matter-of-fact voice. You went off to bed and I had to help Leo upstairs. We stopped outside the door of the bedroom and he turned his face and looked at me and said: "Just fancy, there's a butterfly there, fluttering against the window." When I went back to Helena she was sitting bolt upright in her chair, quite relaxed and calm. There wasn't a trace of her illness. I'll never forget her face, Mother, *I'll never forget her face*. Next day you left for Geneva, four days earlier than we had agreed. There was a snowstorm. Air services were canceled, but you managed to get a berth on the ferry. I drove you down to the harbor. Just before you went on board you said casually: "I've asked Leonardo to stay a little longer, it seems to be doing Helena good." You smiled and we embraced. Leonardo suddenly grew restless and unhappy. He was absentminded and rude and sat in his attic working. On the morning of Easter Day he was drunk and fell down the stairs. It put him in a better humor. He went for a long walk in the rain, and when he came back he was sober. He went over to Helena and said that he must leave in a few hours, that they would meet again and that he'd like to give her the Mozart biography as a memento. Then he put a call through to Geneva and talked to you for half an hour. The same evening he left on the last plane. During the night I was awakened by a horrible sound. It was Helena crying. I went in to her. She complained of terrible pains in her hip and right leg. She didn't think she could stand it until morning. I gave her every painkiller I could find but nothing helped. At five in the morning I had to phone for the ambulance.

CHARLOTTE   So it was my fault that Helena was taken ill.

EVA   I think so.

CHARLOTTE   You mean to say that Helena's illness . . .

EVA   Yes.

CHARLOTTE   You don't seriously mean that . . .

(EVA *is silent;* CHARLOTTE *is speechless*)

EVA   When she was one year old you deserted her. Then you kept deserting her and me all the time. When Helena got seriously ill, you sent her to a home for chronic invalids.

CHARLOTTE   It can't be true that you—

EVA   *(Calmly)* What can't be true? If you've any proof to the contrary, let me hear it. Look at me, Mother. Look at Helena. There are no excuses, Mother. There is only one truth and one lie. There can be no forgiveness.

CHARLOTTE   I've never deliberately—

EVA   No, I don't think you have.

CHARLOTTE   Then you can't blame me.

EVA   You always expect an exception to be made for you. You've set up a sort of discount system with life, but *one day* you'll be forced to see that your agreement is one-sided. You'll be made to realize just how guilty you are, like everyone else.

CHARLOTTE   Guilty of what?

EVA   I don't know. Guilty.

CHARLOTTE   Irrevocably?

(EVA *doesn't answer*)

CHARLOTTE   Won't you come here to me? Won't you put your arms around me? I'm so horribly afraid. Darling, won't you forgive me for all the wrong I've done? I'll try to mend my ways. You must teach me. We'll have lots of long, long talks. But help me. I can't go on any longer, *your hatred is so terrible.* I haven't understood. I've been selfish and childish and anxious. At least touch me! Strike me if you like! Eva dear, help me!

(*A cry is heard through the silent house.* HELENA *is calling for her mother. The two women hurry out into the hall and up the dark staircase.* EVA *gets there first, but her sister pushes her away and holds out her arms to her mother.* CHARLOTTE *presses her head to the sick girl's lap*)

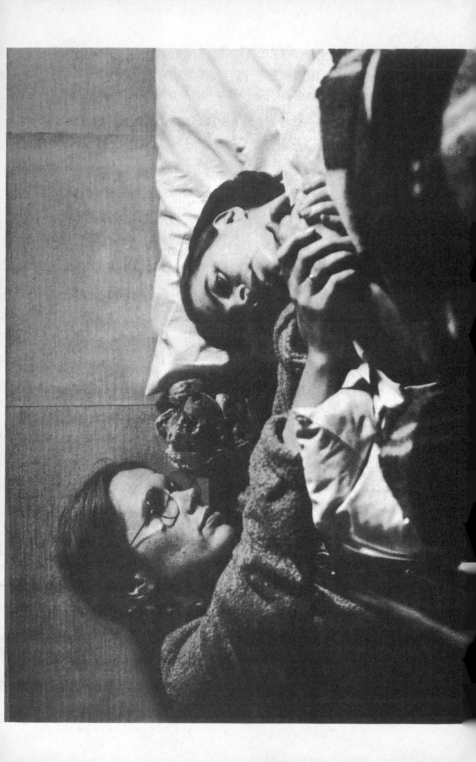

17

CHARLOTTE   *(On the phone)* Paul, my dear, I'm sorry to call you up so early in the morning. I must speak softly so that no one can hear. Will you do me a great favor? When you get to your office, please send me a telegram saying I must go to Paris immediately, or any damn place you like. I can't stand it here one more day, but I can't just leave. I must have a reason. Make up anything at all, Paul, my sweet. You're so good at fairy tales. I must go now, it's expensive too. Bye-bye, my dear. Sweet of you to help me.

*(*CHARLOTTE *creeps back to her room and closes the door.* EVA, *unseen, has overheard the phone call)*

18

CHARLOTTE *(On the train)* It was good of you, Paul, to come with me to Brittany. I couldn't have stood being alone. I think I got a slight shock up at Bindal. My daughter Helena was there, quite unexpectedly, and she was sicker than ever. Why can't she die? Do you think it's cruel of me to talk like that, Paul? You know me pretty well, don't you? I've never let you down, never canceled a concert. You can rely on me, can't you?

EVA *(Alone)* I'll just have to console myself, I can't always count on other people being on hand when I'm miserable. In fact, we nearly always do have to cry quietly, so that no one will hear.

CHARLOTTE *(On the train)* Paul, listen a minute. No, don't go to sleep! The critics always say I'm a generous musician. No one plays Schumann's piano concerto with a warmer tone. Or the big Brahms sonata. I'm not mean with myself. Or am I? All these idiotic thoughts suddenly racing round in my head. Paul, you're not just agreeing with me because you can't be bothered contradicting me?

EVA *(Alone)* Poor little Mother, rushing off like that. She looked so frightened, and suddenly so old and

tired. Her face had shrunk and her nose was red with weeping. Now I'll never see her again. I've scared her away.

CHARLOTTE   *(On the train)* Paul! See that little village? The lights are already on in the houses, people are going about their evening duties, someone's getting dinner ready, the children are doing their homework. I feel so shut out. I'm always homesick, but when I get home I realize it must be something else I long for.

EVA   *(Alone)* It will soon be dark and it's getting cold. I must go home and get dinner for Viktor and Helena. I can't die now. I'm afraid to commit suicide. Maybe God will want to use me one day, and then he'll set me free from my prison. I must be prepared.

CHARLOTTE   *(On the train)* You know, Paul, my daughter Helena has beautiful eyes, clear and bright. She has Josef's eyes, and when I hold her head she can focus them. How can she bear to live with her suffering? My life has been wonderful on the whole, but *hers?* Things have gone well for me, Paul. I feel a bit depressed, of course, I don't mind owning, but at the same time I feel all right. I can't be bothered about self-knowledge. I'll have to live without it.

EVA   *(Checking herself)* Are you stroking my cheek? Are you whispering in my ear? Are you with me now? We'll never leave each other, you and I.

CHARLOTTE   *(Smiles)* You're a kind soul, Paul. What would I do without you? And what would you do without me? You know what a trying time you have with your violinists, how they grumble. And think of the filthy noise they make when they practice.

EVA   There's a light in Helena's room. Viktor's there, talking to her. That's good. Kind of him—he's telling her that Mother has gone away.

19

VIKTOR   Helena, there's something I must tell you. Charlotte left this morning. We didn't want to wake you. You were in a deep sleep from those pills, and the night was rather distressing. So as I said, we didn't want to wake you.

(HELENA *says something*)

VIKTOR   Your mother sent her love. She was anxious and miserable. She'd been crying.

(HELENA *says something*)

VIKTOR   Eva has gone for a walk in the twilight. She's quite calm, almost cheerful. I think she's glad Charlotte has gone.

(HELENA *says something*)

VIKTOR   Dearest Helena, I don't know. She was looking forward so much to this meeting with her mother. She hoped for too much. I hadn't the heart to warn her. So it went wrong.

(HELENA *says something with great difficulty*)

VIKTOR   I can't understand what you say.

(HELENA *trembles, repeats her question*)

VIKTOR   You say you want to . . . What is it you want?

(HELENA, *still more agitated, says the same thing*)

VIKTOR   You must try to talk calmly, Helena, my dear, otherwise I can't possibly understand.

(HELENA *begins to scream. She is shaken by increasingly violent convulsions, snatches of sentences are heard between the screams. She bites her lips till they bleed, her eyes are pleading*)

VIKTOR   Eva! Come at once! Helena has had an attack! Hurry!

(HELENA's *screams get more and more shrill and inhuman. She throws herself about in the chair so violently that it tips over and she falls to the floor. The body contracts, the arms are turned outwards, white foam and blood trickle from her mouth.* EVA *enters, and she and* VIKTOR *try in vain to calm* HELENA, *pressing medicine in between her clenched teeth*)

EPILOGUE

VIKTOR Sometimes I stand out here looking at my wife without her knowing. She's in such distress. The last few nights have been terrible. She hasn't been able to sleep. She says she can never forgive herself for driving her mother away. If only I could talk to her, but it's all just a lot of dusty words and empty phrases. I have to stand looking on at her suffering, without being able to help.

EVA Are you going out?

VIKTOR Just down to the post office to fetch a parcel of books.

EVA Be a dear and post this letter at the same time.

VIKTOR By all means. Oh, it's to Charlotte!

EVA You may read it if you like. I'm going up to Lena for a while.

VIKTOR (Reads) "I have realized that I wronged you. I met you with demands instead of with affection. I tormented you with an old soured hatred which is no longer real. Everything I did was wrong and I want to ask your forgiveness. Helena's insight is much greater than mine. She gave, where I demanded. She was near you, when I kept my distance. Suddenly it dawned on me that I was to take care of you, that bygones are bygones, that I will never let you go again. I will never leave you alone again. I've no idea whether this letter will reach you, I don't even know if you will read it. Perhaps everything is already too late. But I hope *all the same* that my discovery will not be in vain. There is a kind of mercy after all. I mean the enormous chance of looking after each other, of helping each other, of showing affection. I want you to know that I will never let you go again or let you vanish out of my life. I'm going to persist! I won't give up, even if it should be too late. I don't think it is too late. It must not be too late."

PANTHEON MODERN WRITERS ORIGINALS

THE VICE CONSUL
by Marguerite Duras, translated from the French by Eileen Ellenbogen

The first American edition ever of the "masterful novel"*(Chicago Tribune)*that Duras considers her best—a tale of passion and desperation set in India and Southeast Asia.

0-394-55898-7 cloth, $10.95   0-394-75026-8 paper, $6.95

MAPS
by Nuruddin Farah

The unforgettable story of one man's coming of age in the turmoil of modern Africa, by "one of the finest contemporary African writers" (Salman Rushdie).

0-394-56325-5 cloth, $11.95   0-394-75548-0 paper, $7.95

DREAMING JUNGLES
by Michel Rio, translated from the French by William Carlson

"A subtle philosophical excursion embodied in a story of travel and aventure...it succeeds extremely well."—*New York Times Book Review*

0-394-55661-5 cloth, $10.95   0-394-75035-7 paper, $6.95

BURNING PATIENCE
by Antonio Skármeta, translated from the Spanish by Katherine Silver

A charming story about the friendship that develops between Pablo Neruda, Latin America's greatest poet, and the postman who stops to receive his advice about love.

"The mix of the fictional and the real is masterful, and...gives the book its special appeal and brilliance."—*Christian Science Monitor*

0-394-55576-7 cloth, $10.95   0-394-75033-0 paper, $6.95

YOU CAN'T GET LOST IN CAPE TOWN
by Zoë Wicomb

A "superb first collection" *(New York Times Book Review)* of stories about a young black woman's upbringing in South Africa.

0-394-56030-2 cloth, $10.95   0-394-75309-7 paper, $6.95

THE SHOOTING GALLERY
by Yūko Tsushima, compiled and translated from the Japanese by Geraldine Harcourt

Eight stories about modern Japanese women by "a subtle, surprising, elegant writer who courageously tells unexpected truths."—Margaret Drabble

0-394-75743-2 paper, $7.95

NELLY'S VERSION

An ingenious thriller of identity by the author of *Waking* and *The Seven Ages*.

"A taunting, captivating novel."—*Times Literary Supplement*

0-679-72035-9 paper, $8.95

ALSO FROM THE PANTHEON MODERN WRITERS SERIES

L'AMANTE ANGLAISE

by Marguerite Duras, translated from the French by Barbara Bray

A gripping novel about a savage murder in small-town France.

"Astonishing...a small gem."—Lynne Sharon Schwartz
0-394-55897-7 cloth, $10.95   0-394-75022-5 paper, $6.95

THE RAVISHING OF LOL STEIN

by Marguerite Duras, translated from the French by Richard Seaver

"Brilliant...shoots vertical shafts down into the dark morass of human love."
—*The New York Times Book Review*
0-394-74304-0 paper, $6.95

THE SAILOR FROM GIBRALTAR

by Marguerite Duras, translated from the French by Barbara Bray

By the author of The Lover, "a haunting tale of strange and random passion."
—*The New York Times Book Review*
0-394-74451-9 paper, $8.95

THE WAR: A MEMOIR

by Marguerite Duras, translated from the French by Barbara Bray

"Autobiographical narrative of the highest order."—Philip Roth

"This meditation on the horrors of World War II [is] a complex and extraordinary book."   —Francine du Plessix Gray, *The New York Times Book Review*
0-394-75039-X paper, $6.95

ALL FIRES THE FIRE AND OTHER STORIES

by Julio Cortázar, translated from the Spanish by Suzanne Jill Levine

"One of the most adventurous and rewarding collections since the publication of Cortázar's own *Blow-Up*."   —*Los Angeles Times*
0-394-75358-5 paper, $7.95

BLOW-UP AND OTHER STORIES

by Julio Cortázar, translated from the Spanish by Paul Blackburn

A celebrated masterpiece: fifteen eerie and brilliant short stories.

"A splendid collection."—*The New Yorker*
0-394-72881-5 paper, $6.95

HOPSCOTCH

by Julio Cortázar, translated from the Spanish by Gregory Rabassa

The legendary novel of bohemian life in Paris and Buenos Aires.

"The most magnificent novel I have ever read."
—C.D.B. Bryan, *The New York Times Book Review*
0-394-75284-8 paper, $8.95

THE WINNERS
by Julio Cortázar, translated from the Spanish by Elaine Kerrigan
Julio Cortázar's superb first novel about a South American luxury cruise.

"Irresistibly readable...introduces a dazzling writer."
—*The New York Times Book Review*
0-394-72301-5 paper, $8.95

THE LEOPARD
by Giuseppe di Lampedusa, translated from the Italian by Archibald Colquhoun
The world-renowned novel of a Sicilian prince in the turbulent Italy of the 1860s.

"The genius of its author and the thrill it gives the reader are probably for all time."
—*The New York Times Book Review*
0-394-74949-9 paper, $7.95

YOUNG TÖRLESS
by Robert Musil, translated from the German by Eithne Williams and Ernst Kaiser
A classic novel by the author of *The Man Without Qualities*, about students at an Austrian military academy and their brutality to one another.

"An illumination of the dark places of the heart."—*The Washington Post*
0-394-71015-0 paper, $6.95

ADIEUX: A FAREWELL TO SARTRE
by Simone de Beauvoir, translated from the French by Patrick O'Brian
Simone de Beauvoir's moving farewell to Jean-Paul Sartre: "an intimate, personal, and honest portrait of a relationship unlike any other in literary history."
—Deirdre Bair

0-394-72898-X paper, $8.95

THE BLOOD OF OTHERS
by Simone de Beauvoir, translated from the French by Roger Senhouse and Yvonne Moyse
A brilliant existentialist novel about the French resistance, "with a remarkably sustained note of suspense and mounting excitement."—*Saturday Review*
0-394-72411-9 paper, $7.95

A VERY EASY DEATH
by Simone de Beauvoir, translated from the French by Patrick O'Brian
The profoundly moving, day-by-day account of the death of the author's mother.

"A beautiful book, sincere and sensitive."—Pierre-Henri Simon
0-394-72899-8 paper, $4.95

WHEN THINGS OF THE SPIRIT COME FIRST: FIVE EARLY TALES
by Simone de Beauvoir, translated from the French by Patrick O'Brian
The first paperback edition of the marvelous early fiction of Simone de Beauvoir.

"An event for celebration."—*The New York Times Book Review*
0-394-72235-3 paper, $6.95

Look at your local bookstore for other Pantheon Modern Writers titles